STAMPEDE

Center Point
Large Print

**This Large Print Book carries the
Seal of Approval of N.A.V.H.**

STAMPEDE

GOLD FEVER
and
DISASTER
IN THE KLONDIKE

BRIAN CASTNER

CENTER POINT LARGE PRINT
THORNDIKE, MAINE

For my father, who told me stories
of his own youthful adventures in Alaska,
and my mother, who stoked my love of books
through endless visits to the local library.

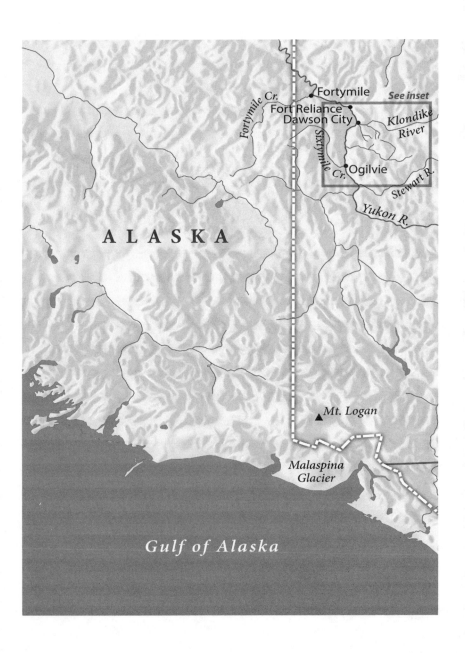

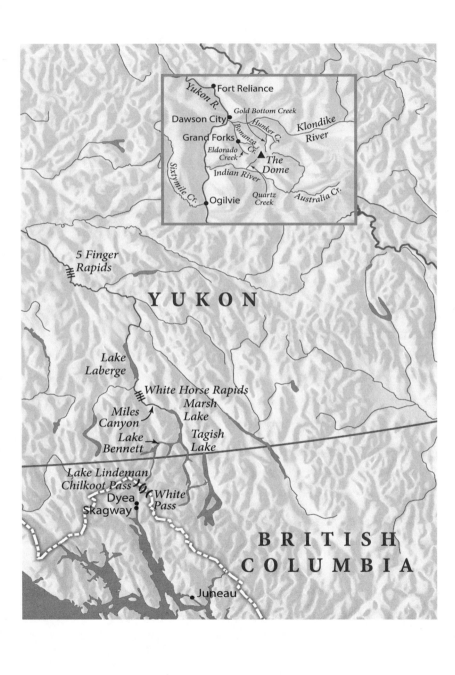

Fort Reliance

Yukon R.

Gold Bottom Creek

Dawson City

Hunker Cr.

Grand Forks

Bonanza Cr.

Klondike River

Eldorado Creek

The Dome

Sixtymile Cr.

Indian River

Ogilvie

Quartz Creek

Australia Cr.

5 Finger Rapids

YUKON

Lake Laberge

White Horse Rapids

Marsh Lake

Miles Canyon

Lake Bennett

Tagish Lake

Lake Lindeman
Chilkoot Pass

White Pass

Dyea

Skagway

BRITISH COLUMBIA

Juneau

Men, it has been well said, think in herds; it will be seen that they go mad in herds, while they only recover their senses slowly, and one by one.

—Charles Mackay,
*Extraordinary Popular Delusions
and the Madness of Crowds*, 1841

Cast of Characters
(in order of appearance)

Robert Henderson . . . *a prospector
from Nova Scotia*

Joe Ladue . . . *a promoter and outfitter
for the Alaska Commercial Company*

George Carmack . . . *a shunned American
who avoided white man's work*

Kate Carmack . . . *a Tagish woman,
George's wife and Jim's sister*

Skookum Jim . . . *a Tagish man
of great strength*

Tagish Charlie . . . *Jim's nephew*

Clarence and Ethel Berry . . . *a husband-
and-wife mining team from California*

Tappan Adney . . . *a journalist and
naturalist from New York*

Jack London . . . *a stampeder looking to
escape factory work*

Arthur Arnold Dietz . . . *founder of the New York and Bridgeport Mining Company*

Samuel Steele . . . *commander of the North-West Mounted Police*

Belinda Mulrooney . . . *owner of the Grand Forks and Fairview hotels*

John J. Healy . . . *a merchant who roamed the West*

Jefferson "Soapy" Smith . . . *a gangster and notorious bunco man*

Anna DeGraf . . . *a veteran stampeder whom everyone called "Mother"*

Author's Note

The end of the nineteenth century was a deeply racist and violent era that I attempt to portray authentically, using language of the time. To that end, many characters in this book express a number of racial stereotypes and use a variety of epithets that many readers will find deeply offensive. I find them offensive as well. I repeat them only as required, and in service of a historically accurate story.

As a basic guide, throughout this book multiply all historic monetary values by 30 to make an approximate comparison to modern currency. So a 10-cent hourly wage in 1895 would convert to about $3 in 2021.

STAMPEDE

CHAPTER ONE
1895

I am not fit to live among civilized men.
—ROBERT HENDERSON

In those days the men who panned for gold in the streambeds of the Yukon valley would often work with a partner, to avert lonesomeness or starvation or worse, but Robert Henderson was his own man, never could find another who matched his endurance for misery, and so when he slipped while crossing an icy creek there was no one there to right him, and he fell, fell hard, and impaled himself upon the broken shards of a downed pine.

Henderson had been working his way across a tree trunk that he had dropped for a makeshift bridge, axe in his right hand, bracing himself against a limb with his left. Below, the stream rushed as a snowmelt cataract. He swung and chopped away the branches that barred his path but then the limb in his hand snapped and his feet came out from under him in a flash.

Henderson tumbled toward the torrent of water. Then sudden blinding pain as the jagged stump of a branch speared the flesh of his calf and wrenched him to a halt midair. There he hung on a hook, like an animal snared in a toothed foot-trap, dangling head-down over the flooded stream.

He was all alone. His axe was still in his hand.

With a lurch Henderson yanked himself up, the bloody stake straining against the tendons in his leg, and he swung hard with his axe. The blade bit and held and Henderson pulled and his chest met the trunk and he clutched it in a bear hug. His leg was somehow free but he dared not fall, and inch by inch he pulled himself to the bank.

Henderson sat in the muddy slush on the creek edge. "A bad wound," he thought. He lowered his mangled leg into the ice-cold water and it numbed immediately. The creek went pink, then clear, and he pulled out the leg. He knew he could not walk. It was May, the days were long now, the sun warming, and yet snow still lay thick and the frozen Yukon River had not yet broken.

He was stranded, cut off, hungry, and lame. No one knew where he was, and even if they did, no one could reach him. Fifty hard miles to the nearest settlement, and the rapidly melting rivers were ready to rupture at any moment.

He set camp and prepared for a long wait. He carried very little. Flour, sugar, salt, a small bit of tea. Rifle, pistol, shovel, and pan. His clothes were rags, patches of wool and furs and buckskin, and his hobnailed boots were held together with burlap sacks. His last resupply at the trading post at Ogilvie, the last time he had seen another man, was the year before.

Henderson was blue-eyed, tanned, tall and lean like timber. He was nearly forty years old, no longer a young man, and his face was sunken, overcooked, all the fat drained off. He wore a long mustache that drooped at the corners of his mouth and occasionally got caught in his teeth. Old-timers called him a born prospector. He had the gold fever. He must, to spend the winter cutting trail from the Indian River all the way up Australia Creek, melting snow to wash gravel in the darkness. And for nothing but a few colors, a few specks of gold, two cents to the pan.

The muscles in the calf were torn, and soon the whole leg swelled and turned bright red, hot to the touch. Henderson's only relief was to crawl, on two hands and one knee, to the creek bank and dip the mangled leg in the icy bath. The never-setting sun was fierce off the snows, and Henderson could find no relief from the glare. He pulled his flat-brimmed felt hat down low to his eyes, but it made no difference. His vision went blurry and pained, and he knew snow blindness was coming on, so he rubbed his eyes with salt and water hoping to stave off the worst of it. Like most prospectors, Henderson shaved in winter, as a beard would solidify into a hazardous mass of ice, but now he grew his whiskers to keep the mosquitoes off. It made little difference. Breeding in the shallows, the insects were ferocious, and Henderson took to wearing a hood of cheesecloth. Even so, the mosquitoes would smother themselves so thickly upon it that he had trouble breathing.

Just before he fell crossing the creek, Henderson had shot a caribou and strung up the haunches in a nearby tree. Now he sawed through the forequarters and moved that section of raw meat to his tent, to a hole he dug to the permafrost. Then he dug a second hole in the ground, also inside the tent but a little away from the first, and packed the sides with clay. He broke a few twigs into kindling and struck a sulfur match and made a small fire in the hole, and the clay dried and hardened. Every day he cut off a piece of the caribou carcass and made a small fire and put both of them in the little clay oven and cooked the meat and this was all he ate for the day. The oven's smoke clogged the air of the tent, but that was okay, it kept off the mosquitoes.

Wolves prowled along the edge of the camp every night. Henderson had no medicines, no poultice to draw out the bilious fluids in his leg, and so he laid strips of bacon across the wound until they were heavy with pus. "These have done duty," he thought, as he carefully pulled them off one by one and threw them outside the tent, where the wolves would leap on them, gobble them down, and then back off, temporarily satiated.

Henderson tried to count the number of wolves outside his door. "Their hideous howling continues both day and night," he rued. Trapped, he imagined hundreds of the animals, their calls echoing in the valley. Other beasts came to the tent flap as well. Moose. Caribou. And then, the very embodiment of his fears.

One day he heard grunts and huffs as a broad brown paw pushed through the flap. Henderson recoiled and pulled out his six-shooter and fired and blood splattered across the canvas. The bear retreated into the forest but Henderson lay uneasy, wary, watching. The bear would come back. The only way to kill these Yukon bear was to shoot them through the spine. You could empty two pistols into a grizzly's chest and they'd still fight on with a shredded heart. He'd seen it himself. Henderson listened and waited, vigilant, but the bear never returned.

Robert Henderson lay in that tent, among the wolves and mosquitoes, for twenty-two days. He starved until his skin hung loose, like ill-fitting clothes. Finally, desperately hungry, and thinking his leg at last well enough to take his weight, he packed his gear and pushed on.

The sickbed cost him forty pounds, and he walked with a limp for the rest of his life.

That country in the upper Yukon valley consists

of a mix of rounded rolling hills veined with tight streambeds and wide U-shaped valleys dug by glaciers that left silty floors and moraines strewn along the shoulders. Henderson picked his way down among the conifers until he struck the Indian River, at its icy spring-melt flood. Henderson had no boat, so he shot a moose and skinned it and stretched the hide over a frame of sticks he lashed together, and with this he floated down the Indian. He didn't want to waste a minute of summer light, and he figured his leg was usable enough, so rather than return to Ogilvie for resupply he instead paddled to a place called Quartz Creek, in search of his next prospect.

Henderson stashed his boat on the bank and packed his moose meat up the rocky shoulder of the creek bed. Gold followed quartz, so this could be a lucky spot. He found a place where the waters ran clear and dipped his pan in the gravel and pulled up a mixture of water and rock and dark soil. He shook shook shook the pan and the water splashed over the side and ran down his fingers and forearms. The chunks of gravel scraped and scratched a racket and he used the tips of his fingers to rake out the largest rocks so he could pick them by hand and toss them aside. Then he took more water in the pan and shook and swirled it so the sand and rock separated. Gold is twenty times heavier than water, and eight times heavier than the sediment with which it mingles, so it is only a matter of patience and skill to slowly clean a pan.

As Henderson shook the pan he gently tipped it away from himself so the gravel collected on the far side. With every shake, the gold invisibly worked its way down into the deepest crease. He carefully dipped the working edge of the pan in the water and as he pulled it out the top layer of lightest sand floated away. He dipped again, and a third time, and once more. Every dip, more bits of gravel slipped off, until all that remained were fine black grains. Pay dirt.

Henderson poured off most of the water except for a small pool, opposite the pay dirt. Then he swirled that slug of water around the bottom crease of the pan, like a marble ringing a bowl, and as it circled the well of the pan it swept off the sand, leaving behind the heavier grains of gold. The flecks emerged like buried treasure in the retreating surf on a beach.

A flash. Two. But nothing more. Only colors. A disappointment.

Undaunted, Henderson hobbled further up the ridge, and panned again, and again, and again, and again.

The Yukon. Long had the promise of its buried riches tingled the imaginations of white men. That name, Yukon, always signified more than a river. It meant a place of absolutes. Endless summer sun followed by bottomless night. Mosquito-blackened heat and bone-shaking cold. Herds of stags and flocks of eagles and ferocious predators like outsiders had never seen. The highest mountains of the continent, monstrous sentinels guarding the northern rim of the world. All in the remotest domain conceivable. The greatest privations for the greatest rewards. So much rocky wilderness, men asked, how could it not hide gold?

The native people of that land knew of the gold but had little use for it, and so it sat untouched in the mountain creeks for thousands of years, until white men came. First the Russians in the early nineteenth century, all trappers and traders. They brought missionaries and the pox and left with furs, and as they remained largely on the coasts they heard only the faintest whispered rumors of gold. Then the Hudson's Bay Company, whose voyageurs entered from the broad Mackenzie River valley to the east, setting up fur-trading forts in the 1840s. The Russians never attempted to breach the gates of the icy Alaskan fortress and prospect the distant valleys of the inner sanctum, and the practical Canadian traders saw furs as more reliable than treasure hunting, and so the gold remained undisturbed. When the czar sold Alaska to the United States in 1867, little changed for a time. Seward's Folly, said rival politicians in Washington.

Alaska cost seven million dollars, two cents an acre, but for what? A polar bear garden. Alaska wasn't even a territory. It was classified as a military district, with few lawmen and no elected officials and no system to produce any.

At first, only a few outsiders seeped in. A handful of gold seekers followed the path of the Hudson's Bay Company and reached the Yukon River in 1873. One party was led by an American named Leroy Napoleon Jack McQuesten, a veteran of the California goldfields. The next year he established a new post in the upper Yukon valley and took a fourteen-year-old Indian girl as a wife and began to trade flour and gunpowder for pelts. McQuesten called his compound Fort Reliance, and he renamed the nearby creeks—Fortymile to the north, Sixtymile to the south—for their distance from his home. McQuesten found little gold, as he was forced to spend most of his time trading furs to pay for grub, but more miners would follow him.

Outsiders first used the Chilkoot Pass, the Indians' traditional trading route from the sea, to reach Fort Reliance in 1880. Twenty-five men made the journey that year. Fifty breached the narrow pass in 1882, then nearly eighty in 1884. The first white woman over the Chilkoot was Dutch Kate, a good-time girl who crossed wearing men's clothes in 1887. By twos and fews, over the years the numbers slowly increased.

For the world was starving for gold. Silver too, and precious gems, but gold most of all because the currencies of all the leading economies and great powers were backed by it. The total amount of paper money in circulation was limited by the reserves in capital vaults, and so in a very real way, wealth could be created only when more gold came out of the ground.

For most of the nineteenth century, fortune hunters could slake their thirst in softer, warmer places far to the south of Alaska. California in 1849, then New Mexico and Colorado and Nevada, and then up the Rockies and Pacific coast. All this gold panning and boomtown rushing forged a new archetype: the prospector. Loners and small crews of men followed the news of the latest big strike and in so doing kept the coffers of American banks filled. Over the decades, these men came to embody an ethos, an ideal combination of hardiness, diligence, labor, and greed.

In time, though, the American West became settled and domesticated, all the frontier run out. The coastal destiny was finally manifest. Oregon was a state, not a trail. The Indian tribes of the Great Plains had been defeated and rounded up. All the lands of the inter-mountain basin had been picked over, Deadwood and Tombstone were old news. Only the Yukon remained as a reservoir of golden dreams. A secret depository. Nature's own vault. The mountains hid a dragon's hoard of gold, in tiny grains dusted over the landscape.

In the American mind, Alaska stood as the last place. The last place without a railroad and telegraph. The last place with Indians who had not met a white man. The last open country. The last place without laws. The last place a man could still find his own fortune, free of other men.

Once the West was seemingly stripped of novel discoveries, the prospectors' focus shifted to Alaska and the Yukon River. The kind of man who once went west now went north instead.

Robert Henderson was just that kind of man.

That Henderson would pan for gold alone in the Arctic wilderness was either inevitable predestination or wish fulfillment or both. The son of Nova Scotian lighthouse keepers, Henderson was infected by terminal wanderlust from an early age. As a poor young man he sat in solitude on a rock and thought of what he wanted in life. He thought of all that he had heard about the Jews and their gold and decided he wanted some of his own and so he ran away from home in search for it. He sailed around Cape Horn to prospect in Australia and Patagonia, and then he returned to North America to try his luck in the Rockies of Colorado, but all that time he dreamed of the north.

Henderson was living in Aspen with his wife and children, prospecting and chopping trees and full of discontent, when in the spring of 1894 his younger brother Henry returned from the Yukon and told tales of hunger and dancing women and gold above all. Robert felt it then, the yearning of his restless spirit.

"That is a rich country," he said. "I am going there and nothing will stop me this time."

He sailed to Alaska a month later, without his wife or brother or even a partner to work the mine, and immediately set out alone. But by the time he fell at the creek and injured his leg, Henderson had labored for a full year with little to show for it, certainly not finding anything that he thought he could turn into a productive paying claim.

All that summer of 1895, Henderson prospected on creeks up and down the Indian River valley. When the snows passed he gathered leeks and huckleberries, and rhubarb leaves when he could get them. These burned his throat and gave him diarrhea and made his urine red, but at least they looked a little like cabbage and kept away scurvy. After the solstice the harsh sun proved unrelenting and the Yukon dried into a labyrinth of shallow channels, sandbars, marshes, and stony banks. Henderson slept outside or under trees, and hunted caribou and mountain goats and fished for pike and grayling. And the surrounding hills were alight with wildflowers, wild roses, and bumbling bees the size of his thumb.

But still his luck remained poor, no more than two- and three-cent pans. So in early fall, when the birch leaves faded to pale yellow, he returned to the trading post at Ogilvie, to restock his supply of grub for the next year.

In 1895 there were about three thousand Indians and a thousand white men and exactly twenty-eight white women—a few wives but mostly sporting girls selling themselves at the pleasure palaces far from Ogilvie—in the entire Yukon valley, an area larger than Texas. The Indians belonged to various tribes though the prospectors mostly called them all Siwashes, a bastardized derivation of "savage." The sourdoughs, the white men who came to that country, belonged to one of two classes: the miners on the creeks, and the traders in town who ran the post office, brought news from the outside, and sold the essentials: bacon, beans, flour, alcohol.

The upper watershed, where Henderson worked, hosted two such outposts, mathematically and geographically about a hundred miles apart. The settlements of Fortymile and Sixtymile were named for McQuesten's creeks that they had grown up beside. Sixtymile was the smaller of the two, and was also sometimes called Ogilvie, after the land's original Canadian surveyor. McQuesten's old Fort Reliance, on the other hand, had been abandoned for nearly a decade by the time Henderson arrived. The creek names stuck, the fort rotted.

Ogilvie consisted of a sawmill and the main trading post for the Alaska Commercial Company and a few dozen rough log cabins squatting in the frozen mud. The sod-roofed hovels were cold and smoke-choked in the winter and leaky with rains and mosquitoes in the summer; Henderson stayed in his tent whenever he could. Dogs lay everywhere in the streets, underfoot, refusing to be moved when sleeping. No one fed the sled dogs when they weren't working in the summer, so the mutts resorted to stealing food. They broke into cabins and larders and every man's outfit and ate anything they found: soap, snowshoes, leather harnesses, greasy dishrags. A candle, still lit. A dead baby, prepped for burial. Each other.

About a hundred men wintered over at Ogilvie each year, a mix of Americans and Canadians and men from the old country, Swedes and Norwegians and Italians. Technically, Ogilvie lay within Canada; the border between the North-West Territories and Alaska, and thus the United States and the Dominion, had only been formally surveyed in 1888. But the prospectors did not care for the arbitrary boundary. The border was unguarded, and no natural feature blocked their way. And so they largely carried on as if the cartographer's line did not exist, nor the laws or regulations of either nation, and instead they followed their own rule and code and banished any soul who did not abide and keep it so.

And that miners' code was very simple. Never steal. Share food. Tell every other man about any discovery. And most importantly, do as you would be done by.

The code was enforced at the miners' meetings, which were held whenever sufficient men were gathered. If a man had a grievance, he brought it before the group. A chairman was chosen, as well as advocates for and against. The remaining men in attendance formed both judge and jury, one vote each, majority rule.

The miners' meetings embodied the fiercest elements of democracy and mob domination. Rulings and punishments were final and applied immediately, no appeal possible. Minor offenses, such as claims disputes, were solved with restitution. The typical punishment for major offenses was either hanging or exile, and both sentences usually achieved the same end. The miners' meetings nearly eliminated violence among white men, as duels were forbidden. When an Englishman and a Frenchman agreed to use Winchesters to settle a dispute over an Indian woman, the president of the meeting arrived at the contest with a coil of rope, to hang the winner. Both men were banished. Similarly, get caught stealing, you were sent out on a boat. If no boat was available, then floated out on a log. In winter you had to walk.

In Ogilvie, the premier man-about-town was a gregarious sawmill operator, grubstake investor, trading post owner, and general business booster named Joe Ladue. He first established his office of the Alaska Commercial Company, the region's main outfitter, at the Sixtymile River in 1890 and was always known to share scuttlebutt and hot tips of the latest strike, or his prediction and prognosis of fertile ground for the next one. No carnival barker could best him in promotion, nor any mystic entice a man with richer golden daydreams.

Henderson first met Ladue when he entered the country in 1894, and thought the huckster a most genial chap. It was Ladue who gave Henderson the idea to go to the Indian River, twenty-five miles downstream of Ogilvie. Until then, gold was known to be found only on the west side of the Yukon, on the creeks that dumped into the Fortymile and Sixtymile rivers. But it seemed only a matter a time before gold was discovered on the east side as well, and Henderson took on the challenge.

"I'm a determined man," he had told Ladue. "I won't starve. Let me prospect for you. If it's good for me, it's good for you." Henderson was broke, but Ladue was so sure of the prospects, he grubstaked Henderson's entire outfit, providing supplies and gear in exchange for a portion of the miner's future earnings.

That had been the year prior, though, and thus far Henderson had nothing to show for Ladue's investment. Hat in hand, Henderson had to ask again for the same terms and grubstake. Ladue granted it, another year's worth of food.

So in the fall of 1895, via boat and rough trail, a burdened and worn Robert Henderson returned to Quartz Creek.

A poor man with sufficient gold fever can pan a ton of gravel a day. Doing so required a complete obsession with the gamble of turning up colors, to the detriment and breakdown of one's own body. Henderson had the work ethic and mania to strike this devil's bargain, but Quartz Creek was over six miles long. Where to begin?

In those northern reaches, gold finds its genesis deep belowground but its release at altitude. Under great heat and pressure the mother lode grows in a vein from the center of the earth up to the highest peaks, where it is slowly slowly ground to dust by time's millstone and carried down the cleft gulches and gullies by trickling streams. Eventually, this placer gold, free alluvial grains, comes to rest in the sandbars of the wide shallow rivers, floods washing it to the sea. But any man with strong hands and back can interrupt the cycle, catch the grains amidrift, in the bottom of creeks with names like Quartz, Australia, and Dominion.

Henderson knew that any gold to be found in the lower river was ground to dust finer than frog's hair. But if you ascended the creeks, got up on the mountainsides, the gold was still coarse and unworn, whole nuggets to be retrieved from the gravel.

He worked his way up the creek until he found a place with a few vague colors, plus quartz and purplish porphyrites, which were known to bind to gold. Could be a telltale, Henderson thought. Then he set to build out his operation for the winter.

The chill air of fall came quickly; Henderson did not have much time. He took his axe and felled a tree and another and then he wedged the tree trunks in a brace and began to saw lumber. First he cut long boards and joined them together into a sluice box. He set in wooden strips as riffles in the twelve-foot-long chute and dammed the stream with rocks and fitted the sluice box to the outflow of the basin. He shoveled gravel into the flume and let the water run and the rock and gold separate as water flowed downhill. The lighter dirt and soil washed away first, then the heavier rocks of assorted varieties, until only the gold dust was left behind.

Eventually, the water in the bony creek got low and then froze, and so Henderson built himself a rocker box. A rocker looks like a baby's cradle: a crate, four feet by two feet, mounted on twin curved sections of wood. Henderson put a wool blanket in the bottom of the rocker, and then an iron plate with holes on top of the blanket. He dug gravel from icy muck and dumped it in the hopper and then he melted snow and ladled the water overtop, seesawing the box back and forth. The heaviest sand passed through the iron plate, and the fine gold dust got caught in the wool, while the gravel rolled off and away. Several times a day he pulled out the wool blanket and washed out the bright gold dust in a basin and put it in his poke, a small pouch, for safekeeping.

Henderson spent that whole winter on Quartz Creek. The veil of darkness broke only a few hours a day, when the sun briefly slipped over the ridgeline and the snowy mountains reflected the pale rose of morning. No companions, no birds, no sounds; the kind of solitude that lent eloquence to canned food labels and trademarks on pick handles. Melting snow and rocking gravel was hard, slow work. His world shrank in dimensions. Fire, tent, rocker, hemmed in by the hills clad in tall, snow-choked trees. That winter proved especially cold, and on the coldest nights even the wind would stop blowing. All was perfectly still, the snow and ice cracking and popping, like a dropped crystal cup.

The calendar turned, unnoticed, to 1896.

One day, in the deep winter, Henderson needed to restock the provisions at his work site, so he struggled through the drifts to reach his food cache, where he had laid down the carcasses of two moose he had killed for winter meat, and the main portion of his outside store-bought grub besides. But when he got there, and worked off the layers of snow and ice that covered the hole in the ground, he found that his larder was empty.

Not only the two moose, but all the rest of his food. Flour, salt, bacon, all of it. All his grub for which he owed Joe Ladue.

Henderson looked at his empty cache. He knew who had done it. There were no white men for miles around. And he knew the punishment for the Indians when they were caught.

The miners' code treated murder and robbery the same. Steal a man's food and he was good as dead, and so thieves got hoisted, the jig-in-air at the end of a rope. White man's justice.

Years back, an Indian had not just stolen from a white man, he had killed him too. And so after the miners' meeting the old-timers went to the Indian's village and seized him and then took a rope and covered it in axle grease and eased it over a branch on a tall tree by the river. They slipped the noose over the Indian's neck and every man grabbed the line to heave to and when the work was done they got back in their boats and left for home.

They lynched that Indian and left his body to

hang and slowly twist in the eternal Yukon sun. A warning. A promise.

Henderson never caught the Indians who stole from him. The remainder of the winter passed slowly, a time of deprivation and hunger. Henderson had to spend as much time hunting as he did mining. He managed to shoot a moose and a caribou and roasted their flesh to eat, and still he nearly starved that winter. His teeth loosened and his gums bled. As spring broke two men came from Ogilvie and saw him washing his dump in the sluice and then they pressed on and Henderson kept working alone.

That whole winter and spring cleanup, Henderson washed out a total of thirty-six ounces of gold. Six hundred twenty dollars. Barely enough to pay back his grubstake to Joe Ladue.

It was June. By then Henderson had spent more than two years in the country. His face was black with frostbite and soot. He scraped insects from his skin with pitted fingernails. His leg ached. His food cache had been robbed. And he had nothing to show for it; only enough gold dust to break even.

So instead of returning to Ogilvie to pay back Ladue, Henderson decided to try something new.

The highest point, for miles around, was known as the Dome, a 4,300-foot massif from which sprang many long arms, ridges that separated one creek bed from another, and, at the highest elevation, the Indian River from other major tributaries of the Yukon.

At his work site on Quartz Creek's upper waters, Henderson was standing on the edge of the Dome. So instead of descending to the Indian River to the south, he decided to climb to the north, up the steep ridge, and in so doing, cross into a new watershed. He had never worked this valley before. It was known as a moose pasture, a place to hunt and fish, but no gold of any consequence had been pulled out of that land. All of these waters flowed into a river that the Indians called Thron-diuck, and all the white men called the Klondike.

Henderson worked his way down the Dome and spotted a gulley starting to bite into the land and he followed it until the streambed filled with water. He began his prospecting there, making his way along the creek, stopping every so often to drop his pan and scoop a little gravel and swish and swirl, carefully cleaning as he went. He panned just as he had on a dozen creeks a thousand times before. The gold flashed as the sand was swept aside. A few flecks of color. And then, all of a sudden, more. A bright comet's tail along the bottom lip. All told, about an eight-cent pan.

Eight cents! Henderson hadn't found an eight-cent pan since he came to the Yukon. Four times what he found on any of the surrounding creeks.

Eight cents was working wages; a man could get ahead on such pans. He couldn't believe his fortune, he was beside himself, and would have given a hoot if anyone was around to hear.

Henderson named the creek Gold Bottom, and he pounded four posts into the ground. On one he scratched his name, the date, and the dimension of the claim, one thousand feet of creek bed, twice the typical distance, as he was allowed double as the discoverer.

But he had to spread the news. That was the rule of the miners' code, to always tell any man when you staked on a new discovery. This social compact built trust between miners, let everyone share in the labor of the whole. A man could legally stake only a limited amount of creek anyway, so you lost nothing and had plenty to gain by doing as you wanted to be done by.

Henderson retraced his steps back over the ridge and returned to Joe Ladue's trading post via the Indian River. The claims office was in Fortymile, not Ogilvie, and nothing would be official on Gold Bottom Creek until he did the paperwork with the government. But Henderson figured he had time to finalize legalities later. He needed food, if he was to work his claim and not spend his time hunting, and for that he needed Ladue's continued investment in his grubstake. Only now he could report with confidence that the trust the trader had placed in him was worth it.

Back in Ogilvie, Ladue was ecstatic to hear Henderson's news; all his promotional tales about the east side of the Yukon had been right all along. Before he left, Henderson sent a letter to his younger brother Henry, who had convinced him to go north in the first place. The letter was dated June 20, 1896.

"Dear Brother, I am well and have struck it at last," he wrote.

Robert told his brother that the creek ran into the Klondike and he named it Gold Bottom. By next spring he expected to be cleaning up a fortune. At that time Henry Henderson was living in Nova Scotia, and it took many many months for the letter to reach him.

Ladue promised to tell every prospector he met about Henderson's find on Gold Bottom, adding that if the lode were as big as Henderson said, he'd plan to pack up Sixtymile and move his base camp to the Klondike.

Eighteen prospectors followed Henderson back to Gold Bottom, though all but four of them found the pace of Henderson's toil, not to mention the maddening incessant mosquitoes, too much to bear and so quit and soon returned to Ogilvie. That left five of them—Henderson, Munson, Swanson, Dalton, and Liberati—to do the work that summer to open the spot as a proper mining claim. They felled hearty trees and used long two-man whipsaws to cut proper lumber, for proper sluice boxes, and shoveled gravel and began to work real gold out of the earth. In just a few weeks' time, they pulled out $750, more than Henderson had seen in an entire season on Quartz Creek, and they divided it equally among themselves.

But five mouths ate far more food than one, and soon Henderson had to make the trip to Ogilvie again. By now it was late July, and the water was low, and Henderson knew he'd never get a fully laden boat up the Indian River. So after resupplying his grub, he decided to return to Gold Bottom via the Klondike River, which was known to be a deeper salmon stream. Not only would there be more water for his boat, but the trip would be faster than climbing the length of Quartz Creek, crossing the Dome, and then descending to the claim.

Henderson's hunch proved correct, there was plenty of water in the Klondike, and where it joined the Yukon he saw a small party of Indians fishing. Thron-diuck means "Hammer Water" in the local tongue, for the pounding required to drive stakes into the riverbed that held the netting of the salmon weirs strung across the mouth. The Indians had set up a small salmon-smoking operation, selling dried fish and bone butter, which they made from boiling skulls and horns and adding salt until the substance congealed.

On that day at the fishing station, Henderson

saw a small group of Indians and a hawk-nosed white man named George Washington Carmack. Fitting, to find Carmack engaged so, as he was known as a "squaw man," having taken an Indian for a wife. A fair number of men did this, in and of itself it was no source of shame. But Carmack was different. He seemed to have converted, gone over to their side somehow. Everyone knew Carmack wasn't a real miner.

"There is a poor devil who hasn't struck it," Henderson thought.

All the sourdoughs considered Carmack a lazy quitter who shunned respectable white man's work, choosing to be a packer and trapper with the Indians rather than a prospector with the whites. Which is why they all called him Siwash George, or Stick George, or Lying George. That's the one that counted. Lying George Carmack, for the undependability of his tall tales. Henderson knew you couldn't trust an Indian lover any more than the Indians themselves.

Fishing with Carmack was his wife, a dour dark-haired woman whom he had renamed Kate, as he found her Indian name unpronounceable. Joining them were several other Indians, including Skookum Jim and his nephews, Patsy and Tagish Charlie, sometimes also called No Good Charlie. Jim was a tall broad man of great physical strength. He had earned the name Skookum Jim, Strong Jim, when he carried

156 pounds of bacon over the sheer summit of the Chilkoot Pass for the chief surveyor Mr. William Ogilvie himself. On easier ground, he carried even more. Jim was Kate's brother, and along with Charlie and Patsy, plus each sibling's children, they all formed a family, traveling along the Yukon.

Henderson stopped to speak to Carmack as a courtesy alone.

"There has been a prospect found in a small creek that heads up against the Dome," said Henderson. "When I left the boys were running up an open cut to get to the bedrock."

"What are the chances to locate up there?" Carmack asked. "Everything staked?"

Henderson looked at Jim and Charlie. He thought of the miners' code that said that every man should tell another man when and where he's found a prospect. That everything should be shared. That every man should be done as they'd want done to them.

Henderson thought of what had been done to him. He thought of his empty belly the winter before. Of what had been taken from him. Of the Indians that other sourdoughs had strung up, for stealing from white men. Do as need be done.

Henderson shook his head. "Well, there's a chance for you, George," he said, "but I don't want any damn Siwashes staking on that creek." Then he pushed the boat off and paddled away.

Behind him, Jim and Charlie began to get angry. "What's the matter with that white man," Jim said. "He kills Indian moose, catches gold in Indian country, but doesn't like Indians to stake claims?" But Carmack soothed them quick.

"Never mind, Jim," he said. "This is a big country. We'll go find a creek of our own."

Henderson worked his way up the Klondike River to the point where Gold Bottom entered, and then limped his grub up the wash. It was late July and hot and he and the four other men continued their labors.

Several days later, as he worked his sluice, Henderson saw Carmack and Jim and Charlie approaching his camp on Gold Bottom. Carmack said they had been felling logs, to float down to the mill at Fortymile, and with nothing to eat but dried fish they were very hungry. Skookum Jim carried nothing but a Winchester rifle and a hatchet—one provided food, the other shelter—but they had no time for hunting, had no other supplies, and so they asked for spare grub and pipe tobacco.

Henderson refused.

Skookum Jim offered to pay, and this caused shame and embarrassment for both men. Henderson knew that under the miners' code he should give it up free, and Jim knew this as well; he was hard put to it, and needed the tobacco.

Henderson remembered again how hungry he

had been the year before, when the Indians had stolen his cache.

The anger hadn't gone away. No, he wouldn't budge, and without qualms. "They only get the same taste as I got," he thought.

Henderson told Carmack he had nothing to spare. The Indians and their Indian lover hefted their gear and turned around, but before they left Henderson called to them.

"Are you going to prospect on Rabbit Creek?" he asked Carmack. Rabbit Creek also fed the Klondike River, but was closer to the mouth where they fished.

"I think all those creeks are good," Henderson went on. "If you find anything better than mine let me know."

He needn't even have said this, though. Every prospector was honor bound to tell all others about a strike.

Carmack, Jim, and Charlie took their empty bellies back up over the hill. Henderson didn't hear another word about George Carmack for some time.

Work continued on Gold Bottom. Henderson and his companions shoveled out the creek bed and mounded the dumps, content in their eight-cent pans until, many weeks later at the end of September, two white men came down off the Dome. It was Charles Johnson and Andy Hunker, the first new faces Henderson had seen in some time. He called to them and asked where they had come from.

"Bonanza Creek," Hunker said.

Two and a half years in that country, the name was unknown to Henderson. His skin suddenly prickled, and he felt a great hole open in his guts.

"Bonanza Creek?" he replied, atremble. "Never heard of it. Where is it?"

They pointed back over the hill.

"What have you got there?" Henderson asked.

"We have the biggest thing in the world."

"Who found it?"

"Carmack."

CHAPTER TWO
1896

Good hard work is the most effectual
remedy for discontent.

—ETHEL BERRY

For many years to follow, Lying George Carmack told the story of the Klondike discovery this way:

When he and Skookum Jim and Charlie left Henderson, they followed the ridgeline west, off the Dome and back toward Rabbit Creek. It was slow going, a swamp of grass tussocks and half-frozen muck, sinking to their thighs in glacial ooze as they swatted mosquitoes. These were the murky headwaters of a series of creeks that fed the Klondike, and upon following one feeder stream, Carmack began to find pools of black sand that glinted in the sunlight. He led them down this creek, where they came to a major fork and then worked their way lower again. Carmack was in charge and ahead of Jim and Charlie, his head down like a bloodhound following a trail, when suddenly through the clear cold water he saw bare bedrock and a knowing flash.

"Look down there, boys," Carmack called. "If

this creek is good for anything at all, we surely ought to find gold down there."

Mixed in with the sand and gravel were gold flakes like grained wood shavings, and oblong and irregular lumps that had the look of something molten and cooled. Carmack dropped his pack, rubbed his misty eyes, leaned over, and picked up a gold nugget the size of a dime. There was so much gold layered between the slabs of bedrock, he thought they looked like cheese sandwiches.

Carmack figured they had somehow made it to an upper section of Rabbit Creek, one they hadn't explored before. He and Jim and Charlie moved up and down the stream, panning for the densest concentration of gold. They camped several days along that creek, and when he was satisfied they had found the best place, Carmack took a hatchet and chopped a blaze in a spruce tree and wrote this with a pencil in the exposed heartwood:

"TO WHOM IT MAY CONCERN: I do, this day, locate and claim, by right of discovery, five hundred feet, running upstream from this notice. Located this 17th day of August, 1896. G.W. Carmack."

Carmack then pulled out a rope, measured five hundred feet up the creek, and set another stake to mark his claim. Then he repeated the process, marking the section known as One Above discovery, which would be for Jim. Then

Carmack did the same downstream of his original marker, One Below for himself again—as the discoverer, he was allowed two claims—and then Two Below for Charlie. Two thousand feet in all, of what Carmack had decided to call Bonanza Creek.

Carmack told Skookum Jim to stay and guard the claim, as he and Charlie would go to Fortymile right away and file the legal paperwork. But as they made their way down to the Klondike River, they saw four white men coming up the ridge: McGilvray, McKay, Edwards, and Waugh, all experienced prospectors.

"Where do you think you're bound for?" Carmack asked.

"Well, we've just come down from upriver and heard at Ogilvie that a prospect has been found," said one of the men. They had obviously been sent by Joe Ladue to meet up with Henderson at Gold Bottom. "Do you know anything about it?"

"Yes, I left there three days ago."

"What do you think about it?" one asked.

"Well," Carmack said, and paused, drawing it out. In later years, he always liked telling this part of his story best. "I don't like to be a knocker, but I don't think much of it, and I wouldn't advise you to go up there."

The faces of the four men dropped in disappointment, until Carmack continued.

"I've got something better for you," he said,

49

and showed them his handful of gold nuggets.

So ends Carmack's version of the tale.

And that was how the miners' code was broken. Henderson's reprisal, Carmack's spite. Not only did Carmack never tell Henderson about the strike, he stopped anyone else from telling Henderson until it was far too late.

When Carmack strode into the saloon in Fortymile three days later, on August 20, 1896, he did so with a conceited air about him, the like of which was wholly out of character and, the assembled miners agreed, unbecoming as well.

Carmack's uppity tone did not seem to match his environs. Fortymile was a dreary collection of whiskey dens and moldering log cabins tossed about with no order or reason. Trash filled the streets, starving dogs ran rampant, and the dance hall generously known as the "opera house" was a place where the only singing consisted of barroom chants, and the only dancing partners to be had were Indians nursing infants on the tit or sporting girls turning tricks.

But Fortymile was also a place that provided every kind of service a miner could need, from blacksmiths to outfitters to druggists to barbers. And on the day Carmack arrived, the saloon was full, as miners had returned to town to gather their supplies for the coming winter. In town was Big Alex MacDonald, a land purchaser for the Alaska Commercial Company, who was also called the Big Moose for his enormous bulk, big lips, and sloping forehead. Also Swiftwater Bill, so named because he preferred to walk around rapids rather than run his boat through. Cannibal Ike, who liked to eat his kills raw. Howard Hamilton spent the winter chipping away the wood from the inside walls of his cabin; he said the thinned two-inch logs let in more light. Plus Crooked-Leg Louie, Slobbery Tom, and Pete the Pig, crazy old codgers all. Robert Henderson had never spent enough time with any of the men to earn a sobriquet; the other miners just called him Bob.

Carmack's name, on the other hand, was well known. Lying George.

The only man missing was the saloon's owner, Bill McPhee, who was temporarily all the way up in Circle City, many days' journey to the north. In his place, a bull-shaped young man named Clarence Jesse Berry was tending bar. New to the district, he had also earned no nickname as yet, and merely went by C.J. Like all Berry men, Clarence was bald, with a broad shiny cupola of a forehead and square foundational jaw, silhouette of a cathedral. He was a reluctant barkeep, but having just returned from a five-week failed prospecting trip, he needed the steady pay.

In this, Berry was typical. As a general rule, the men of Fortymile—some six hundred of them, mostly American—made only bare wages on their claims, just enough to keep them in the country another season, enough to order a drink at Bill McPhee's saloon but not enough to stay reliably drunk.

And so these sober-minded prospectors were suspicious of Carmack, as their common impression of him was less than complimentary. When Carmack strutted in, one miner turned to him and called out. "Hello there, you damned old meat-eating Siwash, how's fishing? Got any dried salmon to sell?"

The room laughed, for while they all would gladly eat Carmack's grub, they knew that even the unluckiest prospector was more reputable than a fishing squaw man like Siwash George.

"Boys, I've got some news to tell you," Carmack said. "There's a big strike up the river."

The men in the saloon were not interested in such talk, barely pausing their billiard games to scoff. They had heard all of Joe Ladue's confidence schemes already, and anyway, no one would believe that Carmack knew anything about prospecting.

So they mocked him again, laughed at Lying George, until he reached into his pocket and pulled out a brass cylinder the size of his little finger. It was one of Skookum Jim's Winchester cartridges, corked with a stick. Carmack removed the plug and poured out a small pile of gold sinker nuggets onto the bar.

"Well, how does that look to you, eh?" said Carmack.

"Is that some Miller Creek gold Ladue gave you?" the first man said, and everyone laughed again, but not as hearty and rough as before.

They all examined the nuggets. Every creek hosted its own particular combination of rock and water, and so ground gold according to its own unique signature that any miner with time in the country could read like handwriting. The prospectors crowded around to look.

This was not Miller Creek gold. This was gold of a shape and cast as they had never seen before.

It really was a new strike. A liar had just announced the truth.

"$2.50 to the pan," Carmack said. Two dollars and fifty cents was an almost insane boast, twenty times what any man would call a rich prospect. And none of them would have believed it, except there was Carmack, of all men, holding the proof.

Somehow, Lying George had discovered Klondike gold.

The stampede was on.

Fortymile emptied as if touched by the plague. Miners clambered into skiffs to pole their way back upstream on the Yukon River, or blistered their hands to pull a towline against the current. The inebriated were scooped up by their less tipsy brethren and dumped into boats like flour sacks. Nearly every inhabitant, and all their worldly possessions, would eventually move from Fortymile to the Klondike. After a few months, the several hundred miners of far northern Circle City would abandon their town as well, leaving behind only three invalids, two men and a woman.

No one was immune from the call of Carmack's gold; even Fortymile's priest left. Father Judge was an old-timer Jesuit missionary, sourdough as any miner, and for years he had watched men cripple themselves in frozen holes for a pitiful earthly reward. "If Men would only work for the kingdom of heaven with a little of that wonderful energy, how many saints we would have," he once said. But in Alaska all the treasure was to be found down below, not in heaven above, and few saints emerged. Father Judge made the move himself that winter, a solitary feeble man with a sled rope over his shoulder and a single dog breaking trail.

One of the last miners to leave Fortymile was Clarence Berry. And he left only at the urging of his wife, Ethel. For unlike nearly all other prospectors in the Yukon valley, the Berrys had come north as a team.

Clarence and Ethel grew up on nearby farms in the Central Valley of California, south of Fresno. At a certain age, the children stopped playing charades and spin-the-plate games, and Ethel started to wear a ruffling hoopskirt with a bustle whenever Clarence came calling at the house. Ethel had dark hair and round blue eyes as big and wide as those of the calves on the farm.

Clarence owned some land and worked a threshing machine, but wild swings in the prices of wheat and raisins had nearly driven his whole family to bankruptcy. And Clarence had no desire to move east and work for wages in the factories of the robber barons and tycoons. Ten cents an hour to pour steel or pack meat, only to be mangled in machinery or choked by coke dust. No, Clarence wanted none of it. He wanted to work for himself. So in the spring of 1894, he sold forty acres to pay for an outfit and boarded a steamer for Alaska, about the same time as Robert Henderson. Clarence was twenty-six years old, determined to return home rich so he could marry Ethel.

He arrived in Fortymile with only $3.60 left in his pocket, which he promptly spent on a round of whiskeys at the bar, in a successful attempt to ingratiate himself with the sourdoughs. First he worked another man's claim on Franklin Gulch, and then the next spring staked his own on Glacier Creek.

Berry was a tough fighter who worked hard and tried not to complain, but in one short season he saw his share of disappointment and death. Two men in his party drowned when they broke through river ice. Another froze to death, pneumonia took a fourth. Not every quarrel was solved at the miners' meetings, and as a big man, Berry found himself using his fists to solve disputes. "There are men that insist on trouble," he thought, "and the ones that I try to avoid are generally the ones I would have to accommodate."

But those accommodations wore on him, and afterward, he was full of regret. "I never got bested, I could understand why," he thought. "My, but I hate myself." That was not the man he wanted to be.

When the cold came on Clarence returned to California, no wealthier than when he left the year before, and he spent the early months of 1896 preparing for his next prospect. By far his best business decision was marrying Ethel, a wedding that went ahead despite his lack of gold. Unlike most miner's wives, living in a Victorian culture that prized feigned meekness and fragility, Ethel was intent on facing the north. She was built for hardship and work; her father called her Big Eth. She planned their Arctic journey with precision, packing unusually large quantities of ham, dried fruit, and tinned food, including vegetables. She also acquired knickerbockers, woolen stockings, high mukluk moccasins with the sealskin on the inside, and flannel dresses cut short—reaching only to below the knee, a scandal—so she could hike through snow.

Ethel, Clarence, and the youngest Berry brother, named Fred, arrived in that country in June 1896, and Clarence immediately set out with a partner to American Creek, about sixty miles further down the Yukon, leaving Ethel in Fortymile. But the venture quickly proved a failure. Berry was a farmer, not a hunter, and after a month they ran out of food, forcing them to head back to Ethel's cache. The boat trip upstream was demoralizing, the current of the Yukon relentlessly pushing against their efforts to pole forward. The last three days they had nothing whatsoever to eat.

Ethel met Clarence in tears.

The loneliness of his time away had nearly crushed her. "Nothing, absolutely nothing to do," Ethel lamented. The relentless misery of waiting and wondering, staring out a sham of a window made from stacked glass bottles and a bit of sackcloth. "I can not bear another minute, the utter blankness." She knew no one, had no work, no industry, and on the lowest days, she went to walk in Fortymile's small cemetery. It had almost broken her.

From then on, the Berrys decided that whatever they would do in the Yukon, they would do together.

But their money and supplies were running out fast. The first claim was fruitless. Clarence was impatient working for any other man, and while he appreciated his job at Bill McPhee's saloon, it was a temporary proposition. They needed a new plan.

After Carmack showed off his discovery and Fortymile wizened into a ghost town, Clarence kept his solitary post at the saloon, waiting for McPhee to return. He was reluctant to go, discouraged by his prospecting failures thus far. Even if they wanted to go, the Berrys lacked the money for a full winter's outfit. When McPhee did make it back to Fortymile a few days later, Clarence remained too depressed to do more than tend bar.

In the end, it was Ethel who pushed Clarence to ask McPhee for the grubstake and join the stampede. She told Clarence to go ahead without her, while she packed their few meager belongings and would follow soon after.

And so Clarence and his younger brother Fred went to the Klondike River, carrying as little as possible, to move quickly. On arrival they found a swarm of activity like they had never seen before.

Carmack's Bonanza Creek was wallpapered with the anxious and fevered. All about them, men were climbing the rock faces, slipping and sliding as they worked their way higher, amid the windswept scrub, to stake their claims. When a man fell asleep from exhaustion, he was awakened by another boatful of whooping prospectors, scrambling to reach a patch of unclaimed gulch.

At Number One Bonanza, the discovery claim, George Carmack and Skookum Jim and Tagish Charlie all worked the open pit, amateurishly, with crude sluice boxes. Jim and Charlie dug out virgin muck while George worked the bottom of the flume, the tail end, shoveling up those tailings and running them through again. A stampeder asked him why he did this, as normally tailings were nothing but worthless sand and gravel, but Carmack said the dirt was so full of gold he still got $5 a pan off the second run. He put his hand in his pocket and pulled out three nuggets.

"Fished 'em out of the bottom of the creek with a shovel," Carmack said. The three alone were worth about $25.

"Jimminy-crickets," said one man.

"Well, I'll be hanged," said another.

Then the two ran off to stake their claims.

Clarence and Fred Berry looked for a stretch of unclaimed creek, and found that Bonanza had already been completely staked below Carmack's discovery claim. This was typical. Gold dust accumulates as it runs downhill—collecting at the bottom faster than it was mysteriously ground free up top, or so men believed—so lower claims were prized. With all six miles below already spoken for, Clarence moved uphill, past other stampeders' claims, and staked at the next available spot, Forty Above discovery. Forty claims from Carmack's find, or nearly four miles farther up the ridge. By the end, stampeders would stake a total of eight miles above the initial discovery, almost to the Dome itself.

When Bonanza was all taken, men started staking the creek's branches, the gullies and feeder creeks known as pups. One of those pups came in from the south, at Seven Above discovery, less than a mile from Carmack's claim. Even from the first days, there was mud in the water, meaning at least one man was already working, having judged it the best prospect from the beginning. Some said the pup was full of five-cent pans and some said it would be richer than Bonanza.

Old man Whipple wanted to name the pup Whipple Creek but everyone knew Whipple was nothing but a claims jumper, and so when one of the Swedes suggested they name it Eldorado, everyone agreed to that. Where Bonanza and Eldorado joined together was the heart of the mining district and would soon be called Grand Forks.

Not everyone on the stampede was enthusiastic. Some old-timers arrived at the Klondike, looked around, and then left, dissatisfied. That Joe Ladue seemed involved suggested the whole thing was likely one of his promotional schemes. Plus the signs were all wrong, gold would never come out of that place. They said the water didn't taste right and the willows leaned the wrong way.

"I'll leave it to the Swedes," said one sourdough, as everyone knew the Scandinavians were willing to work the most meager prospects. Let the outsiders and tenderfeet have their moose pasture, they'd slink back as failures soon enough. Plenty staked and left; one traded half of his claim for a sack of flour. Many a sourdough declared the Klondike nothing but a bunco.

After Clarence and Fred drove their stakes into the ground they returned immediately to Fortymile to file the legal paperwork. While there Clarence met a man named Anton Stander, who had filed a claim on Eldorado but was now so broke he couldn't buy an outfit and could find no one to grubstake him. Clarence stepped up and with bravado and nothing else, as his pocketbook was empty as well, swore that he'd back up Anton and guarantee the bill.

The ruse worked, and in gratitude, Anton offered to trade half his Number Six Eldorado claim for half of Berry's Forty Above discovery. In so doing, each man was hedging his bet, though both men knew Berry was likely getting the better end of the deal. Stander had said he got $6 a pan on Eldorado. Six dollars. That was a week's worth of wages back in California in just a single pan.

Fred and Clarence hurried back to Bonanza, leaving Ethel to finish packing and catch the first steamer upstream. More waiting. "Patience is a virtue which I am fast attaining," she thought.

She hoped it would all be worth it somehow, just a few lucky pans.

By the time Ethel arrived, a rude village was already growing out of the floodplain at the mouth of the Klondike River. At the suggestion of Robert Henderson, Joe Ladue had packed up his post at Ogilvie and gone downstream at the earliest opportunity. He arrived soon after Carmack's announcement in Fortymile, and instead of staking a claim, he began to survey a townsite for the hundreds of miners flooding in from Ogilvie, Fortymile, and Circle City.

The only flat space of any size in the region was a muskeg bog of mud and rotting deadfalls on the north side of the Klondike, right where it emptied into the Yukon. The bank was twenty feet above the river, fronting a large eddy that collected late-summer scum. Ladue laid out a town of 160 acres, a mile by a mile and a half. To the north, the town was bounded by Moose-Hide Mountain, named on account of the rock slide that had left a great gray scar upon its face. To the west, across the river, rose steep bare slopes. To the south lay the Indians' small salmon-drying camp, though they had already been run off, as a stampeder's raft of logs had destroyed their fish weirs. To the east lay opportunity, the Elysian fields of gold.

Less than a month after Carmack walked into that saloon in Fortymile, most of the white men in the Yukon valley, a thousand strong, had converged on Ladue's tent camp. The place would be named for the director of the Canadian Geological Survey, a man who would never set foot there: Dawson City.

Robert Henderson passed through Dawson just after its founding. He was headed to Fortymile, where the government mining office was still located, to file his claim on Gold Bottom Creek. But when he arrived, the office told him it was too late. New government regulations said he had to file within sixty days, and his time was up.

Henderson's discovery claim had gone to another man, who decided he didn't like the name Gold Bottom Creek, he wanted to name it something else. The mining commissioner told Henderson that the stream was called Hunker Creek, after Andy Hunker, the man who was credited with its discovery. It was Andy Hunker who months before had crossed the Dome and told Henderson about Bonanza and Carmack and the biggest rush he had ever seen.

Henderson had missed the stampede, and now he wasn't even permitted to work his eight-cent pans. The commissioner allowed him to make a compensatory claim up Hunker Creek, but Henderson's crippled leg was raw from overwork and as winter came on he found himself waylaid in another sickbed.

Henderson would never stake a share of Klondike gold.

．．．

About six hundred claims were posted in the initial euphoric wave, and at first no one knew what they had. The claims were all anticipation, no realization. Anything could be hidden in the ground. Or nothing.

But as they worked, men began to call out their finds. Ten dollars a pan here and five dollars there, then a nugget worth twelve. The first to build a sluice box were McGilvray, McKay, Edwards, and Waugh, the four men Carmack had met on his way to Fortymile and told of his discovery. They staked Number Thirteen, Fourteen, Fifteen, and Sixteen Below, and decided to work together to use the last of autumn's flowing water to wring the surface gravel. They found coarse gold that stuck, and lots of it. The men quickly put the gold in sacks and ran to Joe Ladue so he could weigh it.

Nearly fifteen pounds of the stuff, worth over $4,000.

"How's that for two and half days shoveling," said Ladue.

The days were growing cold, though, and mining had to be put on hold, at least temporarily, to build shelter and stash away grub to survive the coming snow. At first, Ethel Berry pitched her tent on the edge of Dawson, in an open area she heard was an Indian graveyard. She told Clarence it made her nervous, but he said not to worry, that if they were buried deep enough, the bodies were frozen tight.

Stampeders began requesting lumber, to build cabins, and the always entrepreneurial Ladue returned to Ogilvie to break down his sawmill and float it downstream. Timber was scarce and food was already growing short too. The flat-bottomed stern-wheeled steamer that had delivered Ethel in September was the only cargo vessel to resupply the new town that fall. Soon after ice began to form and the ship was caught on its way back downriver. Attempts to remove the steamer, using dynamite, would result in the boat's destruction. Joe Ladue's sawmill ran full out cutting lumber, but it was expensive, nails and hardware more so. One man remarked that it cost as much to build a cabin in Dawson as a brownstone in New York City.

In the Klondike, everything was scarce except gold.

In November, the temperature fell below zero and stayed there. Snow came in, the Klondike and Yukon froze, and Ethel was finally able to move up to their claim on Eldorado, where Clarence and Fred were sawing wood for a cabin. The trip was nineteen miles, the air temperature 13 degrees below zero, and it took her two days of hard climbing to reach the site.

Clarence and Fred built the cabin from logs chinked with mud and moss, to keep out cold drafts and mosquitoes alike. Near their cabins, many miners set in poles, or boats cut in half, to prop up little boxes accessible by ladders. This is where everyone put their caches of food, so dogs and bears wouldn't get in them. At first, the Berry cabin consisted of a single main room, sixteen by twenty feet, but on initial construction Clarence did not put in a door, so Ethel had to wait while he sawed a hole. In time they put in a window as well, an old sack again, to let in a feeble light.

By now, there was little sun to be had, though. Their cabin was ringed by hills, and so the sun hardly showed its face, spending most of its day below the horizon or behind the surrounding ridges. "Dark, dreary country," thought Ethel. At about half-past one, when the skimming sun sank for the night, she lit the oil lamps.

Ethel worked hard to improve the home where she spent so much time. She acquired some calico cloth and covered the ceiling and sectioned off part of the cabin for a bedroom, where she made a bed of pine boughs. A tub of water squatted near the door, to clean up some pay dirt each day, and near a small window she hung frying pans from nails and set a shelf with a little gold scale. She spent much of her day keeping the fire going in the narrow, sheet-iron stove. "Turn your back on the fire for a moment it burns up and goes out." A bucket left even a few feet away from the woodstove would freeze. Every day the food had to be thawed before it could be cooked, and the inside walls, being made of green logs, were rimed with ice, as the moisture was slowly drawn out. On the coldest days, the nails in the cabin walls popped and snapped like gunfire. The whole place smelled of woodsmoke, wet hair and fur, bodies grimed from weeks of exertion, soiled clothes.

Ethel felt that she had only one friend available to her, as there was only one other woman in her circumstances. Her name was Salome. She was married to Tom Lippy, from Seattle, and lived in a cabin about a mile away. They were the only two wives in the Klondike.

Well, other than Kate Carmack and the other Indian wives, of course. But Ethel stayed away and didn't talk to Kate. To her, the Indians just seemed so dirty, and hard to understand. Ethel only spoke to them long enough to show off her mirror and a few trinkets, and it took her a long time to even eat the caribou the Indians killed.

The extreme cold elicited laziness among many sourdoughs. They passed the winter the way they always had. Taking an Indian woman. Telling lies. Betting on every trifle, like whether a man would enter a room with his left foot or right. Holding miners' meetings over this or that petty infraction. Drinking. First the whiskey, and then a hooch distilled from black molasses, boiled in old kerosene cans with a worm box made from shabby rubber boots. That rotgut tasted like pickled carrion, but some said it cured scurvy.

As winter set in, many moved on. Experienced prospectors who had worked Fortymile Creek and other rockier sites were discouraged by the quicksand gravel and depth of the muck; they sold their claims for a song and left that country. Others arrived too poor to work, lacked the outfit to survive the winter on the creeks, and retreated to Dawson to huddle against the cold and do labor for better-prepared men. Of the six hundred claims, only about twenty saw significant production that winter.

Ethel couldn't stake a claim herself because it was illegal for a woman to do so. For the Berrys to acquire more claims then, Clarence kept trading portions of his existing holdings, acquiring stakes in other sections of creek bed from less-business-minded prospectors. He and Anton Stander, whose grubstake Clarence guaranteed at the start of the stampede, eventually bought Number Four and Five Eldorado, and a sliver of land between Five and Six besides. In all, Clarence then owned a controlling interest in over 1,500 feet of Eldorado Creek. This section became known as the Berry Claims.

Clarence and Ethel were determined to work that winter. But Clarence didn't dig into the earth. He burned his way in, mining with fire.

In summer, the sun's rays were sufficiently

strong to every day thaw the first foot of frozen earth, which a miner could remove with a shovel and dump in his rocker. But as October turned to November, and the days shortened, and the creeks froze and the snow piled up, a black hood fell over the lonely valley, with only four dismal hours of thin starved sun a day. As shadow and darkness ruled, a miner could gain nothing except through ceaseless toil. A pick could break the first layer of muck, but once the primordial frozen gravel was reached, nothing dented it. Mattocks and shovels bounced off. Dynamite left empty holes and tightened rock. To delve any deeper they had to burn a path into the gloom.

The shaft was six feet by four feet, a grave. At the bottom miners piled wood on the gravel and started the fire with a candle and pitch pine. They added dry spruce, then heavy dried logs, then green wood on top. The green lumber burned slower and held the heat in the pit.

They were burning to bedrock, twelve or twenty or even fifty feet deep. On the way down they found all manner of skeletons and ancient secrets. In the top layers were pieces of caribou and moose, but as they got lower, strange animals emerged that had not been seen in that land in thousands of years. The horns of great bison, and mastodon tusks, and other fantastical creatures, freeze-dried flesh still clinging to bone.

When they reached bedrock, the miner began

a drift, a horizontal tunnel along the rock face to find the paystreak, the narrow concentrated path of gold dust. But the paystreak followed the direction of the stream in eons past, not its present course, and so there was no way to predict exactly where it would be found. The miners burned their drifts at right angles to the inclined creek bed so the paystreak could be intercepted crosswise. But after twenty-five feet of burrowing, the air would grow foul and vertiginous. In the winter, fresh cold air would naturally drop into the shaft, warmer stale smoke rising and drifting away, but dig too deep and the holes filled with head-spinning fatal vapors, enough to choke and overcome a man. Then you had to drop a new shaft, to search for the paystreak anew, like a rifleman hoping to hit the target with his eyes closed.

Once they found the streak, they followed it like a royal edict, as it contained the vast share of the claim's gold. Every night they burned the drift, and in the morning when the smoke cleared they shoveled among the slushy wet ashes and acrid fumes, stockpiling the most valuable gravel in a dump near the top of the shaft. Yet even on a paying claim the gold is not equally dispersed, and fractured bedrock or an old landslide could steer the streak wildly or cut it off entirely. So some miners would open a series of galleries along the paystreak, with occasional pillars of frozen ground left to support the roof. This was tough, dangerous work, and yet easier than open-pit excavation, as only the richest dirt was removed. And still, it often took a month to hit bedrock, and another month to burn a drift across the streak, the muck and gravel so sodden that fires stayed weak and smoky and never penetrated far.

At least two men were required to work a winter claim, one to dig underground and fill the bucket with gravel, the other to crank the windlass to pull the bucket up and then pile the dump. In some ways, the man at the bottom of the shaft, standing in the mire and shoveling last night's embers in the foul stifling air, had it easy. The temperature in the shaft, while barely above freezing, was significantly warmer than outside. The man at the top, working the windlass, took the full winter blast all day. In the deepest cold, eyelids can freeze shut, and one can hear his own breath as he exhales warm air and it crystallizes into ice shards on contact. They took to wearing long Indian parkas, not inferior white man's denim but thick animal skins, plus trousers made of seal, boots of walrus, mittens of bear, and hoods of dog.

The job was this: dig the dirt, fill the bucket, crank the windlass, one hundred times a day. Two shovels make one pan, sixteen shovels make one bucket, sixteen hundred shovels a day make honest work. Every day.

Clarence Berry woke in darkness, ate in darkness, mined in darkness. He spent his days in that icy poisoned pit, and when at the end of his labors he finally ascended to the surface he could look across the night-black valley and see, claim by claim, Dante's Ninth Circle come to life, glowing fires burning in a frozen hell. Each hole looked like a belching smokestack, and come morning thick dark woodsmoke hung in the valley like a noxious fog.

One day in November, twelve feet deep into his claim on Eldorado, Clarence put his shovel in the half-frozen muck as he had ten thousand times before. Except this time when he turned over the dirt it was so thick with gold dust it shone in the candlelight.

Frank Keller, who shared the claim via one of Berry's trading schemes, was at the top of the shaft. Clarence called to him.

"What do you want?" Keller asked.

"Get a gold pan," he said.

Clarence filled the pan and told Keller to take it to Ethel so she could wash it proper. Keller did, and when he returned he said it was a $3 pan.

They were onto something.

Clarence climbed out of the black hole into the black night. The air above was 80 degrees colder than in the shaft, and his sweat instantly froze to his body. It was late, time for bed, and Clarence returned to his cabin and tried to sleep but found himself tossing and turning and soon he was back up again, in the hole, filling the bucket with dirt and then climbing out and pulling it up with the windlass and heaping it on the dump. He worked all night and into the morning darkness, and when the sun rose for a few weak hours, he labored on. The farther he dug, the more gold he saw.

Fred Berry returned to camp, hauling a cache of food they had stashed on the riverbank. Clarence came up to him and shook his hand and the older brother's eyes went wet. Fred looked uncertain, a hedge against hope and misinterpretation of his brother's emotion. But then Clarence simply filled a pan with new dirt from the dump and cleaned it with water Ethel had just boiled and handed it to Fred.

Mounds of gold. A $50 pan.

The Berry family would never want for money ever again.

Gold came in every possible shape and size and consistency. Leaf gold, flour gold, wire gold, gold dust, gold flakes, coarse gold, nuggets. That fall, all up and down Bonanza and Eldorado, miners found all those kinds of gold, in quantities that boggled the mind. Eight-dollar pans here, $10 there. On November 23, a miner by the name of Rhodes, on Twenty-One Above discovery, got a $65.30 pan. The pans kept coming. Fifty-dollar pans, then $116, then $212 off Number Sixteen Eldorado.

The first claim to reach bedrock was Number Fourteen Eldorado, in December. Men discarded $5-a-pan dirt to get to the $100-a-pan variety. By Christmas, men were pulling out $500 pans and $200 nuggets. It was like nothing the world had ever seen. In the California rush of '49, the best pans ran 35 or 40 cents.

That winter, the Yukon valley froze tight until mid-April; for three weeks in March the high temperature never broke 50 below. The cold killed the soft pretenders and merely violent, leaving only those toughened by the crucible. Despite the high earnings, some men quit for the winter, it was so dark and cold. A few dug through the floors of their cabins, fifteen feet down, to see if a paystreak happened to lie right below them. But most simply hunkered against the elements, praying for the worst to pass.

But not the Berrys. Both Clarence and Ethel excelled at the dogged adherence to chores, a farmer's work ethic that served both well. Digging and hauling, boiling water, cooking, laundry, day after day after day. To drift that winter, Clarence burned thirty cords of wood, a wall of split timber four feet thick, eight feet high, and 120 feet long. In the mine, his arms were like iron bands, his broad chest a kiln. He excavated by hand half a ton of gravel a day, frost crusting his stubbled whiskers, shoveling in ankle-deep water and mud.

All winter, he didn't stop. He didn't quit early. He didn't get cold feet.

If Clarence was the grunt labor, Ethel was a one-woman logistics battalion. She tended fires day and night. She kept the books for their own claims, and then became the de facto accountant for the other miners on Eldorado. She made moose sausage. Delicate as chicken, it was said. Her presence was a great, almost unique, advantage for the Berrys. Other miners worked all day underground and then collapsed at night, too exhausted to kick a dog for stealing food. They had little energy to eat or care for themselves, and so grew thin and dirty and prone to disease and want.

Meanwhile, Ethel cooked all day to feed Clarence and Fred and their crews. "Even before we have a table to eat from, we have nine to a luncheon," she said. With so many claims, Clarence needed help to pull all their gold out of the ground, so he began to hire men for $15 a day, an extraordinary wage. Ethel's kitchen allowed this expansion of the operation, and Clarence knew how lucky he was to have her. "Beans without grease might be alright for a while, but try it for three months," he thought, remembering his time alone the year before.

And on nights when the temperature fell below 40 degrees of frost, and the mercury in the thermometers froze, the Berrys clung to each other for warmth while up and down the valley solitary men shivered to shake the dead. The coldest night was minus 72 degrees.

When Ethel was done with her cabin chores for the day, she would join Clarence at the dumps, to hunt the creek edge for coarse gold nuggets and hide them in her apron pocket. Then she'd fill a bucket from the dumps and take it back to the cabin, where she boiled water to melt the silty gravel and pan out the gold. She got so skilled that she became paymaster for the crew, often cleaning up $150 worth of pans a day to settle with the men. In all, she washed $7,000 worth of gold that winter. Her best single pan contained $195 in bright gold dust.

By the end of April, the beating sun broke Bonanza and Eldorado creeks, quenching the fires and flooding the drifts. Until the frost returned in September, men could work only the surface dumps, and so it was time for spring cleanup. The sawmill at Dawson again ran full tilt, to keep up with the demand for board to build sluice boxes to clear the dumps and discover the sum total of what each miner had collected all winter. Most claims had enough gold in them to buy a quantity of alcohol sufficient to kill the man who mined it. Meanwhile, some miners burned five or six shafts and never found the paystreak. All the claims past Forty-Two Above discovery on Bonanza ended up being worthless, though no one knew that at the time.

Spring cleanup created a new class of prospecting royalty: the Klondike King. All agreed that Big Alex MacDonald was the richest man, with interests in twenty-eight claims. Instead of spending his time digging, MacDonald had used his experience as a former agent of the Alaska Commercial Company to become a land-swapper. Speculation ruled, and he knew that actually working a claim almost always decreased its value. MacDonald was $150,000 in debt, borrowing money to purchase more claims, but it bothered him none as he said he could dig $150,000 out of the ground anytime he wanted.

Professor Lippy, on Number Sixteen Eldorado, was judged second richest, and the Berrys were deemed to be third. Clarence's crews dropped twenty shafts, and found a paystreak nine feet thick, 150 feet wide, and 500 feet long. Every pan contained at least a dollar in gold, and one time Clarence cleaned $560 in a single go. That spring Ethel filled every baking powder can and old pot and jar with gold dust, and Clarence put aside three glass bottles that, he said, each contained the gold from a single memorable pan. The far upper end of Number Five Eldorado proved especially rich; every shovel of dirt in the streak held $250 in gold, and paid, on average, $1,000 a foot.

As Clarence wished to keep his money, he knew he needed to leave. Grub and gear were expensive but life was cheap, and none of them were really worth anything until they got the gold out. It was time to go home.

They had to wait until the ice floes in the Yukon cleared and the steamships arrived. When the river breaks up, it does so in fits and starts. Great platters of ice float and crash into one another and form a jam, slide overtop then tip so they stand ten feet in the air, and then burst apart as the pressure of the flood builds behind them.

Finally in late May the Yukon was free of ice, and two paddle-wheel steamers left Dawson, bearing about eighty miners who had struck it rich. The Berrys were on board, as well as Joe Ladue. Gold dust was stuffed in suitcases and sealed jam jars and tight wooden boxes. Ethel wore a string of nuggets as a necklace.

The riverboat dropped them at the tiny port of St. Michael, on the Bering Sea, where two other ships awaited, the *Portland* and the *Excelsior*, both bound for the American West Coast. The Berrys chose the *Portland*, as it was departing first. The *Excelsior*, however, made better headway, and landed in San Francisco before them. By the time the Berrys reached Seattle, on July 17, 1897, the news of the strike in the Klondike had already spread, and a crowd of five thousand people awaited them on the docks.

Armed bank guards met the *Portland* and carried off four thousand pounds of gold dust worth over a million dollars. About five hundred pounds of it belonged to the Berrys. They were worth $130,000, the richest on the ship.

The newspaper reporters asked Clarence how he did it.

"I question seriously whether I would have done so well if it had not been for the excellent advice and aid of my wife," he told them. "I want to give her all the credit that is due to her, and I can assure you that it is a great deal."

Naturally, the reporters swarmed Ethel. She was wearing a ragged dress, a man's necktie as a belt, and shoes whose soles flapped when she walked. The reporters asked her over and over why she went to the Yukon. Ethel answered as if the reason should have been intuitively obvious to all.

"I went because my husband went, and I wanted to be with him," she said.

From then on, in all the newspapers, Ethel Berry was known as the Bride of the Klondike.

CHAPTER THREE
1897

One does not fully comprehend the
helplessness of average mankind until he
meets some of these men on the streets.
—TAPPAN ADNEY

America's Gilded Age was always rotten at the
core. Glittering estates and palaces of commerce
for the Vanderbilts and the Carnegies, the squalid
tenement and factory floor for the masses. Two
entire generations of workers had been sacrificed
to that grinder to make the Rockefellers rich. But
when the gleaming veneer cracked, the whole
system fell apart, and the country lapsed into
a stupor like it had never known. The Panic of
1893 was the worst depression the United States
had yet endured.

The railroads—the revolutionary technology
of the age, and engine of overnight trade and
communication—had been overvalued and over-
built, growth fueled through acquisitions that
hid inherent instability. Companies like Union
Pacific were so big, no one thought they could
fail, and yet one by one they crumbled. Over 150
railroads would go bankrupt by the end.

Entrepreneurs had borrowed heavily to fuel their expansions, but eventually the speculative financing imploded. Wall Street suddenly realized it was overleveraged and many companies' paper worth far exceeded the reality. Bankers got spooked and stopped lending money, businesses of all kinds started to go broke, workers lost jobs, homeowners defaulted, and then the banks fell too. In 1893 alone, nearly six hundred banks and fifteen thousand businesses went bankrupt.

Those who lost their homes went west. They settled in Seattle, Portland, San Francisco, Los Angeles. They went west because Americans had always gone west for opportunity but this time they didn't find any, because the Panic had hit the fragile new economies in Washington and California especially hard. Machines took jobs from skilled workers, as everything from shoes to wagon wheels was now made in factories. Global markets were increasingly tied together, and while business owners made record profits, real wages for average workers declined. Homes lost so much of their value that across the country mortgage debt far outstripped equity. The unemployment rate hit nearly 20 percent. A deep and wide depression took hold of the country and did not shake its grip for years.

When these pillars toppled, the public lost faith in institutions of all kinds. The Senate was so packed with the wealthy elite that it was known as the Millionaires Club. The politicians were seen as protectors of the monopolies, the banks, and the Wall Street magnates, and the gap between rich and poor was a widening chasm.

There was a great uprising. The movement was called Populism, and in their call to action they proclaimed that "The fruits of the toil of millions are boldly stolen to build up the colossal fortunes for a few." William Jennings Bryan, their firebrand senator, crisscrossed the country, packing halls with the power of his oration, railing against businessmen and government inaction alike. The "soldiers" of Coxey's Army—hundreds of out-of-work protesters demanding jobs—marched on Washington in 1894, and St. Louis and Baltimore were set ablaze by rioters after young men on union picket lines were shot in the streets by police.

The contrast between tycoons and tramps was embodied in the dual financial systems that existed simultaneously. The United States used two types of dollars, those backed by gold and those backed by silver. While the two should nominally have been worth the same, in practice there was one system for the rich and another for the poor. A gold dollar was worth more than a silver dollar. The government set a firm exchange rate of sixteen ounces of silver for one ounce of gold, but while silver was available widely, gold was scarce on commodity markets and in government treasuries. So for all practical purposes, a silver dollar was worth only 85 cents, and thus the rich hoarded the full-worth gold dollars for themselves, and left the cheap silver for everyone else.

When the Panic originally struck, the Congress and President Grover Cleveland moved to restore business confidence at the expense of workers. The Populists called corporations the root of the problem, acting as overlords and masters of the people, and said that Washington had sold out to J. P. Morgan and the rest of the Wall Street bankers, who only grew wealthier making personal loans to the government.

The old-time political machines and pundits got nervous, as the Populists gained in the polls. In a rebuke to the party establishment, the Populist hero Senator Bryan gained the Democratic nomination for president in 1896. In response, massive corporations like Standard Oil and the Chicago meatpackers funded William McKinley, the Republican nominee who promised to keep the strong gold dollar and impose high tariffs to protect American businesses. John D. Rockefeller and his fellow industrialists spent unprecedented millions of dollars in an effort to put their man in office.

It worked. The old line held. The Populists lost in the presidential election of 1896, and the depression dragged on.

In a last gasp America's Gilded Age had finally come to an end. A subdued and burdened malaise smothered the nation. The country had lost hope. And the desperate poor seemingly powerless to change their fate.

And then, in July of 1897, the answer to all of America's problems appeared on the front page of every newspaper in the country.

The papers said there was gold in the Klondike.

Tappan Adney was in New York City when he first saw the headlines like everyone else.

The front page of the July 18 edition of the *New York Journal* read: "TON AND A HALF MORE YUKON GOLD."

More? How much was there before?

And then right below: "Second Treasure Ship Arrives from the Frozen Klondyke Placers."

A second ship? What about the first? Adney and every other reader was missing out already, though on what he was not yet precisely sure.

Adney paid attention to headlines because he was a reporter, though a peculiar one. In truth, he was at heart a naturalist, inclined to spend weeks and months out-of-doors in remote wilderness, all to write stories of rugged adventure for genteel salon-bound readers back home. So this Klondike bit struck a nerve.

From then on Adney followed the stories, day by day, as did seemingly the whole country.

William Randolph Hearst's *Journal* and *San Francisco Examiner* had missed the initial wire reports of Clarence Berry's disembarkation, and so for many weeks to come, they made up for that out-of-character lapse in sensationalism by trumpeting every bit of Klondike minutiae thereafter as if it were breaking news.

All that summer, the *Journal* had run depressing headlines: coal miners on strike, gas monopolies growing and raising prices, widespread economic collapse.

So what a jarring change on July 19 a dual deadline was. While the right side of the paper contained the same heartache Adney had read since the Panic—"2000 Strikers March: Bloodshed Is Feared"—the left side beamed hope: "Pacific Coast Is Gold Mad." The lead column—"Miners Who Have Returned Predict Death and Starvation in Dawson City"—was classic Hearst, coy titillation wrapped in a dare.

The outlines of the story seemed simple enough. Recent returnees called the Klondike the richest goldfield ever discovered, "$70,000,000 in sight," as if it was right there, lying on the ground. And it was all tenderfeet who hit the jackpot, lucky greenhorns who went north as a "last resort" and couldn't help but succeed as the gold was "yards deep and yards wide." Clarence Berry was listed as the richest of these prospectors, and when asked by reporters about the opportunity for others, he said: "Grit, perseverance and luck will probably reward a hard worker with a comfortable income for life." The papers claimed Berry himself was now worth $135,000. The average man working at the standard 10-cent hourly wage would have to labor every day for two and a half centuries to make that kind of money.

Adney could feel it, this craze was different from California in 1849. There, in the Sierra Nevada, you needed a big crew and hydraulic pumps to wash away the side of the hill, to reach the little bit of hidden gold. This placer mining, on the other hand, seemed like a one-man job. Not for wages from a master, but to build something, on one's own, by himself for himself. A man could become his own J. P. Morgan or Vanderbilt up there. Clarence Berry already had. Take a little journey and work hard and dig in the ground just a bit and you too could have what had been denied to the common man the whole Gilded Age.

And back in '49, the whole rush to San Francisco was only partially about the gold anyway. Everyone seemed to want to go to fair paradisal California, take the land from Mexico and open the West. The gold just provided a good excuse and motivation to do it quick. No, this time the stories were different. No one dreamed of homesteading in Alaska. Enduring the faraway cold seemed like a small price to pay, though, to pick up all that gold just lying there.

And magnifying it all, a modern invention. "Nowadays," Adney thought, "the news is carried by telegraph and newspaper to all parts of the world." Almost instantaneously, in fact; being first with the story was now the most important consideration of all, far outweighing the facts.

By the end of that week, newspapers across the country were full of advertisements for stampeder supplies, outfitters and steamship passage, and palm readers, astrologists, Egyptian occultists, and clairvoyants to predict where the gold was to be found. Women who were unencumbered and matrimonially inclined took out want ads, advertising a desire to go to the Klondike. One was blunt: "I have read everything in the papers about the gold up there, and I am free to confess I want some of it." Another said she was twenty-eight years old, "young enough to see a good bit of happiness, and yet old enough to have gotten over romancing," and so she was "willing to chance it—you, marriage, Alaska and all." The women's mailboxes filled with applications.

On July 21, only four days after the first *San Francisco Chronicle* headline, herds of men already gathered on the docks in Seattle, jamming every steamship bound for Alaska. The wire dispatch called it "a crowd at once weird, strange, and picturesque." Adney was entranced by the spectacle. "The country has gone mad over this Klondike business," he decided. Klondicitis, they called it. An affliction, a disease of the mind that drove a man north. While all occupations seemed susceptible to the contagion, reports said streetcar drivers and policemen were leaving in the greatest numbers. Not the most destitute; a person needed a little money to afford the fare and outfit. Instead, Klondicitis seemed to particularly infect those who, by virtue of their class or race or station of birth, thought they deserved more. Bankrupt proprietors and clerks, failed bankers, farmers kicked off their land. Plus famous men: ex-governors, failed Senate candidates, retired generals, the graybeard "Poet of the Sierras" Joaquin Miller, former cowboys and Civil War veterans, all grasping for reclaimed glory.

Soon passage was sold out. Every leaking tub and rusty steamer up and down the West Coast was being pressed into service, wharves in Seattle and San Francisco sagging under the weight of the crowds elbowing their way on board. You had to believe the hype, people said. This wasn't some fantasy. You had to believe the stories because the miners had brought back proof. The gold. You had to believe in the gold.

The contrast in the daily headlines could not be more stark. While hungry tramps staged a "Midnight March for Bread," and "Congress Betrays the People to the Trusts" by making backroom deals with Wall Street speculators and Standard Oil millionaires, in Alaska, "It's Gold, Gold, Gold Everywhere." The front pages were for hype; caveats did not come until the inner folds. Often quoted was a man named Joe Ladue, who was described as the founder of Dawson City. He gave a long interview to the *New York Journal* that was summarily ignored.

"I am appalled at the prospect," he said. "Everybody seems to be gold mad, and if one third of those who have talked about going to the Klondike reach there, death in its most horrible form will surely follow." He did not expect his advice to be heeded, however. "To these warnings the populace is dumb."

Tappan Adney was one of the very few urbanites not dumb to the dangers. While he had carefully parted hair and the stylish full mustache of the time, his bookish demeanor belied a sturdy frame, a tolerance to wretched struggle of all types, and a preference for raw mountainsides over sidewalks. An uneasy city dweller, yet ever the New Yorker: a moose he had shot, dismembered, and reassembled from the bones out was on display at the city's American Museum of Natural History.

But Adney also understood the Klondike's draw among average citizens, the desire to break free of the ceaseless toil required by the great Panic and depression. One year, Adney earned his keep by making boxes for plums. He was paid one cent a box, and often made 150 a day. Later, he got a job pulling a rope to tow boats across a river. He was paid $1.25 a day, but since four meals were included, he figured it was a raise; his hands soon were blistered and bloody raw.

The mass of men and women assembling to migrate north—when measured in terms of size, haste, and single-mindedness—was like none the world had yet seen. Thousands left in the first two weeks alone, packed in overburdened steamers. Some newspapers tried to call the crowd back. "TIME TO CALL A HALT." The mob was already so gold-hungry, another headline writer felt the need to state the obvious: "WINTER WILL SOON SET IN THERE: Suffering Seems Inevitable." The *San Francisco Chronicle* ran a story titled "Miners Cannot Eat Gold," and Adney read another that began, "Thousands Starve in the Klondike: Almost 2000 Graves Made in Three Years." This last report came from a prospector who claimed to have just returned, and as a cripple too, due to the intense hardships. This miner said he saw the graves himself, and that the richest gold streak was known as the Black Hole of Calcutta and worked only by murderers from Bohemia.

"The tide is too great to turn," Adney thought. The mob was not interested in warnings. It was interested in gold and stories about gold.

Newspapers began dispatching teams of reporters to Alaska, some already under way on ships. The *San Francisco Examiner* chose four men and a woman, Helen Dare, who said the gold "draws men on and pranks with them like a mocking devil." Hearst began a special Klondike edition of the *New York Journal*, and the *Times* of London, the Toronto *Globe*, and the Paris *Le Temps* all announced they were sending special correspondents north.

Adney could not help feeling like he was missing out. He was a more qualified reporter than any of them. He had spent months living on the land in remote eastern Canada, unsuccessfully searching for gold on the Tobique River. Packed in the flour, blankets, picks, drills, chests of dynamite and powder. All the experience and knowledge required for a Klondike expedition, he had it.

The temptation was too much. Adney always got excited about the chance to explore new landscapes. At the same time, only a fool would get on a boat for Alaska so late in the year. So what did that make him? Another victim of Klondicitis, perhaps. He pestered newspaper and magazine editors until one finally took him on.

On the 28th of July, Adney received his assignment from *Harper's Weekly*, to cover the wonder of the age, a mass migration of humanity into a frozen land of gold and pain, America's last march into an unknown frontier.

. . .

Two weeks after Clarence and Ethel Berry stepped off the *Portland*, Adney walked into the Canadian Pacific Railway office in Manhattan and purchased a ticket to Alaska, via railroad and the steamer *Islander*. The printed stub read "New York to Dyea." On paper, it seemed so simple. Adney knew better. He was well familiar with the challenge of penetrating wilderness.

Adney was born in Athens, Ohio, in 1868. His father was a professor of agriculture, and as he moved the family often, from job to job, he tutored his son at home. Adney was a quick student, enrolling in the University of North Carolina at Chapel Hill at age thirteen. After his father was killed in a farm accident, Adney's mother settled them in New York City, and he attended Trinity, a finishing school focused on Greek and Latin and classical literature. His next stop should have been Columbia. But then, just before his nineteenth birthday, Adney went north on summer holiday to New Brunswick, that rugged stretch of coast just past Maine, and didn't return for nearly two years.

Adney spent that time in the forests and river valleys, hunting and fishing, learning to build canoes, absorbing the old knowledge of the native Maliseet people. It was not an unexpected diversion; at Trinity, when he should have been studying, Adney spent much of his time sketching birds in Central Park instead. And in New Brunswick, he skipped church to spend Sunday mornings on the Bay of Fundy, drawing everything he saw. Before, in the city, he had been aimless. Distracted. He couldn't follow through to finish a task. But now Adney had found his niche in the world.

He would consider himself a commercial artist first and a journalist second, and for good reason, as he made $25 a drawing. He sketched wherever he traveled, intent on the smallest details, and learned to navigate in the wilderness through physical cues, like the direction of the wind. He made lists of Maliseet words and collected the stories of old hunters who were stalked by phantoms they called Indian Devils. He caught bears in traps and hung them from trees by a chain and as he skinned them he drew pictures. "Killing is but a small part of the pleasure of hunting," he thought. It was easy. "Give it a tap between the eyes and that's the end of it."

He spent his time with trappers and lumberjacks and wrote about their lives and what they knew. In 1890, he published two stories with *Harper's Young People*: "How to Make a Birchbark Canoe" and "What Can Be Done on Snowshoes." This led to illustrations and stories of adventure for some of the most high-profile periodicals in New York. And eventually, to a commission by Harper and Brothers, to cover the biggest story around.

Adney's steamship was to embark from Victoria, British Columbia, on August 15, giving him two weeks to acquire all the necessary equipment and ride a train three thousand miles to the coast. While en route he commenced with his meticulous planning, telegraphing orders of equipment purchases to meet him at the port. He packed a typewriter, his sketchbooks, and a camera and several spools of 4-by-5-inch daylight film. During a brief stop in Winnipeg, Adney ran to the Hudson's Bay Company post and tried to buy furs for winter clothing. But even so far from the Klondike, outfitters were sold out. The fever had infected the whole continent. So instead he bought the only hooded wool coat they had, knee-high moose-hide moccasins that he could have stitched himself, and a red and black toque for his head.

Years in the wilderness had taught Adney what to pack, but most other stampeders relied on guides of dubious authority. The books were produced so quickly they contained more fantasy than facts, making up in volume for what they lacked in quality; the *Chicago Record's Book for Gold Seekers*, which materialized in the fall of 1897, was 555 pages, promised $50 pans of fine black sand at twenty-three feet below ground, and offered no fewer than six separate lists of indispensable requirements for any outfit. As a safeguard against famine, flour made up nearly half the weight of the standard thousand-pound outfit, though mustard, ginger, and evaporated vinegar made it on some lists as well.

In the end, Adney's outfit proved typical. Seventy-six individual line items, including a granite saucepan, sixteen pounds of nails, and a sheet-iron stove. He kept his food choices limited to pork, flour, beans, and tea; his time towing boats taught him that anything else made a man grow fat. "It takes work and air to make a man hungry," he thought. "We don't eat at all in the city. We mince and fuss and coax our jaded appetites, and in the end die of indigestion."

On August 8, a week before his ship was set to steam out, Adney finally reached Victoria, the small Canadian port across the sound from Seattle. He found it jammed with migrants from all over the world. "Men from every station in life," he thought, "but all of one mind, actuated by one purpose." Like a flock of starlings. Or swarm of ants. Leaderless, rudderless, persistent, inexorable.

But also quite ignorant and naive. Few confidently knew the route to Dawson City, nor what was required to get them there. Adney considered two thirds of these men so hopeless as to be a danger to themselves and others. They didn't know how to hitch outfits to horses or sail a boat, much less make one.

In New Brunswick, Adney had become quite

good at building and paddling birchbark canoes, handling them in whitewater even while standing, the boat dancing under him. So while in Victoria, Adney cut the lumber for a boat before he left. Using his own plans, he sawed and chiseled out the ribs and siding for a twenty-three-foot bateau, easy to handle with either oars or pole. That is, if he could get it to the Yukon River, packing it over the mountain passes. "It may never get over," he thought. "Hundreds of boats, it is said, are being left behind." Still, better to be ready. "It is unsafe to leave any precaution untaken." And hardly the oddest addition to an outfit; one man was bringing a lawn tennis set. Another planned to bring an ox, to eat. Was he mad? Maybe not. "Some say we shall have to eat our horses."

Adney himself knew only the basic oft-repeated route details—a ship to Alaska, a trek up one of the gorges, an assault to the summit and over the Canadian border, and then sail downstream from the Yukon headwaters—but at least he was confident in his mountaineering and survival skills. He had slept outside in snow. Few of the others were so prepared, though, and Adney wasn't sure how many would get through. Hundreds of men might be stuck for the winter in the alpine passes.

But which pass to take? All the talk said there were two: the standard footpath up the Chilkoot, from the port at Dyea. And the new White

Pass, starting in Skagway. Dyea and Skagway were only a few miles apart, and rumors said the residents of both towns were nothing but cutthroats, brigands, and evildoers of every variety. Also, the narrow Chilkoot was already jammed with traffic, and so all who could were choosing the White Pass, which supposedly had been improved by entrepreneurs in the last few months, in anticipation of the hordes of treasure seekers. "News is contradictory, when it is to be had at all," Adney noted, with suspicion. Since the White Pass was advertised in all the papers as a horse trail, seemingly every lowly pack animal from miles around was driven to Victoria and put up for sale starting at $25 a head. Adney was not impressed. "Ambulating bone yards. Ribs like the sides of a whiskey-cask and hips to hang hats on." Miserable pathetic creatures, some clearly just rescued from the glue factory. To Adney they looked as if they wouldn't survive the sea journey, much less work a rocky trail; their backs would sag under the weight of their feed alone.

Adney managed to find six horses he thought might suffice. Most were minimally acceptable and nondescript. The black had a bone spavin in his lower hock that threatened to trip him up at a trot, and, as a measure of the attention paid them in their former lives, only one came with a name, an undersized packer called Nelly. He fed them and prepared them for the journey with a skill most of the stampeders lacked; Adney's father had seen great cruelty to horses in the Civil War and had taught his son to always treat the animals with kindness and care.

It did not take long for Adney to realize that many of the men had already organized into clusters of travel mates, pairing off for mutual advantage. Once he purchased his horses, and took on the challenge of corralling them himself, he sought out a few fellows with whom to throw in his lot. His first choice was two men he had eyed during the train ride, when in conversation they revealed Dawson as their ultimate destination. Jim McCarron had been a soldier in the Seventh U.S. Cavalry, Custer's old outfit. Obviously he knew horses. Burghardt was barely more than a boy and called himself a baker because his father was one. McCarron and Burghardt agreed to tend Adney's horses and get his gear over the pass, in exchange for his building them a boat on the other side. With them was a one-eyed Dutchman—"large, thick, and slow"—whom Adney chose to ignore as if there were not a fourth member of their party.

Finally, after much preparation, McCarron, Burghardt, the half-blind lummox, and Adney boarded the *Islander.* So many boats had been commandeered for the rush to Alaska that all that remained were leaky relics with alcoholic captains and green crews. Below, the hold was jammed with horses such that the brutes stood flank to flank, kicking and rearing, unable even to turn or lie down. And above, berthings were chockablock with stampeders, women sleeping in the same room as men, a Victorian outrage.

The ship pushed away from the dock. Onshore, a small crowd gathered to wave and shout. Some of the prospective miners grew teary-eyed as their families faded from view, but there was pride too, chins up and chests out and hot blood in their veins. Every able-bodied man left onshore was thought a coward to miss this march to war. A few dozen young boys on the wharf called "Three cheers for Klondike!" and Adney felt heartened by this, a balm for his anxious melancholy. He turned to McCarron.

"It would have seemed pretty blue if there had been nobody here," the old soldier said.

They sailed into danger and opportunity and lonesomeness and deliverance. Death and fortune and an Arctic winter all balanced upon a scale. What would come of this great adventure? What would come of them?

Even as Adney sailed north, Ambrose Bierce, the acerbic Civil War veteran and journalist, wrote in the *San Francisco Examiner* his caustic prediction for the fate of the Klondikers:

"Nothing will come of him. He is a word in the wind, a brother to the fog. At the scene of his activity no memory of him will remain. The gravel that he thawed and sifted will freeze again. In the shanty that he builded, the she-wolf will raise her poddy litter. The snows will cover his trail and all be as before."

Life on the ship settled into a queasy routine. Adney sketched. Jim McCarron, the former cavalryman, checked on the horses. There were North-West Mounted Police on board, and McCarron wanted to show he knew as much about horses as they. The animals were straining their halters, kicking and biting their neighbors such that they all looked chewed over. Many passengers drank and sang songs to pass the time, ragtime numbers, faster and faster with every verse. "Today is the day we give babies away," went the tune. Of course they had, for the gold of the Klondike.

Adney surveyed his fellow passengers. A dark-skinned man from the Black Hills that everyone called Buckskin Joe and his seven-foot-tall partner who said he was a lawyer. A well-outfitted band with folding canvas canoes. A shocking number of teenage boys. Half the passengers were Americans from Boston and New York still dressed in their city suits and leather shoes. As Alaska approached, one by one they changed into their new costumes of corduroy, pulling and tugging on the itchy uncomfortable roughs to which they were clearly unaccustomed. Those who brought rifles practiced target shooting at the ducks that flocked near the rocky islands of the Salish Sea. Buckskin Joe had a custom firearm with two barrels, a repeating shotgun and 30-40 box-mag Winchester on the same stock, which he used to fell many waterfowl in a bragging display.

The journey up the West Coast and Alaska's Inner Passage took four days. The mornings were foggy but the sun won out by midday, a clear summer cruise. Long thin waterfalls of lace ran down furrows in the rock wall shore, as if a giant beast had raked the mountainside with its claws. Glaciers glowed a sapphire blue. Whales breached. And in the wild backcountry, only one ridge removed from the coast, glaciers filled the valleys like multiheaded snakes, twisting and curling around the peaks, an anaconda squeezing its prey.

On August 19, the *Islander* stopped briefly at Mary Island, just south of Juneau, to let on an American customs official, Mr. P. A. Smith, to address the assembled about what to expect when they reached port. Adney was attentive. It was the first trustworthy news he received since setting out from New York.

"My advice to you is to get organized, and appoint committees to look after the landing in Skagway," Mr. Smith said. "If you do not do this there will be great confusion, for I suppose you are aware that the landing is done in scows." The harbor at Skagway was too shallow to allow the ship to dock, Smith explained, and without self-directed organization, in the chaos of disembarkation every man would be undoubtedly separated from his freight.

"I would say another thing to you," he went on. "There are persons in Skagway who gather in things." A polite method of saying the town was ripe with thieves; Adney had joined up with Burghardt and McCarron for just such a situation. Then Smith had one further announcement.

"The government of the United States is very strict about bringing whiskey into Alaska," he said. Imprisonment was an option. "If I should find any of you with liquor I should have to arrest him and take him to Juneau, where he would be punished."

Here Buckskin Joe's seven-foot-tall lawyer spoke up, said that between him and his partner they carried several flasks, one as large as a quart. "We don't drink; we are taking it strictly for medical purposes." Others nodded that they too carried such purely pharmaceutical tonics as well.

"The purpose of the law is to prevent the sale of whiskey to the Indians," Smith said, "but, of course, we do not look into people's flasks." To which the crowd again murmured their approval, for such a sensible policy.

"That man's a credit to the country," McCarron whispered to Adney.

Before Smith left, a stampeder in the crowd offered one final question. "What is the penalty for theft at Skagway?" he asked.

"The miners give him twenty-four hours to leave," Smith replied, "and if he doesn't leave, he is shot."

The traditional route to the Yukon, used by the coastal Tlingit people for thousands of years, was the Chilkoot Pass. The Tlingit were traders, and they carried goods to interior tribes. Both men and women grew strong carrying massive loads of fish grease and pelts, mothers even burdened with their babies. The Chilkoot Pass followed a glacier river upstream to a sharp canyon, ever narrowing, until reaching a final wall of loose boulders that had to be summited in the final push. The pass broke at nearly 3,800 feet, and while known for snow and avalanches, was the quickest and most direct route to the alpine lakes that feed the Yukon.

But there was a second option, recently touted by the newspapers and so-called experts. The White Pass trail started at the port of Skagway, and like the Chilkoot, followed a gorge into the mountains. But the climb was reputed to be gradual, no mountaineering required, and so suitable for horses and, eventually, a railroad. Workers had already begun to improve it, a joint venture between the British Yukon Mining, Trading, and Transportation Company, on the Canadian side, and the Alaskan Northwestern Territories Trading Company on the American side. For while the White Pass was longer in distance, it was lower in elevation, topping out at 3,200 feet.

Both trails met at Lake Bennett. After that, they would boat the chain lakes and Yukon River the rest of the way. But how best to get there?

There was no consensus of which trail was best. "Whichever way you go, you will wish you had gone the other," said one man to Adney.

But until they arrived, this was all hearsay. Every man on board had heard his own tale of Alaska. "No two stories agree, save that all tell one story of trouble and hardship past comprehension," mused Adney. Everyone was either a liar or ignorant.

Jim McCarron shrugged it off. "We will know what it is like when we get there, and not before," he said.

By Adney's estimation, of the *Islander*'s 140 passengers, every single one intended to attempt the White Pass out of Skagway. Although to Adney it seemed incredible, and more than a little suspicious, that such a supposedly easy pass would exist so close to the Chilkoot. If the White Pass was truly fairer, why wasn't it the traditional route?

At Juneau, the rain moved in, a slow and steady drizzle, the Inner Passage enveloped with fog. Adney's heart sank—he lacked sufficient equipment to take photos without strong direct sunlight—but as they steamed north the sun broke through. The surrounding peaks thrust into the clouds, the valleys so deep they were lost in the haze, and there, distantly, along the bay, Skagway emerged as a pale film, a smear of white tents upon the landscape.

In planning their disembarkation, the passengers on Adney's craft were supremely well organized. They voted for a committee of three gentlemen, who in turn appointed a chairman and secretary, to write up minutes of their deliberations. They established an administrative process, complete with logbook and receipts, to tally and distribute the goods, and fifteen men with rifles were deputized as guards to protect the equipment once onshore.

But at the moment of truth, the fundamental entropy of the place intruded. The tides shifted enormously, and the *Islander* had to stay out in deep water or risk grounding on the low beach. Soon canoes crowded the rails of the ship, as Indians offered rides to shore for 25 cents each. Adney took one, and onshore was met with a hubbub like he was back on a wharf in New York; men in salty gumboots shuffling parcels, horses tied up as waves lapped their fetlocks, tents haphazardly erected with no plan or rational thought, men cooking on metal stoves and tossing bacon on skillets in the midst of the throng. Only one path seemed established and well-trod: the entrance to the White Pass. Talk was twenty-five hundred men were already on the trail.

"How many of the 140 odd who are starting from this ship will see the summit of White Pass?" Adney said to himself. "How many will reach their journey's end this year, or ever? The thought is on every one's mind."

Large scows pulled alongside the steamships to unload the horses. Each animal walked the connecting plank, the flat-bottomed boats pushed toward shore, and then the horses were driven out and dumped in the glacier-cold water to swim the rest of the way in. Adney's partners, McCarron and the boy Burghardt, set up a tent in town and packed the horses while Adney fulfilled his reporter duties for *Harper's* by exploring Skagway.

Past the beach, Adney found a mud track, ambitiously named "Broadway," lined with a mishmash of tents and wooden buildings, the largest of which were saloons and gambling halls with names like Pack Train, Bonanza, Grotto, and Nugget. The whiskey was watered-down swill, the cigars stale and sodden. Someone beat away on a piano as men pulled stumbling women around a dance circle. "Not even of the painted sort," Adney thought, disappointed. He set up his bulky camera in the middle of the sloppy trail and shot a photo.

The vast majority of stampeders were men, but not all. Some women were two-stepping and some were selling their favors but some appeared to be companions of prospectors, wives of either love or convenience. Most wore wide full skirts, with a multitude of layered hems and petticoats, whalebone corsets that cinched waists tight and starched collars that stuck chins into the air. They'd drown and freeze if they ever got wet, Adney understood. Bloomers or trousers might get the women through, but to show so much ankle? Unseemly.

Adney was astounded at how quickly taverns and disorderly houses could sprout from the ground. "Men are like wolves; they literally feed upon one another." But even as some men set up shop, many others were already quitting and selling their outfits and going home, having not the money to hire Indian packers, nor horses to carry their loads, nor the will to do the work themselves. Adney heard that horses cost $200 in Skagway but 20 cents at the summit, so hobbled were they by the labor of the ascent.

Though this could all be hearsay. Adney didn't know what he could trust or believe. The Indian packers called them all cheechakos, tenderfoot newcomers, and that's what they were. There were rumors about what food had to be in one's outfit, about import duties, about even which law applied to the soil on which they stood. One fat American customs official, with a sweaty face and his feet on the desk, told Adney that newspaper writers shouldn't be allowed to go to the Klondike at all, because of all the negative reports they'd print. "Everyone seems to have lost his head, and cannot observe or state facts," Adney decided. What passed for news felt fabricated, facetious, and fake.

Even so close to the White Pass, no two stampeders in Skagway could agree on its condition or viability. All day, broken and disheartened men descended the pass, telling stories of horses tumbling over cliff edges, seventeen lost in one slide, impossible packing conditions.

"The road is good for four or five miles—it is a regular cinch; after that hell begins," said one to Adney, as he scribbled in his notebook.

And why is there so much trouble? Adney asked.

"It is the inexperience of those who are trying to go over," said another. "They come from desks and counters; they have never packed, and are not even accustomed to hard labor."

"They have lost their heads and their senses," said a third. "I have never seen men behave as they do here. They have no more idea of what they are going to than that horse has."

No one seemed to know how to secure a harness or pack an outfit or holster a weapon. The horses too seemed infected by the ignorant delirium, resisting their masters in a fever of bucking, rearing, tearing at their bindings and trampling through town, knocking down tents and kicking sparks from cooking fires so the fabric-city nearly burned down. It was a version of the American frontier West as farce, cheechakos unable to handle mounts and pistol alike. "The horses are green, the men are green," Adney saw. It was amazing no one had yet gotten shot.

Some said that not one in ten would get over. Others said the door was shut, the way blocked by crippled caravans. Two stampeders loaded their kit in a half-sunk boat and loudly proclaimed they were paddling to Dyea, to attempt the Chilkoot Pass instead. "Well, boys, we will meet you on the other side of the mountains," they called. "They do not look like strong men," Adney thought, "but they smoke their pipes bravely."

And yet every day some men left and did not return, having, it was presumed, summited, and broken the spell. "This is an army," Adney realized. "Those in front are stubbornly fighting their way." In contrast, Skagway seemed nothing but wannabes and tough-talkers. He was ready to be done with idle speculation. Better to go and pit himself against the mountain and have it done with, judged worthy or no.

Adney was not one to shirk the challenge. The first time he hunted caribou, he and a white friend his own age named Hum and an old Maliseet man named Peter Joe tracked the animals across the snows of a frozen lake. Adney was nineteen. It was December, just before Christmas, and the snow lay everywhere thick and heavy. Adney carried a .57 caliber Snider-Enfield carbine, and the other two carried shotguns with slugs. Between them they had only a dozen rounds. They lay on a bank of that lake, and when the two caribou crossed they opened up. Adney fired and then cocked his rifle and the spent cartridge flew from the breach and he fired again and again until he was out of bullets. The little caribou ran away limping. The big one dropped, hard, a mortal wound for sure. The caribou lifted its head, stumbled to its feet, and then dragged itself into the woods. It could not go far. They would find the body in the morning.

The night passed cold, the kind of weather in which the trees pop open. They awoke and Peter Joe handed Adney an axe and they tracked the animal through the snow. He was easy to follow, though the blood trail was thin. They surprised the caribou and it bolted again. Adney and Peter Joe ran after and they saw the caribou collapse at the base of a tree. Adney had the axe and he charged the caribou and swung but the animal kicked him back into the snow. Peter Joe roared and the caribou roared back and Adney raised himself and swung again and buried the axe in the caribou's head. The fight was over.

Adney and Peter Joe checked the body. How had the animal fought so hard after taking a direct hit? But then they searched the carcass and found no hole, no exit wound from the gunshot. Just a little nick behind the ear, where the hard skull had turned aside the half-inch bullet. The day before, the animal had only been stunned. Adney's axe dealt the first and only true blow.

"Poor old Peter," he thought, remembering his friend. "They don't hunt caribou where he is now, and it is one long Christmas."

In this, and so many other ways, Adney was very much unlike his fellow cheechakos.

Adney quickly grew impatient at the logistical and legal delays in Skagway, and started exploring up the trail on his own without filing the paperwork and paying the duties that were rumored to be required. He left Burghardt with the horses and he and McCarron scouted the way ahead.

White fabric tents ran for a quarter of a mile into the woods, but at last they gave out, and the two men found themselves in a queue of packers. Some of the stampeders used overburdened horses, and two used bicycles, and some were toting carts, narrow but long, able to hold several hundred pounds of gear. It was raining.

"Does it always rain here?" a cheechako asked an Indian packer.

"Snows sometimes," the Indian replied.

They followed the Skagway River, a cold rushing stream surrounded by cloud forest and peaks capped by snow and ice. The land reminded Adney of the Adirondacks in northern New York, that sublime ratio of rock, tree, water, sky, and soaring elevation. The mountains were familiar, and yet magnified in every way: taller, steeper, wilder, colder, deadlier. Spectacular. "Bluer and bluer until they merge into the sky." A continuous flow of clouds off the Pacific produced regular showers, the earth always wet and damp and infused with the smell of rot. Cottonwoods and thorny Devil's Club weeds grew along the bank, spruces and white birch ran up the ridge, and deep moss beds swallowed trees, like a sculptor putting papier-mâché on a wire frame.

Well, what forest remained, anyway. Already much was clear-cut for log homes and fuel.

A few miles in, Adney found a makeshift camp called "The Foot of the Hill," a resting spot before the trail abruptly turned left and ascended the ridge. Men clogged the path, field kitchens and sack flour spilling out across the freshly cut ground. Women were selling biscuits. Nearly everyone had a rifle; Adney heard there was pilfering of unattended outfits, and men were prepared to shoot one another on sight. And yet faced now with the first challenge, even more men were giving up and selling off their food and equipment. The farther inland Adney went, the more prices rose. "It costs a dollar to look a man in the face," Adney scoffed. Many men seemed content to forget mining and instead make their riches packing; some teamsters reported they made $100 a day. More were just heading for home, satisfied that they had seen Alaska, and smart enough to return while still in one piece, vowing never to do it again.

Cheechakos kept asking Adney to use his camera, to take a photograph of them so it might appear in the newspaper someday and prove they were on the great gold rush. Never mind that most had managed to move their thousand pounds of goods only a mile or two, their pack animals weighed down by clods of mud. Some were even discussing the best place to dig in for the winter; it was August 24. "There is no common interest," Adney realized. "The selfish are crowding on, every man for himself. Most of them regret having started." They were too tired to go on and too tired to go back, their legs and feet full of fungus and rot from the incessant slop.

"This is no country for tramps and loafers," thought Adney. In New Brunswick, there were two jobs on the lumber crews. Choppers, who cut down the trees, and swampers, who cleared the path in and hitched the felled timber to horse teams for removal. Adney was a swamper. One day he missed a swing with his axe and bit through his shoe and three pairs of socks, severing the toes from the meat of the foot, right at the knuckles. Three arteries were severed and he tied off his foot with his suspenders and walked out all the way to town. A doctor tried to stitch the arteries back together but they kept slipping out of his fingers and eventually they gave Adney chloroform to knock him out because he kept squirming and kicking. He got blood poisoning. Then he went back to swamping logs. He was no loafer.

Adney ascended the trail on foot. The White Pass was supposed to be an improved road, the future home of a railroad. But this was just a scratch on the ground, a pencil doodle between mammoth granite boulders and the stumps of trees. Where brooks crossed the trail and washed out the loosened dirt, some man had laid sawed logs as corduroy. But not nearly well enough to make straight the path.

Stampeders attempted to drag all manner of horses up the trail. The tall horses were dangerously clumsy, stuck their noses in the air and trusted their footing would be sure. This led to stumbles, falls, broken legs, and rolls down the ravine. Meanwhile, lowly donkeys and mules and little cayuse ponies kept their heads down, watched where they put their hooves, and slowly picked their way about the mud-smeared slickrock on steady feet.

It began to rain again. The weather was inscrutable, capricious; none of Adney's storm-watching experience back east proved applicable. Misery set in, ankle-deep in sloppy, slimy, chocolate-colored mud. The higher they went, the worse the trail, a tiny crack on the side of the cliff. At one fissure of several feet, where the horses had to jump the gap, packers reported fifty pitiful animals a day fell. In some places the slope was 40 degrees. In another cavity Adney found an empty packsaddle and a hole in the underbrush leading over the cliff; the stench from below roiled his stomach. Adney passed a man who lay in the open, eyes closed, still, face to the falling rain, pale as death, yet still breathing.

The path stretched ever upward, ledge to ledge, a thin terrace hanging over the valley. The whole trail was a series of shelves, sheer rock faces below and ever more labor above. Every step was precarious, ankle-breaking slime on smooth rock, with barely space for a man to even stand and breathe.

And then the trees fell away and the view opened and Adney could see the wide sweep of the challenge before them. The river churned endlessly six hundred feet down. Below and behind, smoke-filled Skagway clung to the sea.

Ahead were spires of stone a mile high and the path ever twisting out of sight. Maps said the White Pass was still ten miles distant. Adney guessed five thousand men and half as many horses were laboring within his view, breaking themselves upon the mountain. No one kept tally when a steamer dropped its load. "The trail absorbs them as a sponge drinks up water," Adney thought.

Everywhere lay tales of discouragement. Nerves failing, men quitting, horse legs snapping, whole parties turning aside en masse even as they reached the summit, so demoralized were they by whatever they saw farther on. No one knew for sure what lay ahead. Only that a few men, and two or three women, had gotten through.

The rock sections were calamitous. The mud pits sank horses to their tails. Most greenhorns came from a world of electric streetcars and steam railroads; their ignorance of horses would be the death of the beasts. Men beat the animals every time they stopped moving. With weeks on the trail, no forage, the men too impatient or tired to carry their feed, many of the horses were starving, thin as snakes.

And the rain never let up. Sleep in mud, wake in mud, trudge in mud, die in mud.

The White Pass would forever be known as the Dead Horse Trail. Relentless toil killed uncounted thousands. Some horses died and lay where they fell and the caravans continued and ground their fetid carcasses into the dirt. And others, when they died, rolled down the gulley and lay in the water, where they bloated and burst so their putridity hung like a fog and clouded the mind and men drank disease from their canteens. The corpses made a noise. They hummed from the beating wings of a thousand gorging flies. When the men had the energy, which was rare, they piled the bodies and burned them. The wood was wet, and the horses full of blood and piss, so they smoldered and burned poorly, sooty in the nose.

The trail was dark with the blood of flayed animals. On the rank wind, one heard the braying of asses and cries of tortured dogs, begging for mercy with their yelps but receiving none, whipped in agony to the top of the pass. One man beat his exhausted horse with an axe handle for half an hour. But the horse's will was broken, and still it did not move. So the man took a long rope and tied it around the horse's neck and two hind legs and then hoisted it into the air where it finally began to struggle against slow strangulation. The man cut one ear off the horse and cursed it a final time and left. The animal did not die until morning. Witnesses claimed another horse deliberately walked over the face of Porcupine Hill. Said the men who saw it: "It looked to me, sir, like suicide. I believe a horse will commit suicide, and this is enough to make them."

Adney was aghast. His heart broke for the animals he loved. He tried to imagine the scene next spring, after the snows had come and then melted, the grim trail paved with skulls and ribs ground to dust, and the ravens fat with the feast provided by white men's folly and hubris.

The slaughter was incomprehensible. "As many horses as have come in alive," he thought, "just so many will bleach their bones by the pine-trees and in the gulches, for none will come out."

CHAPTER FOUR
1897

When a man journeys into a far country,
he must be prepared to forget many of the
things he has learned. . . . If he delay too
long, he will surely die.

—JACK LONDON

The wet and muddy way station known as Sheep Camp was a ten-day pack up from the Pacific, and there was still another ten days of hard work to reach the summit of the Chilkoot Pass, and the longer Jack London sat there in the rain, the weaker he became.

It was too warm at the base of the trail at Dyea, and already too cold at Sheep Camp, with a steady drizzle that sucked all heat from his body. Every tree in walking distance had succumbed to the axe, the growing green hacked and racked for firewood to break the chill. The camp itself consisted of a couple dozen tents among the boulders on the creek's edge, plus a few larger shelters for saloons. London was happy to see a saloon, if that's what you could call nothing but a man standing behind a wooden board pouring from a bottle of whiskey. In this place, for London, that was more than sufficient.

In the summer of 1897, Jack London was a twenty-one-year-old nobody tramp from Oakland, California. His mother spoke to ghosts and his father was unknown. The stepfather who raised him was a crippled soldier who spent most of his Civil War service in the hospital with failing lungs. London was a veteran himself, of child labor on ice wagons and newspaper stalls and Hickmott's Cannery, putting pickles in jars for 10 cents an hour. The first time he got fall-down drunk he was seven years old.

London got the money for the grubstake from his brother-in-law, James Shepard, an aging sea captain with a bad heart. London's sister, Eliza, had married Shepard when he was a forty-one-year-old widower with three children and she just sixteen. It was Shepard who had contracted the Klondicitis first. He offered to pay for everything if London did the manual labor to get them to the goldfields. In truth, though, the house was in Eliza's name, and so it was she who took out the mortgage to purchase two outfits for $2,000, an extravagant sum the likes of which London had never seen before, and such a matter of excitement to Shepard that he went all aflutter, suffering a mild heart attack on a San Francisco streetcar while preparing for the journey. Despite that, the two men sailed on July 25, 1897, only eight days after Ethel and Clarence Berry unloaded their cargo of gold.

The old sourdoughs said that when choosing between the White Pass and the Chilkoot Trail, one way led to hell and the other to damnation. But London and Shepard and their fellow argonauts gave no more thought as to which trail to brave than does a flea on a bison's rump consider where the herd might tromp. The mob was moving under its own momentum now. They were dropped at Dyea, at the foot of the Chilkoot, and so that's where they began their journey.

Sheep Camp lay thirteen miles in but just a thousand feet up; London was only barking at the gate guarding an interior far wilder and more inhospitable. The approach to the Chilkoot summit—the most strenuous part of the journey, at times near-vertical—was still four rocky miles away. Already the cheechakos were feeling the strain. Some men attempted to rest for the assault, and some men became entrepreneurs and packed others' outfits to make their fortunes, and some men sold their belongings and left, and some men were so desperate and indebted and hopeless they shot themselves rather than face the trail back home.

"Sons of Adam suffering for Adam's sin," thought London.

Shepard himself lasted only two days before rheumatism and melancholy overtook him. "I give up. Go on without me. I'm catching the first steamer back to San Francisco," he said. The man's heart was weak, but his mind sharp enough to realize he would not survive the journey. London went on.

At Sheep Camp he took a day of rest on the Lord's day, Sunday, August 22, 1897. The whole place was mud, and everything within it was coated in mud, as the rain never ceased; so much energy was required simply to stay warm, there was no real rejuvenation possible. In the morning when he awoke he saw termination dust, snow on the mountain peaks. London left Sheep Camp more worn than when he had entered.

His goal was to carry his eight-hundred-pound outfit one mile each day. That meant thirty-one miles of walking: sixteen loaded with a fifty-pound pack, fifteen unencumbered back for more. He rested often, leaning the load on a rock or stump or just dropping himself to the ground. "Short hauls and short rests," he figured. In those first days, out of Dyea, it was so hot under the August sun that London stripped to his bright red underwear and packed in his long johns alone.

When packing, London threw the weight on his back while many Indians used a wide strap across their foreheads and even the women and children carried twice the load of most white men. London felt the rivalry keenly. To him, dogs and Indians seemed the beasts of burden most suited to Alaska, though he refused to be bested by either. "The aboriginal mind is slow," he believed. He would not be left behind in either body or spirit.

Much of his sense of competition, though, was economic. In Dyea, the Indian packers loitered in front of a general store owned by a Mr. John J. Healy, though the namesake himself was nowhere to be seen. There they weighed packs before the portage, 8 cents a pound the going rate before the stampede; now it had jumped to 40 cents a pound. Complain and it was 45 cents, then 50. Some white men charged less, 30 cents a pound to get an outfit all the way to Lake Lindeman, where everyone said there was wood for a man to build a boat. A little math said you could earn $26 a day, just packing. London had made only $1.20 a day at the pickle factory, and thus had no money to pay someone else to do his work.

On the Chilkoot, the mob was reduced to the most callous and primitive of toil. No advancements of the modern age, no railroads or streetcars or telegraphs, only the brutish labor of men dragging themselves on; muddy, steep ascents over boulders the size of tenement buildings. "They no longer walk upright under the sun, but stoop the body forward and bow the head to the earth," London thought. "Every back has become a pack-saddle."

Men were discarding every heavy thing of dubious value, including their pistols, though some went fishing with the weapons first, firing into the cloudy glacier-fed river. Before leaving

California, London had added a few books—including Marx, *Paradise Lost*, and Dante's *Inferno*—to his outfit, but he didn't leave them behind.

At one stream, London saw a tiny man carrying a hundred pounds of flour. The man tripped and fell face-first in the water and there he quietly drowned, as the flour weighed as much as he. Another crossing consisted of nothing but a bowed pine tree, sagging in the middle so a man stood knee-deep in the rapid. They drowned three or four a day there, that's what everyone said.

Days of rain dogged London on the climb out of Sheep Camp. All the time, the pass remained out of view, hidden behind overlapping cliffs and glacial ledges. The valley narrowed and the country did not reveal itself. The trees were stunted by winter and twisted by avalanches, and the land rose and rose with no relief, a great slope of broken rock. London followed the gray-blue stream, cold and silty. It tasted sharp and crisp.

There was a rhythm to the walking, staring at nothing but the back of the man in front of you, step with the right when he steps, step with the left when he steps, a stairway into the clouds. The air was chill but his body built such a tremendous heat, his head a kettle set to a boil. It pulsed so that he could barely think. He was a thing entirely of exertion and hunger.

The ceaseless rain and gradient took its toll,

and London slowed to half his pace, moving his outfit only a half mile at a time before collapsing in exhaustion. Three days out of Sheep Camp lay the Stone House, an enormous block of granite that served as landmark and oracle, signifying that the final ascent was within reach. The wood was gone, no more fires. The forest had fallen away and was replaced by bush and low cover, and so when the swirling rain clouds broke the view at last widened, to waterfalls dangling from the glacial fastness on either side of the canyon, and beyond, high crumbling peaks flanking the vale's mouth at the sea. Above and all around, icefields perched in the hanging valleys directly over the trail. London peered at them, "dead-white through the driving rain." He quickly moved on.

Several weeks later, the leading edge of those glaciers would collapse and send a slurry of ice and rock and rainwater freight-training through the camps. Tent-loads of men and their outfits were buried asunder. Even the Stone House was uprooted and dashed down into the valley. No one counted the number of bodies entombed in the mud left in its wake. The mob barely paused.

London struggled eight long days to move his goods from Sheep Camp to the Scales, named for the place Indian packers weighed their loads a final time. London did not tarry at this last stop before the summit, though. That tiny camp was little more than Purgatory's foyer, the briefest repose before attempting the soul-scouring assault on the pass, and London was too cold and hungry to delay.

Throughout the journey, all the way from Dyea, the Chilkoot Pass had remained out of sight, always around the next bend, behind a ridge, a false summit. Finally, at the Scales the valley could tighten no further. The stream that had cut the gorge was reduced to its trickling birth, and upon attaining a final lip, London at last gained entrance to the hidden upper sanctum of the Chilkoot.

He stood on the edge of a small basin, and surrounding him in a broad arc the sharp peaks formed an amphitheater, the headwall of the pass. "Ice-marred ribs of earth," he called them, "naked and strenuous in their nakedness." Ahead, the object of all their efforts and desires, the last hurdle, a nearly vertical boulder field known as the Golden Stairs.

All the challenges of the Chilkoot condensed into this one final tableau, a rope of men upon the mountainside, battered by the perpetual winds off the Pacific, crawling on hands and knees up the sheer sides of the bowl. In between stone buttresses and couloirs ran two chutes of loose rock, the stones tipping and wobbling as the stampeders moved from perch to perch. London joined the line. Above, he saw only legs and soles of boots. The view over his shoulder, or between his knees below, was enough to make any man giddy. The rock was cold and sucked the warmth from his hands until they cramped and behind him the line of climbers in the canyon fell away into mists, their world reduced to this theater-in-the-round in the sky.

It took London a full day to relay his outfit over this final leg of the Chilkoot Pass.

The cloven notch that formed the pass's breach was frigid and damp, banks of fog blown in relentlessly. London figured he was a thousand feet above timberline, on the mountain's very backbone. It was nearly lifeless at the summit, only the hardiest green, the meanest sort of lichen and moss tucked into corners. A dead land of rocks in the clouds.

But the view into the land beyond was breathtaking. True, the path finally, mercifully, descended, but it was more than that. The trail started among bare boulders and spectacular translucent lakes, and then progressed into rough tundra, then taller club moss and horsetails, then real grasses, bushes of blueberries, life evolving and growing more complex before his eyes as he worked his way down. The earliest days of creation were displayed in those few miles. It was a magnificent country, and fresh as the first morning.

London packed among unnamed creeks and

braided channels, the most remote headwaters of the Yukon River, cold and steely blue. As they dropped from lake to lake, the forest returned, first Krummholz at the top of a long whitewater gorge, later conifers at the bottom. Finally there was enough wood for a proper warming fire, his first in two and a half weeks.

London spent eight days in this descent, packing his eight hundred pounds in his short steady bursts. On September 8, 1897, he reached the sandy shores of Lake Lindeman, the end of the long carry. The lake was the color of moldy bread, and when the sun dipped below the western peaks the air was wicked cold.

Each day, the snow crept a little farther down the shoulders of the mountains, like a clock ticking to midnight. He knew what was coming: a "man-killing race against winter."

The camp at Lake Lindeman was a place of frayed nerves and desperate haste. The mob of outsiders had survived the rigors of the mountain passes and now had to take to the water, to sail their outfits lake to lake and then down the main Yukon River. Most knew as little about building and sailing boats as they did about horses or packing or gold mining for that matter.

Nearby trees provided the lumber for crafts of all varieties, rowboats and scows and bateaux and dories and skiffs. In truth, though, most of the boats the cheechakos built were of no type, only some city-dweller's concoction of what a boat should look like, memories from a child's picture book. The available spruce was poor and narrow, and yielded equally poor narrow boards that easily split. The greens were pounded together with the scant nails available, and patched with moss and sap, as few men packed in tar and the pitch sold locally by exploitive entrepreneurs cost a dollar a pound. The boats leaked and sat awkwardly in the water. Most were the size and shape of coffins.

There was no mill at Lake Lindeman to tear all those spruce trunks into planks, only whipsaws the stampeders had brought with them. Those who had arrived earliest had built a half dozen whipsaw frames: four tree trunks in a rough rectangle, stripped of branches and topped six feet off the ground, so they could serve as the legs supporting a platform. Cross braces were fixed on the narrower ends, allowing newly hewn logs to be sawn from atop.

Two men worked together to operate the eight-foot saws. One stood above, to guide the saw along a chalk line, to keep the boards straight. The other man below in the pit, his eyes full of sawdust. The man on top, stooped, his back seized in pain, pulled the saw up, sure his partner was doing less than his share. The man below, working above his head, choking and blind, pulled the saw down, sure his partner in the sun was loafing as well.

It was an apparatus designed to foment hate and stoke tempers. The whipsaws ended friendships and lives, as men shot pistols at each other in exasperated rage. Two men grew so angry that when they ended their partnership and went their separate ways they physically cut their outfit in half, down to the last bag of flour.

And yet every day, as many as a dozen boats set sail, bearing five to ten men each. Such a great nervous anxiety, to see men leaving ahead of you. A fear of being left out, a fear of being left behind.

In the mornings, fresh ice encrusted the still corners of the lake.

Jack London spent two weeks at Lake Lindeman building a boat. He worked with four travel companions he had met at various points in the journey. An old man named Martin Tarwater had joined when Shepard had quit, and offered to help with the cooking and repairing of shoes in exchange for food. The other three men London originally met on the steamship north: Big Jim Goodman, a hunter and the only man among them with mining experience. Fred Thompson, a bookish clerk who kept a diary. And Ira Merritt Sloper, a wiry tramp and ne'er-do-well who had just returned from South America. Sloper was thin and hard like a hickory axe handle, and Goodman more than pulled his weight, but Thompson paid a packer to carry his outfit and often sat and watched and wrote their story in his notebook.

London and Sloper were in charge of construction. Sloper had experience building boats and London sailing them, having once served as an able-bodied seaman on a three-masted schooner bound for Japan. The two men had to go five miles up a creek off Lake Lindeman to find adequate trees and fashion the lumber. They worked day and night.

Sloper and London named their boat the *Yukon Belle*. It was sturdy and capable, twenty-seven feet long, and all five men and five thousand pounds of outfit could fit inside. London thought it the best boat in the stampede.

They left the frenetic camp at Lake Lindeman on Tuesday, September 21. Spray froze to the side of the ship as they launched. While Goodman and Thompson manned the oars, London rigged the sail. Around them, other boats foundered in the icy wind even as they pushed off—one had sails made of blankets, sopping wet and top heavy before they were even under way—but not London's craft, which he guided expert and true.

Lake Lindeman itself was only six miles long, and they made quick work of it. "No more than a narrow mountain gorge filled with water," London thought. The far end of the lake's outflow consisted of a small stream, shallow and rock-strewn, running a narrow crease that discharged a mile later into Lake Bennett. They watched boats wrecked as stampeders tried to line their empty craft through, and so London and his comrades didn't even attempt it, and decided to portage their boat and pay some men to pack their outfits to Lake Bennett. The portage trail was sandy, a misplaced California beach. London's feet sank and shifted oddly as he trudged up the slope.

Lake Bennett was a crossroads, where the Chilkoot and White Pass trails joined into one unified stampede route. London could smell Lake Bennett before he saw it. The reek of decaying flesh, the corpses of hundreds of horses stacked in piles, discarded with a bullet in the brainpan when their use had run out. London and his companions heard there were so many dead horses on the White Pass, there were enough to line the trail from end to end. Drowned and shot and broken and beaten and disemboweled by upturned corduroy logs meant to bridge the mud.

The wind was now out of the north and blew in their faces, forcing them to wait at Bennett for the weather to shift. There was much talk and news to be had. Of greatest concern, they heard there was no food in Dawson, it was a place of hunger. They were still more than four hundred miles away and London was dismayed by the number of tales of famine. Too many men like

Tarwater, who had brought no food of his own and relied on others. Rumor was that steamboats full of grub were stuck on sandbars in the Yukon River, hundreds of miles downstream of the Klondike, and there were executions in Dawson on account of the wanton theft. "A man who held out an ounce of grub was shot like a dog." That's what they said, anyway.

Eventually the wind shifted so it came out of the south, and they left and made good time across the lake. After Bennett, they skirted the north rim of Tagish Lake, a corkscrewed body of water that branched into every adjoining valley like the veins and arteries off the earth's own heart. The trip was short but required cutting across the Great Windy Arm, which earned its name. Gales surged up the arm, drove huge waves crosswise amidships. Thompson said the boat was positively humming even as all around them other craft filled with water and were swamped. London saw two boats founder and capsize and everyone on board drowned right in front of him and he would never forget that, not until his dying day.

On Thursday, September 23, they paddled into the six-mile Tagish River, connecting to Lake Marsh, and saw the red flag of the Dominion of Canada onshore. It was the first government authority the men had encountered since the Alaskan coast. They pulled over and paid customs duties on their outfits, $21.50 in total, and managed to sneak Tarwater past, even though he was empty-handed and would only add to the hungry mouths in Dawson.

They made good time, London's seamanship winning the day, and they passed many other boats before camping on the lakeshore. In the morning, they entered the Lewes of the upper Yukon. There was so much silt in the water, it sounded as if the boat was scraping by, not floating. Big Jim Goodman shot a couple of pheasants and the current carried them as they ate and all was well.

On Saturday, though, the cold came on and snow began to fall. They were forced to shore to get warm by the fire, and Goodman found no prey that day. The current ran ever swifter, the river ever tighter. London had studied the route, carried a book called *Alaska* by a man named Miner Bruce that detailed each hazard, and he knew what was ahead. Miles Canyon and the White Horse Rapids.

Rock walls arose from each shore and when the river turned sharply to the left it appeared as if the current was either plunging underground or disobeying all rules of nature and flowing into a dead end. This is why some called it the Box Canyon. "Adequately named," thought London. "It is a box, a trap. Once in it, the only way out is through."

Here all stampeders faced a choice, to roll the dice and run the whitewater with their full outfit, or ease to shore to unpack the boats and portage their gear around. The first option took minutes, the second, days. The peaks above were filling with snow; winter would not wait.

The chasm was a mile long and only fifty feet wide, and halfway down a whirlpool rotated like a river god's unblinking eye. The canyon walls were made of hexagonal basalt, great columns erupting from deep in the earth, and directed all the rushing water to the center, creating a ridge of ten-foot-tall standing waves down the middle of the channel.

As London and his companions approached the rapids, they saw a red flag and a sign that read "Canyon Ahead" and they ground their boat to a halt on the side of the river. They watched other men try to run the canyon and fail. "Collecting its toll of dead," London noted, though he remained undeterred. A quick death in the water or a slow freeze packing in the coming winter? London knew his own mind. So Thompson, Goodman, Sloper, Tarwater, and London all voted, very social and democratic, and unanimously they chose to brave the river with the full boat.

Thompson and Goodman on the oars, Sloper in the nose, London at the stern, they made their run. London was the guide, the captain. He lashed the tiller to the boat, and himself to both, so that the fates of all three were tied.

"Be sure to keep on the ridge," yelled a man on the bank as they pushed off.

The water had a glossy sheen to it until they hit the first rapid, and then all was froth and confusion. London called to Thompson and Goodman to pull in their oars so they wouldn't jam and snap. They entered the chute and London saw "the rock walls dashing by like twin lightning express trains" and it took all of his skill to stay atop that ridge, the razorback of boulder-free waves that ran through the center of the channel. Rather than mount each crest in turn, the heavy boat hung low and cut the water, and a crowd gathered on the canyon rim above them, setting down their packs to watch the daredevils.

London was like Invictus, four souls in his hand. Thompson and Goodman could do little more than cling to the boat. In the bow Sloper swung his paddle with fruitless abandon, trying to steer the nose right or left, but always out of sync with the rise and fall of the craft, first catching nothing but air as the boat rose, then deluged as the nose swamped and Sloper nearly washed away. The thin man turned and yelled some warning to London but the words were lost on the wind and surf and then suddenly the boat pitched and fell off the ridge and water flooded over the gunwale from all sides.

"Caught in a transverse current," London realized, too late. Combers were reflecting off the walls of the canyon, twisting the boat, turning it broadside to the current, a deadly proposition. London leaned on the tiller and heard it creak and start to splinter. Sloper swung his paddle and struck a rock and snapped it off clean. The boat was now hopelessly off the ridge, "flying down the gutter, less than two yards from the wall," as London barely maintained command. They were at the mercy of the river.

And then the *Yukon Belle* broke through the final curtain of water, swung around true, and slowly drifted into the whirlpool circulating at the canyon's meridian.

London took a deep breath. The men relaxed their clenched grips. London ordered the oars back in the water, and after a few tugs, they remounted the ridge and were swept ahead by the inexorable current.

Thompson figured the three-minute run saved them four days of packing. After beaching on a bank off an eddy at the end of the canyon, London walked the mile back to the start, and ran through a second boat, belonging to a Mister and Missus Ret, as an act of charity.

After Miles Canyon they came upon the Squaw Rapids, a three-mile rough ride, then the White Horse Rapids, named for the bristle of surf running along the spine of each cataract. The Yukon was relentless.

London saw a bank of rock rising on the left,

forcing the river and the *Yukon Belle* into the narrowing channel to the right. The water clashed upon itself and threw a wedge of high spray. "The dread Mane of the White Horse," London had heard it called. "Here an even heavier toll of dead had been exacted. On one side of the Mane is a corkscrew curl-over and suck-under, and on the opposite side is the big whirlpool." There was nothing to be done but steer for the high water in the center. Yet even then, London watched a thirty-foot boat ahead of him take the Mane, rise and then drop into a furrow between crests, and get swallowed by the foam.

The *Yukon Belle* was next. It hit the Mane and shuddered as it was thrown in the air like a bath toy, not a boat laden with thousands of pounds of grub and gear. The stern jerked from a broadside hit and the boat began to spin. London had lost control, he couldn't believe it, and then the water came in as they fell off the Mane and into the whirlpool.

London leaned on his tiller and Sloper cracked another paddle but the maelstrom held the boat fast and they began to rotate. London was helpless to turn the nose and remount the Mane but their speed was tremendous, the river screaming through the channel. "The boat still has the bit in her teeth," London realized, and then with a flash of inspiration he changed course and steered into the spin, the boat now moving ever faster with the force of the seething whirlpool. The nose swung near a rocky outcropping and Sloper, thinking they were about to be dashed upon the reef, leapt from the craft to safety. But the bow of the *Yukon Belle* just missed the rock, and now, about to be left behind, Sloper ran along the whirlpool rim and clumsily tossed himself back in. London thought he looked "like a man boarding a comet."

The waves towered overhead and came at them from all sides. As the bow came around London used the whirlpool's momentum to jettison them free. They crested the Mane and were yanked forward by the current, pulled from trough to trough, until finally dumped into an eddy at the rapid's base.

Then London walked back upstream, and once again ran the boat of Mister and Missus Ret through to safety.

They slept well that night, for they thought the worst of the river's dangers were behind them. They were wrong.

The next day, Sunday, September 26, they set back out, headed toward Lake Laberge. Steep, sloping banks of sand and gravel rose along each meandering curve of the river, and beyond the treeline, a vision of frozen white mountains in the distance. In mild weather, this section of river would lie flat and still, nothing like Miles Canyon and the White Horse Rapids, but their luck had run out, and the Arctic north wind came upon them.

A bitter and unrelenting storm drove them onshore for two days. With no way to sail into such a blow, they could do nothing but wait and curse their misfortune, as the snow's leading edge slowly inched down the surrounding mountainsides. On the third day, desperate, they set out to row into the teeth of the wind, only to be caught in a blizzard on the water. Still they pressed on, not stopping even to eat, as the shore seemed nothing but sheer headlands, no safe harbors.

The storm whipped fury the next day as well, and as the whitecaps rose from the lake London and the others were once again pushed off the water. Every few hours they ventured out, only to be forced into another cove after an hour of rowing. On Friday they didn't even try to launch, and Jim Goodman's attempts to hunt fresh game failed. Finally on Saturday the wind died, and they could row the remainder of Lake Laberge, the surface freezing behind them as they oared on. They sailed all night, a skill London learned on San Francisco Bay, pirating oysters at age fifteen.

They were now in the Thirtymile section of the Yukon headwaters. Summer's warmth had not completely left the river but the air smelled of winter and a thick fog settled about them. Frost had come to the mountain creeks as well, and soon London noticed the many tributaries of the

Yukon discharging not water but slush ice. So too rim-ice froze along the gunwale of their boat, and around them bells of anchor ice popped to the surface from the dark and permanently frozen riverbed. Soon the whole Yukon would freeze in place; London and his company had only a few more days to travel before they would be locked down.

On Tuesday, October 5, they reached the Five Finger Rapids, named for the eponymous rocks reaching out of the water. Of the six channels formed, only the right-most was navigable, but easily so, the waves boiling into a simple sweeping V they easily breached. A little farther on, they pushed through the long Rink Rapids as well, and kept going, making good time. The next day the weather was fair and fresh and they made sixty more miles. They stopped only once, briefly, at Fort Selkirk, an Alaska Commercial Company trading post full of Indians and their weaned wolf-pups. Thompson signed the visitor register. He was number 4845, all recorded since the stampede began in August.

The company split up on October 8. Tarwater joined the crew of another boat making for Dawson, while London, Thompson, Goodman, and Sloper considered the rapidly approaching freeze and reports of famine and thought it more wise to pull up short at the Stewart River, bed down there for the winter. They pushed the *Yukon*

Belle a short way up the Stewart, to an island with several abandoned cabins that Thompson thought may have belonged to the Hudson's Bay Company. Nearby, a potentially gold-filled creek joined the larger river. Timber abounded. They had prospects, shelter, wood for perpetual fire. It was a good spot.

Day by day, the Yukon filled with ice.

All the old sourdoughs had told *Harper's* journalist Tappan Adney the same thing: that for each of the last three years the Klondike had frozen tight on October 13.

And yet when that fateful day came Adney had still not even made Miles Canyon. Far from his hoped-for final destination, he could only huddle near the fire and watch ice form along the shore, listen to it grind and groan as the waves lapped underneath. "Creaks and cries for all the world like a hundred frogs in springtime," he thought. "A dismal sound that bodes us no good."

Adney was desperate to make it to Dawson despite the incoming winter, and so for the next several days he and several companions of convenience pressed on in their boat. Adney's strokes broke a film of ice as the oars hit the water. He ran Miles Canyon, and the White Horse as well, with a thousand pounds of outfit and six inches of freeboard, not much but still more than he had running whitewater in his birchbark canoes back in New Brunswick. The boat was heavy and cut the waves and they made it through and as Adney passed the last set of rapids he looked on the bank and saw dozens of memorials to men lost at that place. The remembrances consisted of small bits of paper tacked to a post or written on shattered oar blades or cut into the very trees and all spoke to drowned dreams of gold.

Nature's relentless ticking clock—the line of white descending the mountainsides—had struck winter and the bells had tolled; snow lay in thick blankets where they camped. Creeks vomited great bellyfuls of slush ice into the river. They pushed through Lake Laberge and the Five Fingers, and when they stopped at Fort Selkirk, to hear news of Dawson, the post's old trader said, "The boats are stuck and there is a shortage of grub and a stampede out." Privation lay ahead, but there was no way to retreat now.

The next morning, on October 23, the thermometer said 5 degrees below zero. The Yukon froze, broke free, jammed again, great plates cantilevered and slabs jumbled fifteen feet high. Thick heavy ice encrusted the oars such that they had to stop and break it off with an axe. So too the boat was rimed with ice four inches thick, the craft so ponderous Adney and his companions could barely steer among the ice floes clogging the river.

They weren't alone. Around him, members of the mob would launch their boats in any glimpse of open water, only to be caught, smashed, and entombed in the ice. One large raft so captured bore a heap of animal carcasses that had attracted a flock of ravens, the scavengers gorging themselves before the long hunger. Adney heard another such floe contained an arm still grasping an oar. Dozens of boats were lost. The Yukon claimed and kept its own, secrets hidden until spring.

Adney pressed on anyway, through grinding bergs, past the Stewart River where London was already abed for the winter. On the evening of October 25, Adney made a quick camp with men who had pulled their boats from the water for fear of the ice and anarchy ahead. Adney vowed to go on, but what was waiting there for him? "Disquieting news," he heard, "brought by parties making their way out, that starvation faces the camp at Dawson." Two men had already been shot for thievery, they said. And winter had barely begun.

Wolves prowled the shore, and overhead the ghoul-green aurora danced a nightly haunt.

CHAPTER FIVE

With nothing but the desire for gold in his heart man degenerates into a beast. He sees nothing, appreciates nothing, thinks nothing but gold.
—ARTHUR ARNOLD DIETZ

As the old year came to a close, and 1898 began, tens of thousands of men and women found themselves mired in a self-induced natural disaster that stretched from Seattle to Alaska and across to the vast interior of Canada's North-West Territories. The stampeders attacked the Klondike from nearly every direction, and in so doing suffered every sort of calamity imaginable. Shipwrecks, avalanches, pack ice, meningitis, frostbite, famine, murder.

Most of the mob was entombed along the White Pass and Chilkoot Trail, burrowed into snowbanks to wait out the wind and frost. Cheechakos kept steaming into Dyea and Skagway, only to be stranded in fierce blizzards once they left the relative safety of town. At the Chilkoot Pass, the stampeders cut stairs in the snow and inched along, each in the footsteps of the man ahead of him, but for little gain. Even if they breached the summit and worked their way down to the Yukon watershed, frozen Lake Lindeman halted their advance, an icy plug holding back the masses. An entire industry arose dedicated to feeding and housing these stalled stampeders; one recent German immigrant named Frederick Trump opened a tent restaurant on the White Pass that sold horsemeat dinners. A few months later he moved to Lake Bennett and opened a larger wood frame establishment, the New Arctic Restaurant and Hotel, which developed a reputation as a magnet for single men, owing to the lusty cries of the women from the second floor.

The White Pass and Chilkoot were not the only overland routes, however. There were longer, harsher roads to the Klondike. The main "all-Canadian" route from Edmonton, advertised in the newspapers as an easier overland shortcut, was actually fifteen hundred miles of unbroken forest tracing the entirety of the Canadian Rockies front range. An alternative route from Edmonton was even longer, down the Mackenzie River, a portage over the mountains at the Porcupine River, and then a backtrack south on the Pelly to Dawson. Twenty-six hundred miles.

These trails were marketed as "the back door to the Yukon," and almost two thousand souls were taken in by the scheme. The way was near-impassable, the going so slow that parties ran out of food. One pair of prospectors was found dead, their moccasins frozen in a cooking pot. Another wrote a note that said, "Hell can't be worse than this I think I'll give it a try," and then shot himself.

Other promoted routes were even more suspect. Over a thousand tried the Telegraph Trail, a barely bushwhacked and half-completed cable right-of-way through central British Columbia. The Stikine Trail—named for the route's opening gambit, a bloated glacial river that features a Grand Canyon–like passage with some of the fiercest whitewater on the planet—seemed foolhardy on the face, and yet was attempted by some five thousand desperate men and women convinced that there must be an easier way than the logjam on the Chilkoot and the carcass-strewn White Pass.

For all those reasons, many ill-informed cheechakos with means attempted an "all-water route" instead: north along the Pacific coast, around the Aleutian peninsula to Norton Sound, and then up the lower Yukon River, a trip of over four thousand miles. Those passengers, who hoped to skip the exertion of the trail and instead leisure travel to the Klondike, found themselves trapped that winter, snatched tight by the river ice and then starved. The Yukon was dirty, heavy with rock flour silt and punishing to steamer traffic. The sandbars shifted like huge primordial snakes, with no channel trustworthy, and the paddleboats constantly ran aground. If they could not be unloaded and freed in time, they were crushed to kindling in the spring floods. Some steamers were stuck for as long as eight months and didn't reach Dawson until June of 1898. By then, only five of the forty ships that had been sent north to ply the Yukon River were still in operation, the rest marooned in sandy shallows, sunk, or waylaid for repairs.

Of the 2,500 people in the first wave of the stampede who tried to reach Dawson via riverboat, only forty-three made it before the waterway froze in October. The rest were scattered up and down the Yukon, icebound.

And yet ships still set sail daily from Portland and Seattle and Vancouver, even into the teeth of winter, when icebergs clogged the Bering Sea and the fierce Taku winds scoured the channels and pummeled the Alaskan coast. Such winds can encase a ship in ice in mere hours, or flip listing overloaded vessels and drag them to the bottom. In 1898, ten times as many ships were lost along the Pacific coast than before the stampede began. So many gold rush steamers sank that the *Seattle Post-Intelligencer* eventually stopped listing the wrecks as news on the front page and rather used the death notices as filler between the ads in the back.

Unscrupulous investors pilfered junkyard dry docks, and every ship available, hulks and freighters rotten to the core, was hauled from boneyard to wharf with nary a stop for repairs. Not enough trained sailors were available—some men lied about having naval experience just for the free ride north, then deserted once they hit Skagway—and thus ships were misloaded, unbalanced, their emergency hatches stuffed with goods such that they could not be closed. The steamers were so dark, so jammed, so full of vomit and excrement that travelers compared them to Revolutionary War prison ships or an oubliette in Afghanistan. Other boats were little more than floating brothels, a "hot time in the old town tonight," as the lyric went, dens of drunken rutting by passengers and crew alike.

One such ship was the *Clara Nevada*. On February 5, 1898, after negligently dropping its stampeders into the Alaskan winter, the vessel left Skagway and bore south with a hold full of dynamite and gold. She was a tired ship with a fraudulent and malevolent crew and steamed from the tiny port into a snowy gale of hurricane proportions. Ninety-mile-per-hour winds raised fifteen-foot waves, trying circumstances under any conditions, but especially when the captain was trying to sink the ship and steal the gold.

The *Clara Nevada* was a rusty, iron-hulled, three-masted schooner powered by a worn-out 125-horsepower coal-driven steam engine with neglected boilers constantly on the verge of explosion. In 1897, the United States Coast and Geodetic Survey had declared her too old and worn to be seaworthy. An opportunistic transportation company then purchased and rechristened her the *Clara Nevada*, a misspelled reference to an actress of the time. You could tell a landlubber named her, as all salty sailors knew the ship was cursed from the start, with two names both ending in A.

Ten days before she was caught in the storm out of Skagway, the *Clara Nevada* had left Seattle with eight other ships, bearing thousands north for the Yukon. On her way off the dock, she collided with another boat. The next day she rammed the wharf in Port Townsend. The crew was drunk and stole from the passengers. The food was rancid, coffee made with seawater. Some of the stampeders conspired to abandon ship; a petition was circulated to turn in the belligerent crew to local police. The ship carried smuggled dynamite for the Treadwell Mine at Juneau, but when she docked there, she didn't unload it. The ship's officers didn't want to get caught illegally mixing civilian passengers and dangerous explosives, and anyway, the lazy seamen didn't wish to remove and repack all of the stampeders' gear that had been piled on top; better to drop the dynamite at Juneau on the way back. On the return trip from Skagway she hosted disillusioned cheechakos, a corpse on its way south for burial, and several rich Klondikers who locked away $160,000 in gold dust in the captain's safe.

Running with the north wind, the *Clara Nevada* threaded her way down through the narrow channels that separate the mountainous barrier islands of southeast Alaska from the mainland. But only thirty miles into her voyage, disaster struck. Past Seduction Point, at a place called Eldred Rock, a blast tore out the steamer amidships, a fireball plume of sparks and fiery debris thrown into the swallowing black of the winter night sky. In the morning, after the storm, wreckage washed onshore nearby: pieces of lifeboats, hatch covers, singed blanket rolls, planking with the stenciled name of the *Clara Nevada*. New snow, at least eighteen inches' worth, delayed the search for bodies. In the end, only one was ever found, though a dog who had survived left tracks in the snow.

Search parties eventually found the ship in only four fathoms of clear water, a black hole in her hull. The gold had disappeared, along with every hand on board. No one knew exactly how many died; the passenger list was on the ship. Officials later determined there had been at least fifty-seven souls on board, including three stowaways. None survived. Officially.

Several months later, the *Clara Nevada*'s former captain, Charles H. Lewis of Baltimore, bearing burn scars but still very much alive, invested many thousands of dollars in a new shipping venture. It was not clear where the incompetent and formerly bankrupt sailor got all the cash.

That winter of 1898, the hot blood of the stampede was cooling, hardening, the mob stumbling in a frozen fugue. There were so many travails, scams, and hardships, it is no wonder that some men would shun the crowds and try their own route, a new route. Not up a river or through a mountain pass, but overtop. Over the glaciers.

Arthur Arnold Dietz was the gymnastics director at the Young Men's Christian Association in New York City when he decided to form a mining company and get rich. Dietz was an earnest God-fearing gentleman with soft pale eyes and carefully parted hair and no mining experience whatsoever. He did know how to organize a group activity, though, and in August 1897, in the flush of the mob's madness, he put an ad in the *New York Herald*, looking for business partners. He received forty letters of inquiry on the first day alone.

Dietz was careful and meticulous and considered himself more rational than the horde.

He would not rush off immediately. He would consider and study and prepare. From the dozens of applications he'd received, he constructed an expedition party of nineteen: a mineralogist, a tinsmith, a preacher, two civil engineers, two policemen, three toolmakers, six clerks, plus Dietz, his best friend, and his brother-in-law, who was a physician in Brooklyn. They wore identical sweaters, corduroy trousers, leather boots, and wide-brimmed hats they called sombreros. Each carried a 30-30 Winchester rifle, and together were known as the New York and Bridgeport Mining Company.

To prepare for the expedition, they read the travelogue of North Pole explorer Robert Peary, and purchased four St. Bernards and two Newfoundlands and ran them in dogsleds, an act for which the New York police arrested them for animal abuse. They quickly departed the city.

On February 1, 1898, the company took the Black Diamond Express train to Buffalo, then Chicago, St. Paul, and on to Seattle, where they purchased more dogs and the remainder of their outfit. Dietz was shocked by the city's licentiousness and vice. "I thought nothing could surprise a New Yorker," he thought. "More wicked than Sodom; the devil reigns supreme." Whether it be women, divining rod salesmen, saloonkeepers, or casino gamblers, Dietz felt everyone was trying to reach a hand in his pocketbook. The company's gear cost hundreds of dollars, and Dietz was sure they were being swindled somehow.

Tickets aboard a steamer north proved scarce. Dan Collins, one of the New York City policemen in their company, eventually talked to a customs inspector who gave a tip about an old brig down the bay in Tacoma that could be purchased and retrofitted. The *Blakeley* was dual-masted, square-sailed, 140 feet long, and condemned as unseaworthy two years before. Dietz purchased it for $5,000, added a coat of paint, hired a captain who was visibly inebriated, and sailed north.

A wild impatience tugged at Dietz. He barely recognized himself; he was in "a state of insane madness," hypnotized by lust and desperate to get north.

To defray the cost of purchasing the boat, Dietz took on over one hundred additional passengers, who so badly overloaded the tub it wallowed even in light seas. But then storms came in, waves sloshing up and over the prow, and the deck started pitching like a drunken pendulum and soon nearly everyone besides Dietz became debilitated with seasickness.

At first, those afflicted feared they might die of the nausea. Later, after three days of perpetual tumbling and gyrating, they hoped they would. The pallid men vomited overboard until they grew too weak to stand and then they retched right in their own beds. The stench belowdecks assaulted the unlucky few who—through virtue of their remaining upright, and no other training or qualification—had to work as seamen and pump the flooded bilge by hand. The raucous headwinds so shook the boat, one sailor on the yardarm was washed overboard by a towering wave. Belowdecks, the prone seasick lay soaked in freezing salt water. First the dogs began to die, and then the men.

On March 17, almost a full month after leaving Seattle, they finally entered Alaskan waters. A wet sticky snow clung to the ship and obscured any sight of land. Mast-high icebergs floated by. At last the weather broke, and on the horizon appeared the white massif of Mount Saint Elias. "A pyramid standing there immovable in the sky," Dietz described it. In the distance, cracks and booms, like the report of cannon; giant shards cracking and calving off the glacier. The whiskey-sauced captain informed Dietz that this was the sign they had arrived at their destination. They would pioneer a new way to reach the Klondike: up the broad slope of the Malaspina Glacier.

On the map, it had looked so easy, the shortest overland route. Their embarkation point lay directly south of Dawson, as the raven flies. They had only to scale the glacier, cross the mountains, and float down one of the main washes to the

Yukon. Simple. But now that they were in sight of the thing . . .

Dietz was awestruck by "the great Malaspina Glacier, which seems to smother everything out of existence." Only Mount Saint Elias, whose broad flanks fed the icefield, could withstand the sheer enormity of the monster that lay before them. The Malaspina is a piedmont glacier, one that spills out of a mountain range into a flat plain. In fact, the Malaspina is the largest piedmont glacier in the world, a lobe of ice forty miles wide and twenty-eight miles long, dangling toward the sea. "It looks like a great flat wall of marble of various colors," he thought, a wall five hundred feet tall. But this was an optical illusion disguising the glacier's incline, the swirls of black and white in truth the strata of ice and dirt laid down over hundreds of years.

The company landed at Yakutat, a small Indian village, where they were met by paddlers in kayaks. Only one man spoke English, a Swedish missionary who said he had not seen a white face in thirteen months.

Why are you here? the missionary asked, and Dietz said they were looking for gold. The missionary shook his head. No gold to be found here. And clearly, no gold seekers either. Dietz was far off the stampede trail.

They pulled the ship ashore and let it beach when the tide flowed out. There it listed to the side, spilling seawater from its dank hold, the smell of weeks of vomit and feces wafting on the wind. Dietz abandoned that torturous ship with relief and never saw it again.

But before setting out they had to inventory their supplies. The sea journey had spoiled a large portion of their foodstuffs and corroded their equipment. Even the tin cans of meat and evaporated milk carried a layer of rust. Plus, they discovered they had been swindled in Seattle after all: their powdered eggs turned out to be inedible cornmeal, which they discarded. They greased their tools with fish oil and seal blubber, and upon further investigation saw that much of their flour, which they had thought soaked and ruined, was safe behind a half-inch crust. They tested their equipment and found much of it impractical and useless now that they had entered the country, so from the Indians they purchased forty dogs and sleds, harnesses, snowshoes, and mukluks for each man, nearly every useful thing the village had. They replaced all their gear except their rifles and mining equipment: picks, shovels, block and tackle, braces, bits, and critically, an eight-hundred-pound dynamo engine to power the eventual camp via a waterwheel.

Before they left, Dietz asked directions, as he was not entirely sure where to go. The villagers gestured toward the mountains in the distance, past Disenchantment Bay. Eventually, Dietz convinced two Indian men, Koomanah and Koodleuk, to act as guides, though they had never themselves climbed the glaciers. "The natives are fearful of crossing moving ice," Dietz felt. But not him. He considered the warning silly. "We can easily cross the glacier," he told them. The other hundred-odd passengers and crew from the *Blakeley* disagreed. One party sailed home, the others decided to set off for Dawson on a less vertical route, leaving only Dietz and his eighteen companions to face the Malaspina head-on.

It took a full week to backpack their equipment over the low coastal mountains and attain the foot of the glacier. By then it was mid-April and the days were growing long and warm. They shed their heavy jackets and their shoulders misted with sweat even as their feet numbed along the ice. Beneath them, they heard the gurgling of flowing water cutting crevasses deep and deeper. Four men on snowshoes broke trail, the others following on dogsleds, a thin black train a half mile long. Going was slow, as the snowshoers tested the strength of each section of ice with long poles, and the sleds were no faster. With their masters untrained, the dogs fought constantly. Dietz grew frustrated, "a Chinese puzzle to solve in getting the tangle out of the harnesses," as he struggled to simply keep the dogs in line. They made only a few miles the first day.

Once out on the flat blinding plain of the

glacier, they became hopelessly disoriented. With blue sky above and blue ice below, landmarks were blotted out by the reflected glare that bludgeoned and overwhelmed the smoked goggles worn by the men. Heads bent down to the ice, everyone followed the footsteps of the man ahead, whether the path was smooth or not. Stumbling, some tried to walk with their eyes closed but the waves of ice were uneven and they found it impossible. Dietz braved a squint to peek out and the ice shone like a mirror and engulfed him. Some smeared bacon fat on their eyes, hoping the grease would soothe the burning, but the salt in it only stung harder. Dietz rubbed his burning lids until all the lashes were worn off and he wept blood. Eventually they all wrapped their eyes in handkerchiefs and shuffled forward like a string of blind men, nineteen Sauls on the way to Damascus, led by two Indian guides whose faces were stained with black ash and crushed red berries so that to Dietz they looked like Beelzebub's own demons.

Up, up, always up, the glacier a great ramp into the sky. The dogs stumbled on the rough incline, the only sound their yapping and fighting and the plaited seal-hide lash cracking over their heads, puffs of skin and fur snapping off their backs. The men went silent in the brilliant chill. At night, the company ate flapjacks and beans, cooked over oil lamps that left black soot on every surface. When they packed and moved on, they scraped off the crusted ash and left it to lie on the snow.

"The relief that this one black spot in the landscape gives to my eyes," Dietz said. "More satisfaction out of seeing that dirty black spot of soot than anything else on the glacier."

The ice went on and on. The farther they went, the larger the crevasses grew. Snow bridges filled the gaping holes and they crossed them as an entire party, the pathway sagging under their weight. Koomanah and Koodleuk offered no advice, simply stood and watched the white men proceed and answered no questions. But then they took the snow bridges one by one.

A late-spring blizzard drove them to camp and they awoke to two feet of new snow. Their pace slowed even further. To stop as little as possible they began to eat as they walked, spooning up uncooked evaporated potatoes that wore their throats raw. They stumbled on, day by day, until one plodding afternoon Dietz heard a shout ahead of him.

He looked up to see his physician brother-in-law disappear from view in a single instant.

A sled, four dogs, the party's tonics and medicines, and his sister's husband, all pulled into a crevasse with no warning, as if the earth had sucked them up with a straw.

Dietz and the other men ran to the yawning hole and looked down, terrified about what they might see. It was all a formless darkness, an emptiness the color of the ocean depths. Dietz guessed he could see 250 feet before his eyes failed. Below, they heard a few miserable cries. Someone in the company called for a rope, and they lowered a single man to scout rescue possibilities. Five hundred feet deep, they ran out of rope and never reached the bottom.

There was nothing to do. Pitiful whines rose from the depths. They pulled the rescue man up and turned their backs and left. "What a fate!" Dietz lamented, beside himself. He felt jittery and unnerved and his mind recoiled at telling his sister of this abandonment. Eighteen left in the company.

Fred Weiden, a cheerful pious preacher who had worked for the Young People's Society of Christian Endeavor in New York City, decided they all needed to pray. It was their first worship service since Yakutat, and Dietz found it calming. But from then on he also ordered all the men and sleds tied together.

Several days later, on May 4, after two weeks on the glacier, they thought they finally reached the crest of the massive ice slope. They stopped to make camp and realized the last man in the train was missing. It was Weiden. Three men went back to look for him, and following their trail several miles they found another open trench. This time, there was no talk about lowering a rope. No prayers for the prayer leader. "It has little effect on us," thought Dietz. "Each man a world in himself, and a very narrow world at that." There was a hardening of self-preservation coming over the men, and he could feel the empathy draining, melting away.

The trail was easier now, skating downhill toward a ridgeline ahead. The wind shifted. It was warmer, drier, smelled of the coming mountain summer. They glided for long distances but their way was unclear and sometimes they were blocked by a wide cleft, forcing a backtrack, dragging the gear back up the slope to find a new way. Koomanah and Koodleuk, their guides, continued to stay silent and broke their own trail parallel to the sleds.

As they approached landfall they were blocked by high upthrusts of ice, the glacier crushing and grinding against the range. A maze of columnlike seracs and open fissures and the sound of rushing water. The men were bone weary. Boyden, an old friend of Dietz's, was delirious with exhaustion, and managed only a faint cry as he stumbled on the lip of a crevasse and toppled in. Sixteen remained. But his loss barely registered, for the company was about to attain deliverance.

Ahead and above them a timberline came into view and in that moment they realized they had made it, they had crossed the ice cap, and now only the mountains lay between them and the

Yukon River basin. For fifty days they had experienced only blinding ice and snow, but they now again dreamed there would be dirt under their feet and leaves over their heads. They would reach the Klondike in no time.

"We had not mentioned gold while on the glacier," Dietz realized. "Now, however, we talk of nothing else."

But when they reached the edge of the icefield, they discovered it did not touch the ground. Rather, it ended as a promontory of ice cantilevered over the terra firma, as if they were on the pointed prow of a great ship and the water far below. They followed the crease of the glacier down to where a small stream ran along its edge, and using ropes and pulleys for support, waded to the other side. It took almost a week to move all their goods, including the half-ton dynamo, to dry land.

It was June 1898. They were in the Saint Elias Mountains, home of some of the tallest peaks in North America; directly in their path lay 19,551-foot Mount Logan. Faced with this obstacle, and so desperate were they for gold, that rather than wait until they had completed the two-hundred-mile journey to Dawson they decided to start prospecting right where they stood.

They dug rocks off the hillsides and shook sand in their rusty pans. "Seen any color?" they asked one another, like chatty schoolchildren. With no luck, they moved a few miles farther on, and then again. Their two Indian guides left and Dietz was glad to see them go. "We find our compasses far more reliable than their uncertain ideas," he scoffed. The company fished from glacial lakes and shot woodchuck and ptarmigan and made fine roasts. It was summer and green and they were determined to live on the land and prospect and perhaps go north or not, it mattered little. They had arrived. They would make a strike soon. Dietz felt it, "again comes that insatiable desire for gold."

They worked their way ever north, slowly, digging and prospecting as they went. On July 29, they finally left the dynamo behind, as they could not drag it any farther up the creek beds into the mountains, and after the abandonment they made better time. The men and dogs grew strong on the warm sun and the meat of bear cubs. They were beset by mosquitoes, ate them by the hundreds in their flapjacks, drank them in their coffee grounds. Their pans flashed daily but the mineralogist, Professor Merrill, always declared the sparkles to be quartz and pyrite and fool's gold.

The first man became sick in late August. Andrew Maddis, of Bridgeport, Connecticut, caught a fever and retired to his sleeping bag. All of the team's medicines were with the physician at the bottom of a crevasse. They loaded Maddis on a sled and dragged him and three days later he died. Fifteen.

They skirted Mount Logan to the west and found themselves in an enormous glacial valley. Based on his maps and a rough guess of how far they might have come, Dietz thought they had reached the Tanana River. The days were already turning cold. Mindful of avalanches, they left the sheer mountain slope and found a high point along the river to build a cabin of poplar and plastered mud and a river rock hearth. When the first chimney crumbled, they built a replacement. They cut eight cords of green wood, and made a cache of fish from the river, and as winter came on, the dogs lay fat around the fire.

Blizzards arrived early and heavy. Hunting ceased. So did fishing, wood splitting, prospecting. Snow drifted above the roof. Their world became small, as they retreated to a cabin ten feet by twenty feet.

Halderman, one of the New Yorkers, was the first to panic, and even as the wind whipped he said they must abandon their shelter and move downriver as quickly as possible. Tom Eagen, a police officer, and Henry Bohn, a clerk from Rhode Island, agreed. All day the three spoke of leaving the cabin, finding a mining camp or Indian village, asking directions to Dawson. Dietz couldn't talk them out of it and the more the snow fell the more the men insisted. Eventually, the three took their share of the food, plus a rifle, axe, shovel, and two dogs, and set out into the snow. Dietz never saw them again. Twelve.

Dietz figured the company would be stranded in the cabin for seven months. This void of time— its length, its power, its indifference—gnawed on his mind. "I begin to fear the great unknown darkness ahead of us," he brooded. What would happen to them? They waited in anticipation of the waiting. Dietz prayed for certainty: that they all live, or they all perish, just to know which it would be, rather than being at the perpetual mercy of fate's chance.

He had always been a Christian man but now Dietz felt his fervor rekindled. The whole party felt it. The men took turns reading the Bible continuously. While one man preached aloud, the others cleaned and greased their shovels and picks so that their polished blades gleamed in the firelight.

Inside the cabin, everything was small and petty and quibbled over, the Old Testament word by word. But outside the door? Avalanches, driving winds, plunging temperatures that broke their thermometers. "Nothing but the grandest and most profound demonstrations of nature are left," he thought. "The snow has snuffed out everything but the towering mountains."

They didn't leave their sleeping bags. They didn't change their clothes. They ate once a day, mere crumbs; they had the energy for nothing more. "Time is simply one vast span of eternity—no days, no nights, no weeks, no months," Dietz thought. Some men watched the hands turn on the clock face of their watches, and every twenty-four hours they put a nick in a branch of firewood. But then the watches ran down and they forgot to wind them, and the nicks stopped and the devil's idleness began as the great darkness dragged on.

They plugged every hole and crack in the cabin, so that the chimney's fireplace, home to a flame that could never be allowed to snuff out, was the only vent to the outside. Even so, ice formed two feet from the hearth. Dietz pulled his St. Bernard into his sleeping bag, where neither would move for an entire day. The men developed rheumatism, bedsores, loose teeth that they pulled from their gums by hand. They ate their meat raw, lacking the energy or interest in cooking.

"Behold, the power of gold! Imagine this great army of humanity—the very flower of America's best physical manhood—going down to death for mere gold," he ruminated. Dietz was a godly man. Where had he gone astray? Why were they here? Why so useless and purposeless? What sin had led them to this corporal punishment? Dietz began an examination of conscience.

Each man told every poem he knew, then every hymn, then their genealogy, every root and twig. They whittled wood into lewd shapes. They repeatedly read the tables of weights and measures from the inside cover of their school notebooks. They confessed their sins, simply to have something new to say. They said things they never would have admitted under conventional torture. Time wore them all down to the nub.

After four months of continuous fire, they ran out of wood, and were forced to break their idleness and cut more timber in the depths of winter. The alternative, noted and considered well, was to freeze to death. Rousing themselves to do labor in the cold nearly killed them, so flaccid and weak had they grown in the cabin. After the first outing, they used every excuse not to leave to cut wood again, searching about for other items to burn, including the bones of a bear, the stench of which soaked into every pore.

More months passed. The darkness did not break. Dietz wanted to die but found he could not. "Self-preservation," he thought, "keeps us alive against our wills." Some men offered the theory that the earth had stopped spinning, or the sun had burned out. They said this for something to say. They said this because they believed God and nature had abandoned them to unending frozen night.

Dietz began to question the nature of his existence. Perhaps the Day of Judgment had come and they had been forgotten, overlooked in that unmapped valley? How to persist even one more moment inside those sooty stinking walls. "Life without hope," he declared, "is punishment that will sooner or later drive a person insane."

And then one day a streak of sunlight broke the horizon, and they knew they would live.

Dietz immediately felt the desire for gold stir within him.

Avalanches rang up and down the valley as the men pulled out their nearly forgotten picks and shovels and began to dig through the snow to reach the creek bed gravel near their cabin. Then they cut more timber and made a fire to thaw the earth and dig deeper and deeper. They had been in Alaska over a year and they still had not found gold, and the urgency and anxiety suddenly animated them.

They crafted a windlass and piled a dump of earth and when the river began to run they made a rocker and started washing. Merrill, the mineralogist, contracted a fever and his hair fell out and his teeth fell out but he insisted on supervising the cleanup.

The men found some copper nuggets and a very few fine gold grains in each pan. This was the only gold the Dietz party would recover during their entire expedition.

They wanted more. At this time it entered their minds that they were simply looking in the wrong place for gold, that the foot of the mountains would be more promising terrain. Three men—Horman, Norris, and Harry Davis, an engineer from Brooklyn—set out to scout the creek beds and prospect, find a new camp for the summer. When they did not return for three weeks, Dietz and three other men followed on a rescue. They found the small party's tent abandoned, and nearby a roaring snowmelt river in a deep gorge with a new scar of a rock slide scouring the mountainside. The dogs whined and sniffed; the avalanche had swept away any trace of the three poor souls.

Nine.

At last the terror of the wilderness overcame their avarice. The remaining members of the New York and Bridgeport Mining Company decided to leave Alaska while they could. Their food and ammunition and will were spent, the summer of 1899 nearly so. They would wait until the first snow and then make directly for the coast. No one knew precisely how to get there, and Davis, the engineer who died in the avalanche, had all their maps showing their route in. So they would follow the river, once it froze, in the steps of Halderman, Eagen, and Bohn, who had struck out the year before rather than face the winter marooned in the cabin. This snowy route would be downhill, sure to end at the sea, and allow them to use their sleds to transport the bedbound Merrill.

They killed six of their dogs and fed the carcasses to the remaining teams and stockpiled smoked fish for themselves. They grew weaker and anxiously waited for the snow to come. They needed the snow to move Merrill. The summer ended and the frost arrived and then Merrill died without a whisper. Eight.

The hour had grown late. They set out on the frozen river, a choppy plane of icy ridges and bare rock that frustrated the dogsleds. Early winter squalls harassed them, forced them to seek shelter, snowbound behind a windbreak of sleds. They pierced a canyon and then entered a wide valley and unexpectedly bumped into an Indian settlement. The Indians offered seal meat for the men to eat but Dietz found that he was too weak to chew.

The Indians directed the party south. The long night had resettled over the country. The dogs were reduced to shadows of ribs and loose skin. Frostbite mangled their feet and stole their toes. And then, after several days of rough labor, they made a terrifying discovery.

They found themselves, inexplicably, back on the far western arm of the mammoth glacier that they had escaped eighteen months before.

The thought of crossing the glacier again was almost too much to bear. One man, Evans, saw his frostbitten feet swell to twice their normal size; he lay down on his sled and never moved again. Seven. The dogs pulled until their paws stained the ice red and then the men started to kill the dogs and eat them. They stumbled for weeks down the slope of the glacier until one day the field of white ahead turned blue, and they noticed sand beneath their feet, and they realized they had reached the Pacific Ocean.

They burned the sleds for warmth and killed the rest of the dogs. The last to die was Dietz's St. Bernard, who had shared his sleeping bag in the cabin the winter before. When the dog meat ran out, they ate dead fish that washed up on the beach. They put driftwood and the dog skins on the fire and crawled in their sleeping bags and the party slowly and quietly started to die one by one.

Of the nineteen who set out in the original company, only Dietz and three other men survived. They were picked up by the USS *Wolcott*, a Coast Guard cutter, in the spring of 1900, a full two years after they originally set out from Yakutat. The ship's crew saw the smoke from their signal fire and followed it and in an unnamed cove discovered the horrific camp of rotting fish and dog bones and dead men so stretched and skeletal as to be mummified. Three corpses lay stiff in their sleeping bags, and of the four who lived, two were struck permanently blind from the snow glare and at least one went mad.

When Dietz arrived back in New York City his wife did not recognize him. She thought his return a hoax, then an uncanny resurrection and she shrank from his sunken Lazaran face until Dietz's little six-year-old son ran up and reached for his father.

Like Dietz and the members of his failed mining company, Jack London passed many lonesome months shut away in a poor cabin in the northern wilderness. Slowly, hungrily, 1897 drew to a close, and the long dark days of 1898 began.

It was the silence that unnerved him. He had never before experienced a place with no insects, no birds, no sun, no sounds save for his own breathing and the creaking of the frozen birches.

"The world sleeps," he thought. "Like the sleep of death."

It was London's own fault that he passed much of that winter alone, though it didn't start that way. At first, he bunked with his shipmates from the *Yukon Belle*, Goodman and Sloper and Thompson. Soon they were joined by other stampeders who had been waylaid and stuck on their journey to Dawson. The cloister consisted of a huddle of cabins on a small wooded island, a mound of glacial sand in a low swampy delta where the Yukon and Stewart rivers join in a confused, multi-channeled jumble. It was Thompson who had first identified the camp, figuring it an old Hudson's Bay Company post. As winter settled in, the men in those dilapidated shacks turned inward, and only the daily routine of chores broke the black monotony: chop ice, gather firewood, cook, sleep.

They hunkered down against the frightening cold, the red-hot stove powerless to heat any part of the body not directly facing the fire. Sweat across the forehead and feet solid blocks of ice. London read books by the feeble light of a slush lamp, which everyone called the bitch and burned enough bacon grease to leave a film on every surface of the cabin.

That winter of quiet, London did nearly all of the talking. He was an unceasing emitter of smoke and speech, rolling cigarettes one after the other with his stained fingers and telling magnificent tales, of visiting Japan and riding the rails as a hobo and getting locked in jail in Buffalo and his attempt to march on Washington with Coxey's Army. London was younger than his companions and they endured his monologues with amusement. He had a tangle of brown hair and two missing teeth lost during a fight on a ship and he said that back home he was known as "the Boy Socialist of Oakland."

London told them that after the Panic of 1893 he got a job in a jute mill, replacing bobbins of thread that would be woven into burlap bags. He made a dollar a day. Then he got a job in a coal plant, where he was paid by the load, not the hour, shoveling until the last pile was clear no matter how long it took. London had replaced a man who quit because of the exploitive conditions, and then, when he couldn't find a new job, killed himself. That's why London joined the Oakland regiment of the Industrial Army of the Unemployed, to go to Washington and demand better jobs. He made it only to Des Moines, though, before they all ran out of food and London struck out on his own. "The wanderlust in my blood that will not let me rest," he said. He ran the rails on the Southern Pacific without compunction because the Octopus, as they all called it, owed him a ride.

He drank to oblivion and got in bar fights. In July 1894 he was arrested for vagrancy while hoboing in Niagara Falls and was tossed in a dungeon for a month. His police record described him as a "sailor" and an "atheist" and a "tramp." When London tried to plead not guilty the judge told him to shut up.

He saw horrors there. Walls, floors, ceiling swarming with insects. A man who trapped sparrows and ate them. A mulatto boy who was thrown down eight flights of stairs and kicked and beaten until naked and bloody as freshly butchered offal. "Hereditary inefficients, degenerates, wrecks, lunatics, addled intelligences, epileptics, monsters, weaklings," that's who London said ended up in the Buffalo jail. They fought each other in cages, their only weapons broom handles, used by the men to beat each other or far worse.

On the Stewart River, stuck inside their cabins and playing endless games of cards, London tried to convince them all that only through collective action and racial separation could white men free themselves of their oppressors. London read Kipling's *The Seven Seas* and Milton's *Paradise Lost* and Darwin's *On the Origin of Species* again and again. Evolution had scientifically proved the falsity of God, London said, and implied the requirement of men to raise their station and free themselves from the infested sties within which modern society penned them.

"What is truth? Is there justice in this world?" London asked, as if he did not already have a ready answer.

Eventually these sermons wore on even the most patient man. Through the twin burdens of time and proximity, London realized how unlike his cabinmates he was. "Save existence, we have nothing in common," he thought. Life on Stewart Island deteriorated. They stopped washing and started quarreling, fighting over trifles and slights. Worried that food would grow scarce, they began stuffing themselves, to make sure they ate their share. One day, while trying to chop ice from the river, London damaged Sloper's axe, and when Sloper went for his rifle, that's when the Boy Socialist knew it was time to find other sleeping arrangements for the winter.

In October, before they began their long hibernation, Big Jim Goodman had reported that he got some good colors on a creek not too far away. The creek was named for some old sourdough called Robert Henderson, though no one knew who that was. Everyone went up the draw and staked a section. London's claim was Number Fifty-Four, two and a half miles up the left fork of Henderson Creek.

London found a little abandoned cabin up near his claim, seventeen miles from the main camp at the Stewart River, in an isolated valley where he could hunt moose. The walls of the cabin were twelve logs high, dovetailed at the corners, and bore two windows, each two feet square. A couple of bunks lay along the far wall and a sheet-iron stove stood near the door. The cabin sat in the middle of a flat marshy area, a swamp made up of clumps of grass and sod that many men called "niggerheads." There was no way to walk on the tussocks, they swayed and fell apart and he stumbled into the mud and muck hiding permanent black ice beneath. London cursed the niggerheads and sat by the fire to dry out.

To avoid the ire of his bunkmates, London spent much of early 1898 in that small cabin, thinking about the land and the wolves and the gold in his claim. "Beyond this bleak sky-line there stretch vast solitudes, and beyond these still vaster solitudes," he thought, with a certain circularity that induced a stupor. Lethargy hung on him like a chained collar, his refuge felt like a crypt.

He was stalked by the demons of cold and silence and darkness. Superstition ruled. London's imagination took hold of him. Every dark corner held a secret. And a threat. London felt suspended in a void, meditating on "the absence of light and motion; the infinite peace of the brooding land; the ghastly silence." Sometimes he just sat and listened to his heart beat in his breast.

It was at this time that scurvy, the Klondike plague, first came on him. Lassitude. Swollen, stiffened joints. Pustules. A loathsome, purplish rash. His skin started to turn black; his mouth, gums, and lips went white. As a former sailor, London understood the affliction was brought on by lack of fresh vegetables, but this knowledge did not allow him to conjure the cure. The disease had arrived at the Stewart River as well, each man mocking the other's symptoms. They wore rags and their whiskers grew long and they pushed needles into their toes to make sure they were not frostbit.

Up at his little cabin on Henderson Creek, London lay in a stasis by the stove, the mice nibbling at his nose, running under his clothes.

"Quit this horrid dream," he begged. The California sun felt centuries away. Death lay as his bunkmate. It hurt to move, but the firebox had a ravenous hunger and he dare not let it grow cold. London chopped wood on his knees when he could no longer stand.

On January days, London would spit outside and listen for the crackle. If it froze, if his warm spit burst into ice before it hit the ground, then the temperature was more than 50 degrees below zero.

It was a struggle, just to move, to breathe. To build a fire. How could any living thing survive such a place? He felt like the "sole speck of life journeying across the ghostly wastes of a dead world." The frozen stillness was overwhelming; he was so small. "A maggot's life, nothing more."

One long night that winter, lying on his hard bunk in the endless darkness, body failing him, London made a decision, a resolution even. No more jute mills or coal yards. No more pickle factories or dollar-a-day jobs. No more slaving for another man's capital. He would do what he had long dreamed of. He would set his own way.

London pulled out a pencil and, standing awkwardly on his weakened legs, wrote a message on the icy log next to his bed:

"Jack London, Miner, author, Jan 27, 1898."

From then on, he was determined to be a writer. He had staked his claim.

CHAPTER SIX
1898

Neither law nor order prevailed, honest persons had no protection from the gangs of rascals who plied their nefarious trade. Might was right.
—LIEUTENANT COLONEL SAMUEL STEELE, NORTH-WEST MOUNTED POLICE

The day after Jack London scrawled his name on the inside of a Yukon cabin, a letter arrived at the North-West Mounted Police barracks at Fort Macleod, an outpost on the Canadian prairie almost fifteen hundred miles to the southeast. The letter was addressed to the garrison commander, Samuel Steele, who was snug at home with his wife and small children. Steele was a proper, upright Victorian officer. Fastidious. Particular. Well-groomed. He was a forty-one-year-old up-and-comer who had fought Indians and hanged smugglers and was awaiting his next promotion and assignment.

The letter was a set of military orders. He would leave the next day to report for duty in the Klondike. The chaos caused by the mob moving north had reached such a tumult that the Canadian government planned to send hundreds of armed men to tame it.

Up until then, there was very little police or military presence in the Yukon valley. Inspector Charles Constantine, a veteran lawman, and a single sergeant had arrived in 1894. They documented the influx of American prospectors and rampant bootlegging but between the two of them could do little but write reports to Ottawa. More North-West Mounted Police officers had been sent in the three years since, but still only a baker's dozen patrolled that enormous wilderness in early 1897.

But now Steele would be put in command of a force of two hundred men and horse. It was the largest expedition in the history of the Mounted Police, and yet dwarfed by the swarm of tens of thousands of cheechakos they were meant to protect.

Steele had work to do. Equipment, food, transportation. "Get things in shape for that country," he thought.

Sam Steele was a natural military man who came by the work honestly. His much older father served in the Royal Navy, first fighting Napoleon and then the United States in the opening skirmishes of the War of 1812. Steele's mother died when he was very young, his elderly father soon after. Ambition and a youthful naive wanderlust led him to the military profession, first the army, in the infantry, and then the newly established North-West Mounted Police in 1873; he was the third man to swear the oath.

The Mounted Police would be more soldiers than constables, clad in dark grim coats and jackboots. They were a light cavalry regiment, in truth, equipped to cover the vast distances of the Western frontier, with field guns to engage the well-armed and organized Indian nations they would encounter. Across the high plains Steele would track whiskey smugglers and lynch mobs and the reviled "wolfers" who poisoned the animals for their pelts.

Steele took to the work and excelled. He thrived in that unique environment: part field expedition to make war, part showing-the-flag pomp and ceremony in which they wore bright red in honor of their British heritage and to distinguish themselves from the traditional blue of the police. A prodigious writer of letters and a daily journal, Steele kept a fine understated record of garrison life, an inexhaustible series of inspections, summary judgments, and correspondence sent and received. A typical entry: "Very busy. Decided several cases and looked after a lot of work. Wrote many letters to people, and gave a great deal of advice." A respected pillar of reticence, and a fine specimen of his era.

But Steele could lead and fight as well. After

Sitting Bull defeated Custer at the Battle of Little Bighorn, the Lakota chief brought three thousand of his warriors and their families north to Canada, where Steele was part of the delegation that negotiated his extradition back to the United States. And at the head of a mounted column known as Steele's Scouts, he chased the Cree across the prairie, eventually fighting them on a small isthmus between two lakes and forcing their retreat.

The assignment to the Yukon came at an opportune time. Steele was at a nadir. After eight years at Fort Macleod, he was listless, and had not made a journal entry for five months. A silver mine he'd invested in had failed, falling prey to American political divisions over currency backing and the upper class's stranglehold on the gold supply. He needed a new challenge.

Steele's orders were twofold. First, to secure the border against American incursions, by establishing two new posts along the White and Chilkoot passes. Both Canada and the United States claimed the land between the coast and the inland lakes, from Skagway and Dyea all the way up to Lake Bennett, and the Ottawa government wanted a bright borderline set and held. Second, Steele would move to Dawson and establish a barracks and headquarters for the region. They would promote him to lieutenant colonel to do it. Steele accepted the assignment with relish.

The commandeered SS *Thistle*, a former seal hunting boat, left Vancouver with Steele aboard on February 6, 1898. Steele was at home on a horse, not a pitching boat, but by his own reckoning he endured the voyage better than most. Snowy hurricanes lashed the seas, their small boat rolling like a bobbing cork amongst the fresh remains of ships wrecked upon hidden reefs. More concerning to a gentleman, the food was hurried and subpar, and Steele thought his wretched berth smelled like ancient cheese.

By the time Steele arrived, in the middle of February, the stampede was six months old, and Skagway no longer a muddy tidal flat filled with haphazard tents, as Tappan Adney and the first wave of cheechakos had known it. Skagway had grown into a town of thousands, with packed rutted streets and wood-plank saloons and flop-houses full of charlatans and good-time girls. A classic boomtown, with all the disorder that implied.

Steele spent six weeks in Skagway, waiting for the bulk of his police forces to arrive by boat, and he found the town intolerably chaotic. "About the roughest place in the world," he thought. Extortion, kidnapping, robbery, stabbings, shootings. Steele met with a U.S. Army captain who claimed to be in charge but in reality was inept and overmatched. One of the packers Steele hired to carry his freight over the White

Pass was swindled in a dance hall to the tune of $3,750 in drinks and cigars. When the proprietor complained to Steele that the man didn't pay his whole bill, Steele told him no payment was forthcoming and to stay on the American side of the border.

The lawlessness extended up and down the stampede trails. In Sheep Camp, a long day's hike up the Chilkoot, two men were caught stealing and the mob sentenced them to trail justice. One of the men, Wellington, escaped from his captors and tried to run but as he was about to be caught he pulled out a revolver and shot himself in the head. The other man, Hansen, was held firm and given no chance to flee. He was a young man, with a light beard. The mob stripped him naked to the waist, blindfolded him, strung him up to a truss, and gave him the lash. Fifty strokes with a knotted rope and then they untied him from the whipping post and hung a sign around his neck that read "thief" and sent him back down the trail.

At this time, Major A. Bowen Perry, who had arrived in Alaska a few months earlier, was passing through Sheep Camp on his way out to Skagway to meet with Steele. Perry watched the whole scene, and then descended the rest of the way to the coast in a horse-drawn cart, sitting on Wellington's corpse.

Again, the U.S. Army didn't seem too bothered

by mob rule. "Horrible," Steele thought. And fundamentally unprofessional.

In this, and every other way, Skagway was too much. Steele had no proper company. He couldn't sleep, all night long listening to "the howling of dogs, women, pistol shots, shrieks, yells and curses." And the poker dens and pleasure palaces hosted acts tawdry and undignified. "In the dance hall the girl with the straw-coloured hair trips the light fantastic at a dollar a set," he thought, untempted.

To Steele, the source of the licentiousness was obvious: Soapy Smith and his gang of pimps, confidence men, shell game swindlers, and common thugs. "150 ruffians," Steele guessed, "run the town and do what they please." One night his quarters were in the line of fire, bullets passing through the wood plank walls as the running gunfight moved up and down the street. If Steele had not been lying on the floor, he would have been hit. Soapy Smith was an old-fashioned outlaw from the American West, and his posse robbed and murdered at will. Steele saw the body from one execution in a back alley, "powder marks on his back and his pockets inside out."

Steele and the stampeders alike were trapped with Soapy Smith's gang due to the heavy snow that fell in the mountain passes all the late winter and into early spring. Steele himself was so desperate to get out of Skagway—move over the pass into Canada, before the crowds stuck there killed themselves too—that in mid-March he and a few of his men went to Dyea and set off up the Chilkoot right into the teeth of a blizzard. They moved slowly, hunched, from boulder to boulder, holding on so as not to be swept from the mountain.

On the Chilkoot, Steele saw unprepared cheechakos in every state of misery. The stampeders were like a swarm of locusts drawing a curtain over the land, swallowing every tree for firewood and every exposed twig and blade of grass for their horses, leaving nothing but the rock and trodden dirt path. Graves lined the trail and the banks of the river. Some people would lie down and simply not get up, the snow soft and inviting like a city dweller's favorite quilt or feather bed back home. One woman dug a hole in the snow for herself and her young baby. She wrapped her body around the child and quietly died and when rescuers found her the cradled baby was unmoving but alive.

A new camp had been established, Canyon City, at the river fork where the steep gorge turned to the northeast and rose to the main pass. By the winter of 1898, over a thousand people lived there in a chilled stasis, the surrounding hills cut bare except for a few useless matchsticks in the steepest draws. There was a large boiler in Canyon City, made by the Union Iron Works of

San Francisco in 1886, but it was there to power a new aerial tramway which would carry freight to the Scales, not heat the town. The cheechakos shivered on.

Steele and his party attempted to summit the Chilkoot, but battered by the wind, they withdrew to a cluster of tents, dug into the drift banks and reachable by a tunnel cut in the snow, where they waited three days for the weather to clear. It never did. Eventually, Steele retreated back to Skagway.

Storms ravaged the pass that spring, and snow clung to the upper cliffs and glaciers, built up in great towering heaps upon the massifs that overhung the trail. But as the days lengthened and the skies cleared, the stampede at last resumed. The crowd was eager to get over the pass and to Lake Bennett. Two of those people in the spring rush were, unexpectedly, part of the original settlement of the Klondike: Clarence and Ethel Berry.

Having spent the fall and winter in California enjoying their wealth and celebrity, the Berrys decided to return to Dawson to meet up with Clarence's brothers, who were already there, and oversee the next spring cleanup. Plus, the trip offered Ethel's younger sister Tot the chance to come and experience the adventure of the age that she had read about in all the newspapers.

The Berrys sailed to Skagway, took a small

boat to Dyea, and started up the Chilkoot, but then found themselves stuck because their Indian packers refused to go any farther up the mountain.

That the pass might close days at a time was not new. Old-timer sourdoughs knew all the stories, how Bill Stewart was caught in a storm and crawled into his sleeping robe and existed there for nine days eating raw oatmeal and tallow candles. How Sid Wilson and John Reid were trapped even longer, ate raw cornmeal and the dried salmon meant for their dogs. At least Wilson and Reid cut their dogs loose, so the beasts ran off and disappeared forever into the white death. Not Whiskey Thompson. They said Thompson ate his dogs raw.

So when the snow fell too thick, the Indian packers wouldn't move. But now that the snow had stopped, and the hot sun beat on the mountainside, they wouldn't move either. Clarence Berry checked when they would leave and the Indian packers said "Not yet, big snow comes fast." Clarence became frustrated, but deferred to their verdict.

Ethel and Tot were two of the very few women in the stampede and so attracted a lot of attention. To wash and dress, they hid inside a double-walled tent held together with six-inch safety pins. Men would stand outside and shout at the women to be allowed in and when one man tried to force his way through, Clarence appeared and dropped him with a blow to the jaw, saying, "You are not wanted here." Even so, Tot longed to go to the dance hall, where a few women were swinging and swearing and playing roulette, doing things she had never seen before. But Clarence forbade it.

Ethel was shocked by the decadence—there was too much work and not enough food for such vice in her time on Eldorado Creek—but not Clarence. He knew the temptations of alcohol-fueled dance halls and the demimonde, and in younger years he might have enjoyed it himself. But for some time he had consciously returned to his wife each night, to keep his money and his marriage. "The old saying, easy come easy go," he preached. For Tot's sake, though, they needed to move on.

More time passed. Heavy snow had fallen for weeks, but now warm air blew in from the south. High above the Chilkoot, the snowpack quivered, precarious. The Indian packers wouldn't go. The sourdough white men wouldn't go. The stampeders pressed on.

The Berrys grew increasingly anxious to join the throng. Every day Clarence asked the packers when they could go, and every day got the same response. The sun beat on the heights.

When the weather shifted again, and snow began to fall once more in the high peaks, Berry wondered whether the concern had been for nothing, if any danger had passed. And so on the morning of Palm Sunday, April 3, 1898, Clarence went to the packers one more time.

"Not yet," one of the Indians said. "Sun too hot. Big rush of snow come pretty quick."

Not a few hours later, the avalanche struck.

In truth, there were five separate snowfalls, not one, though the last was so vast and deadly that it would overshadow the others. The night before, two smaller slides dropped on the Scales near the top of the pass, sending stampeders and construction workers, who were trying to install the new electrical aerial tramway, scurrying back down the trail to lower elevations. And thus many hundreds of people, thinking they were fleeing danger, entered a narrow canyon just as warm winds and heavy sleet hit the unstable snowpack perched on ledges hundreds of feet above their heads.

The snow blew sideways and the stampeders could not see the man and woman next to them, much less the trail they hoped to descend. Some held a rope to stay together. Others wandered off on side paths and found themselves in ravines of deep snow even before the mountain did its worst.

Suddenly the gusty leading edge of a storm front struck from the east and then everything happened at once. The entire earth seemed to shake in a heart-tearing crescendo of sound and wind from above and behind and then all around. Air and snow fused as one as the avalanche fell on the line in a roar and in a terrifying moment all was left in muffled choking silence.

The Berrys could hear low thunder in the distance, then gunshots to summon help. A crowd from Sheep Camp ran up the pass in a frantic effort to rescue those buried alive. They dug out one woman and she said her husband was still trapped, so they started to pull him out as well. His head and arms appeared and he breathed free air and then the mountain shook again. Everyone yelled that another slide was coming and ran. The man was still trapped and when the second rush of snow and rock fell he was lost forever.

The avalanche covered an area of ten acres in thirty feet of snow, and all across the field, men and women dug with spades and mattocks from their mining outfits. They exhumed bodies in every possible orientation and state. Some lay peaceful, as if asleep, and some were upside down, as if strung up by their feet, with looks of desperate terror. Bound and slowly suffocated in the dark.

Dozens of corpses came out of the snow. The bodies were taken to a morgue at Sheep Camp where petty thieves stripped them of anything valuable. Clarence helped nail together coffins, and Ethel and Tot lined them with black cloth and included notes about the little that was known of each man or woman. Tot thought the frozen bodies looked natural, like real life. As if they might get up at any moment and walk to the goldfields.

No one knew how many died; every newspaper had different lists of different names. It could have been as many as a hundred. Some bodies weren't found until the snow melted later that spring.

Sam Steele received a report three weeks after the incident, saying that the storm had finally broken, leaving sixty feet of snow on the main trail and adjoining peaks and glaciers. The report listed seventy-two names of the dead: fifty-three stampeders and nineteen construction workers. As was his habit, Steele wrote a personal letter to the next of kin of every person killed.

The Palm Sunday Avalanche was the single greatest calamity of the stampede, and the deadliest such incident the United States had ever known.

Steele himself never made it over the Chilkoot. The daunting snow and ice forced him back to Skagway, and instead he had to ride a horse over the White Pass, which had been the death of so many beasts. He nearly lost his own mount too. Steele was sick and exhausted, too nauseated to eat, and as he descended his horse tumbled and they pitched together down the slope, the horse rolling over him several times. Steele took the horn of the saddle hard in his gut but held on and somehow wasn't crushed.

In this case, the horse survived. As a mounted police officer, Steele was no sentimental horse lover, he worked and used the animals as needed. But to have so many die from negligence and incompetence that the pass earned the Dead Horse Trail stigma? It bothered him as a military professional. "Ill-usage and starvation," he thought. It was just inefficient.

In his first ordered task, to establish and seal the border against American intrusions, Steele succeeded well. After the colonel arrived, the White Pass became a mighty fortress, peaks as turrets, a high wall guarded by snow and cold and men with rifles, .303 Lee-Metford carbines and belt-fed Maxim machine guns. "A wonderful weapon," in Steele's opinion. Despite continuous ice and wind, the Mounted Police built small posts, single cabins and a few tents, at the very summit of the pass; the men shoveled out the doors and chimney all night, lest they be smothered under a heavy strangling blanket of snow. The Mounted Police raised the flag of the Dominion, and the standard of Queen Victoria's empire flew for the world to see.

But when he arrived at Lake Bennett in early April, Steele found that his second task, to save the mob from itself, was far tougher. Crowded on the frozen lakeshore lay a muddled camp of thirty thousand hungry and desperate stampeders, so many white tents like a flock of seagulls on the beach.

His orders were to project an air of calm and sovereignty. What he found was a disaster.

Steele had men to secure the border and keep the gangsters of Skagway at bay, but what he needed was adequate food and a dose of sanity for the tens of thousands of stampeders along the trail. "It seems that some men are more likely to make trouble than to stave it off," Steele thought. He quickly saw that if he couldn't conjure grub into existence, he could at least keep the incipient famine at Dawson from getting worse.

Steele's first major act was to require that any person who passed his camp at Lake Bennett carry a ton of food each, enough for up to a year. By increasing the burden on each individual cheechako, the regulation had the dual benefit of increasing the food supplies in Dawson while also limiting the total influx, turning around many an ill-prepared pretender.

His second act was to send his officers out to the impromptu shipyards and inspect every boat before it could leave Lake Bennett and run the rapids of Miles Canyon and the White Horse. And that day of reckoning, when the mob would suddenly be unshackled, was coming, soon.

"The ice is bad, in fact dangerous now," Steele realized. Under the lake's frozen surface, the liquid water drains away, leaving large air holes that could swallow the unwary. Soon even the upper crust would break. The sun grew hot that spring, and Steele thought the fish ran so thick in the smaller side creeks that a horse might ford a stream by simply stepping on their backs. It was all a sign. The great rivers and lakes were about to bust free.

There was a locomotive coming. A whisper. A tremor. The very earth rumbled and groaned, as up and down the Yukon valley the ice began to crack and split and pitch.

Breakup had come. Jack London knew it was finally time to go.

And not a day too soon.

London's scurvy had almost completely incapacitated him. His stupor and stiff joint pain had progressed to bleeding gums, wobbly teeth, and splotchy purplish skin that was soft and pliable, like bread dough. Pushed in with a finger, it left a sodden dent. Most striking, he was now crippled from the waist down, his palsied right leg limp against his chest. If he didn't get treatment soon, he'd die at the Stewart River. He needed to get to Dawson.

Having worn out his welcome with Sloper and the original boat crew, London found a new traveling companion, a man named Doc Harvey. While he may or may not have been a trained physician, he was, usefully, willing to perform surgery. One man staying in their cluster of cabins on Stewart Island had broken his ankle crossing the Chilkoot and as it never set properly it started to fester with gangrene. Doc Harvey offered to do the work, but they needed anesthetic. All winter London had kept a jug of whiskey in his medicine chest, and though it sorely tempted him every day, he knew he had to save it, if frostbite and scurvy required amputation. Reluctantly, longingly, London handed over the whiskey. Then doctor and patient proceeded to drain the entire bottle and once they were both good and drunk Harvey got down to cutting. The mangled man survived.

Now out of liquor, London was eager for the river to clear and safe passage to open. The ice was rotting away along the shore, leaving gaps where open water rushed, pushing on the floes ahead that stacked and piled sometimes forty feet high. These massive chunks of ice, thousands of pounds each, jumbled into grinding dams that spilled floods over the banks, the pressure behind the ice wall building and building and then breaking free and pouring downstream in torrents, until the next spontaneous jam.

It was exhilarating and terrifying, the water rising and falling a dozen feet every day. "On the breast of a jarring ice flood," London thought, thus would the stampede finally arrive in Dawson.

As the ice broke, objects appeared in the water. Lost outfits and pieces of wrecked boats. An entire boom of logs. Doc Harvey and London commandeered this last find, tearing down their cabin and using the timber and new logs to lash together a simple raft. With London lame, Doc Harvey had to do the construction by himself.

Wracked with pain, London was desperate to get to a doctor in Dawson and be cured. But he was also eager to return home to California, $5 of gold in his pocket and a lode of stories in his head.

On the 8th of May, the river ice in the heart of Yukon gold country, between Fortymile and Sixtymile, broke free. The next day, Lake Laberge cleared of ice. Slowly, slowly the thaw worked its way upstream. The jam at Miles Canyon didn't clear for weeks, but finally the many arms of Tagish Lake freed on May 28, and the next day Lake Bennett opened as well.

Finally, after seven months of hunger, frostbite, and anxious torporous inactivity, the stampede was back on.

Lieutenant Colonel Samuel Steele looked out over the motley collection of skiffs, bateaux, Peterborough Canoes, and rowboats waiting to launch at Lake Bennett. His men had counted

7,142 boats, loaded with thirty million pounds of supplies, all of it carried by hand over the passes. Steele thought it the largest fleet ever assembled in Canadian waters.

The vast majority of these incompetent amateur sailors had never piloted their own boat, much less built one, before heading to the Klondike. Keeping them from killing themselves was now the primary task of Steele and his men. It was a huge job, inspecting every boat for seaworthiness; a week before breakup, the mounted police had duly registered only a fifth of the total fleet. And another seven thousand boats waited to launch upstream at Lake Lindeman. Maybe fifteen thousand total craft in the initial rush alone.

And every day, more cheechakos crossed the Chilkoot and White Pass, fed by steamers constantly dumping loads of passengers in Skagway and Dyea. For even as small local newspapers reported the tragedies that befell their native sons—two dead in a landslide here, seventeen dead in a drowning there—the largest major papers continued to publish "How to Go, What to Take" stories that promoted the wealth and opportunity to be found in the Klondike.

When the main throng set out, Steele thought he counted eight hundred boats sailing across the lake at once, gunwale to gunwale and all headed to Miles Canyon and the White Horse Rapids. Steele himself enjoyed running the breaks in a canoe. It reminded him of days in his youth on the Winnipeg River and the lands of the mythic voyageurs. "A fine and rather exciting thing," he thought, imagining the thrill ride.

But not for the untested greenhorns who had no idea of the challenge that awaited them. "A current which runs like a mill race," leading to a whirlpool's maw, and in the center of the rapid, standing waves taller than any man, a ridge that stood a boat right on its stern. "Many fools are attempting to go down and are losing their stuff through striking rocks," he realized. If they were lucky, that's all they'd lose.

So the following day, Steele boarded a steamer and traveled the hundred miles to the White Horse, overtaking many boats relying on wind and strong backs, to supervise the navigation of the deadly flume.

When Jack London ran those rapids eight months before, in the vanguard of the stampede, grave markers already lined the riverside. In the time since, waves of ignorant cheechakos had thrown themselves at the rapids with predictable results, bodies and broken boats carpeting the river bottom.

Above the canyon, Steele found several thousand boats tied off, waiting to run the chute. A river steamer that had tried to run outfits through the worst of the rapids had already wrecked during the first rush from Lake Bennett the day before. And so impatient stampeders had begun to run the cataract on their own. In only a single day, 150 boats and ten men were lost. Steele's police had rescued women and children from the waters and so a bottleneck formed, as cheechakos weighed their safety against the desire for gold. "Remarkable that more people were not drowned," thought Steele, and he moved to action.

Steele called everyone together. Many appeared to be Americans, rowdy and uncouth. He addressed them in a loud voice.

"There are many of your countrymen who have said that the Mounted Police make the laws as they go along," he said. "And I am going to do so now for your own good."

Steele began by ordering every woman and child out of the boats and forbidding them from running the rapids in the canyon or at the White Horse.

"If they are strong enough to come to the Klondike they can walk the five miles," he said.

His next order required every boat to be drawn to shore to be checked by the police, to ensure sufficient freeboard. That is, that each craft had enough decking above the waterline of the rapids they ran. In addition, the same corporal who inspected the boats would inspect the men who intended to crew them, and if he deemed them deficient in health or skill they were not allowed to pass. In the end, the Mounted Police established a de facto licensing system, allowing only a few qualified pilots to guide the craft through the canyon for $5 each.

After Steele intervened, thousands of boats ran the box canyon and the Mane of the White Horse and not a single one was lost.

Steele returned to Lake Bennett the next day. The snows were melting, the water opening, and the disheveled parade of stampeders continued. He saw every kind of tub and pontoon and proper canoe, carrying every kind of person and all manner of cargo, livestock and sundry supplies, all meant for sale in Dawson. It was a migration to dwarf the Serengeti. A continuous line of women and men, from the shore at Skagway to the dry docks of Lake Lindeman to the flotilla stretching hundreds of miles along the Yukon itself, until the bleeding edge finally approached the Klondike.

There in the distance were fields of white tents, smoking cabins, and saloons. The El Dorado of their dreams. Dawson City.

For months the mob had heard so many stories trickle out of Dawson. It was both a land of deliverance, where gold nuggets lay like Easter eggs upon the very ground, and a land of want, nothing but famine in extreme cold and darkness.

Would Dawson provide bounty and grace, or simply further deprivation?

What those cheechakos found, in May of 1898, was a noisy, crowded, mud-caked, and largely drunken city of flooded streets, rampant typhoid and syphilis, and every bit of prospective gold-filled creek within two dozen miles already staked.

All the best claims were taken. All the businesses were established. All the overworked prostitutes were worn as raw as the stampeders' blistered feet.

They were too late. The mob had come all that way for nothing.

CHAPTER SEVEN

> All wanted a gold mine and wanted us to show them where they could find one right away. We thought we had a foolish mob.
> —BELINDA MULROONEY

That summer, stampeders wandered up and down Dawson City's Front Street in a state of bewilderment, too exhausted and confused to do more than shuffle in a herd and stare at the garish signs of the saloons and dance halls and gambling dens.

The Combination, the Dominion, the Northern, the Pacific, the Green Tree. Games of faro and whiskey and clubs full of good-time girls, all ruled by the Klondike Kings, the men who had arrived in Dawson at the very beginning, made the first mining claims, and reaped the rewards. Big Alex MacDonald. Charlie Anderson, the "Lucky Swede." Swiftwater Bill, who once lost $5,000 a hand at cards, married one dance hall girl after another, including the infamous Gussie Lamore and her two sisters, and opened the Monte Carlo pleasure palace because every fox dreams of owning his own henhouse.

The saloons were open continuously six days a week, closed only for a respite on Sunday, and even so the Salvation Army was particularly exercised by the greed and wickedness and flagrant wrongs. "An angel couldn't keep good in Dawson City," they wrote. The corruption was not limited by gender or class or age. Everyone had the fever. One night a pack of young boys swept up the dirt on the floor of the Northern Saloon and panned out half an ounce of gold dust. And even when the Pioneer Hall advertised "Clean-Cut Family Entertainment," it turned out to be bloody "Moving Pictures of the Spanish-American War," presented in Wondroscope. Tickets were only one dollar.

Gold was worth $17 an ounce and anything could be bought with it. It was considered bad manners to watch the proprietor weigh out the dust, so you turned your back while he swindled you with wet fingers. The mining inspectors had hired the Big Four, all men who weighed at least 250 pounds, to keep the peace through fear and intimidation. Therefore scores between miners, over the jumping of claims or the stolen affections of the sporting girls, were settled in the early mornings, after long lit nights of drinking. Rarely was a man shot in plain sight at the bar or in the open muddy street. No, the violence was properly hidden away, as manners dictated, in the private balconies off the main stage or in the rooms above.

Night was bright as day, with only a brief interlude of twilight as the sun passed behind Moosehide Mountain. So photographers set up their cameras at midnight, when everything glowed. The streets were full. No one wanted to sleep, even the birds.

"What time is it?" a cheechako would say.

"Ten o'clock."

"Morning or evening?"

The hillsides around Dawson City were covered in tents that grew stifling hot in the endless sun, the daylight glaring off their bone-white sides. The new camps were on the highlands outside of town because the greenhorns and old-timers alike were avoiding the worst of the flooding Yukon, the water five feet deep in some areas near the river. Boatmen plied their craft up and down Front Street, delivering miners to saloons for 50 cents a head. Those with cabins stuck underwater slept on the roofs with their outfit, a boat tied up at the eaves.

And when the spring deluge finally receded, Front Street was left a bog all summer, horses slogging through hock-high mud as their carriages sank to the axle. The river dropped and the flood of men rose; every cheechako said the real crowd was behind him. Old-timers tried to estimate the arriving throng by the number of tents. By midsummer, there were fifteen thousand souls and counting, with newcomers arriving every day. When a steamboat whistle sounded, everyone ran out of the saloons and tents, whether their pants were up or not, and joined the dogs—who were all half wolf, anyway—in yowling with delight and anticipation of what new thing would disembark next.

What was there for a stampeder to do? Broke, hungry, all claims staked and no mining prospect available, many stood in the street and tried to sell their outfits for passage home. A dollar a pound was the going rate, but the old-timers just wanted the underwear, tobacco, and tinned food, leaving piles of unneeded pickaxes and cooking pans discarded about the streets.

The saloon- and hotelkeeper Belinda Mulrooney could spot a cheechako as easily as a cherry on an ice cream sundae. "There's standing room only on the streets of Dawson," she thought. Lines were forming outside of saloons. For a day or two, Dawson ran out of whiskey. To Mulrooney, though, it was just a sign of high demand for dinner and drink and gaiety and beds with clean sheets, proof that business was good. Her staff couldn't serve meals fast enough, which suited her just fine.

Mulrooney was short of stature but loud of voice, with a buxom figure and a pile of chestnut hair that she vainly tried to pull into a utilitarian bun. Her brogue and temper were legendary. She owned a guard dog, a St. Bernard named Nero, that she paraded up and down Front Street. It was larger than she, the size of a small horse, and reminded her of her best friend growing up, a donkey she won in a raffle at a church fundraiser. When in 1885, at twelve years old, she sailed to America, she cried for hours. Not for the grandparents who raised her, that she was leaving behind in County Sligo, but for the donkey.

Mulrooney was already in Alaska when she got news of the discovery on Bonanza Creek. She hit the Chilkoot in March of 1897, six months before the mob, and arrived in summer, just as George Carmack and Clarence Berry and the first lucky few were finishing cleanup. The newspapers from outside said the Klondike was no place for women. The labor was too much, they said, and even nurses should stay away, the hardships too extreme for the more delicate sex.

But what did they know? She had been in Alaska longer than just about any of them. She had made it, when so many men had fallen behind and turned back. "After looking around, I saw there was nothing in Dawson I could buy for a quarter. So I threw my last coin into the Yukon and said, 'We'll start clean.'" That's the story she told, anyway, about the day she arrived. There was a lick of truth in it; she was a self-made woman for sure.

When Mulrooney walked the streets of Dawson, she still saw a fortune waiting to be made. At the north end of Front Street were the large supply warehouses owned by local business titan John Healy. At the south end, she had just purchased an empty lot, to build a new hotel, the grandest in Dawson City.

All these rail-thin miners were used to sleeping in bays of open bunks, with vermin-filled rags for blankets and rancid food. Now Mulrooney intended to raise a monument to luxury, with wallpaper, real glass windows, and whiskey that never ran out.

There were easier ways to get rich than mining for gold. The trick was to mine the miners. And as the richest woman in Dawson, Mulrooney knew how to do it well.

For truth be known, Mulrooney had made her riches selling bread to starving men.

After Clarence and Ethel Berry and the other rich lucky few left Dawson following the spring cleanup of 1897, prospectors had continued to trickle in. Over the summer, old sourdoughs from across Alaska, and then the very first stampeders from outside, the first drops of the tidal wave, reached Dawson in the fall, just months after the Berrys stepped on that Seattle dock and sparked the frenzy. Winter set in and the ice on Lake Bennett held back the main flood of men and women, but already far more people had arrived in Dawson than there was sufficient fare to feed them. Even as the first snows hit, the city fathers knew that old horseman known as Famine was lurking on the edge of town.

In June of 1897, six hundred hardy men and women called Dawson City home. Provisioning them was the business of two companies, the established and hated Alaska Commercial Company—known as the ACC, for which Joe Ladue had been an agent in Sixtymile—and the upstart North American Transportation and Trading Company, the NATT.

The owner of the NATT was a belligerent crag of a man named John J. Healy. His pallid face was that of an ancient bull elephant scarred from battle, nose torn from a fight with a dog in an Indian teepee, scalp furrowed from bullets that just missed the mark. He had a hypnotic left eye, craned open and rarely blinking, which made people unsettled and compliant. Healy was short but broad in the chest and shoulders, with thin legs, like a triangle standing on its point. He said he never felt right unless he had a fight on his hands and usually more than one. He had a quick wit and easy trigger finger, and for this men were drawn to him, though by his own admission he never forgot and never forgave.

Long ago Healy learned that the ordeal of searching for gold was not worth the pain and heartache. He called it all "nonsense," his favorite belittlement. Let others break their backs over a pan. Instead, Healy got rich the same as Belinda Mulrooney, one bag of flour at a time. He'd sell anything to anyone, and how. In Montana, Healy sold whiskey and repeating rifles to Indian and white man alike, arming and antagonizing each side against the other. At Fort Whoop-Up, just over the border on the open Canadian high plain, Healy sold the Blackfeet a concoction known as bug juice, or grain alcohol cut with chewing tobacco, Perry's Painkiller, and soap, plus molasses and red ink to get the color just right. Now, in Alaska, he was building a commercial empire based on desperation and want, as traditional economics were turned upside down: plenty of gold and not enough of anything else.

By the time of the Klondike stampede, Healy had spent nearly forty years on the frontier, always moving just ahead of the last railroad stop. He was born in 1840 and started young, lying about his age to enlist in the army in Buffalo in 1858. He was promptly shipped off to Bleeding Kansas, where he escorted wagon trains on their way to Oregon, as the Shoshone made a habit of butchering and desecrating the bodies of those white families who attempted the crossing on their own. "Curdle the blood of a demon," he said, gagging as he stepped his horse through the coyote-gnawed remains.

They kicked Healy out of the army once they discovered he wasn't twenty-one years old, like he had said. Just as well. When the Civil War came his commander defected and put on Rebel gray, while their unit was absorbed into the Union's Army of the Potomac and they bled anew, up and down the coast from Yorktown to Bull Run to Antietam. By that time, Healy was seeking his fortune in the unregulated territories of the Rocky Mountains, a place of anarchy and claims jumpers. From behind the counter of his mercantile he witnessed Indian wars and gold rushes and by playing the long game profited from them all. At Fort Whoop-Up, he stared down bands of Blood and Blackfeet and Flathead, and armed with a sawed-off double-barrel shotgun, a pair of revolvers, and a Winchester repeating rifle faced off alone against eighteen wolf poachers of the roving militia known as the Spitzee Calvary. Each time he survived a standoff his stature grew, and when he ran for sheriff of Chouteau County, Montana, he told the voters, "If any of you are going to steal horses during the next two years, he had better vote against me, for by God, if I catch him, I'll hang him." Healy won.

Now in Dawson City, fifty-seven years old and gray and hard, he found his reputation preceded him. A former lawman, a pioneer of the West of old. "A good horse traveling light, my rifle, a bed roll, a coffee pot and frying pan, a bit of sugar," that's what made him happy. A throwback to another time, not long past but still another age, one of violence and blood and certainly not the era of modern manners and skyscrapers in Chicago and New York that the stampeders had just left.

Healy came to Alaska in 1886, as a trader on the coast, first in Juneau and Haines, then quickly to Dyea, to corner the market supplying Tlingit packers on the Chilkoot. At the time, he and Mrs. Healy were two of the three white people living in the village. The third was George Carmack, the man whose discovery would kick off the rush to the Klondike a decade later. But even early on, Healy had the foresight to see a stampede coming. "This place may in time become an important point," he predicted.

Healy had seen other gold rushes in Alaska. In January 1887, two ghostly figures appeared off the pass, an Indian packer named Bob carrying on his back a white man frozen to his guts and feverish. They had left the Fortymile River six weeks before with news that could not wait. The traders brought the man inside Healy's post. He said his name was Tom Williams, but he was hallucinating, coming in and out of consciousness, and talked about something valuable left on the Chilkoot. Williams died hours later, so the traders asked Bob what was so urgent that they risked the blizzard to travel so far. Bob spoke almost no English, so he reached out a black frostbitten hand and grabbed a bunch of dried kidney beans from a barrel and tossed them on the floor.

"Gold," he said. "All same like this."

Healy himself led an expedition back up the Chilkoot, to find Williams's cache. There, dug into a hole in the snow, was Williams's last dog, dead stiff and curled up around a mailbag of letters that contained the map to the Fortymile strike.

That 1887 rush consisted of only 250 men, and the richest dug out a mere $3,000. Barely worthy to be called a stampede, compared to what would come after.

As Dyea grew, Healy was eventually made the deputy U.S. marshal, though he didn't last long. The whites said he should talk less and hang more. "This part of Alaska can furnish more petty, trifling criminals, and shady men than any other portion of the U.S.," he declared. After a few too many negotiations that required drawn pistols, Healy left the store with his name on the sign and moved inland, to Circle City and then Fortymile.

At the time, only the Alaska Commercial Company served the interior mining towns. The old-timers hated the ACC because the food they sold was too expensive and rotten to boot. Yellow bacon, moldy flour, beans like rocks. In 1892 Healy brought a sternwheeler to the Yukon River to compete with the ACC directly and prices fell like mercury in winter. A hundred-pound sack of flour went from $15 to $8. Still the sourdoughs grumbled, because Healy forced the miners to pay in gold, rather than grubstakes and credit, like when old John Ladue provisioned white men up and down the Yukon.

Healy's inland business grew. He was there in Fortymile the day George Carmack walked into town and bragged about what he found on Bonanza Creek. Healy presided over the selling off of everyone's possessions and then followed the crowd to the Klondike where he quickly established himself as the tycoon of Dawson. He was a man atop the world and without fear. He controlled the levers of commerce in a boom-town that garnered global infatuation. He owned a 241-ton boat named the *John J. Healy*, and a saloon named for himself as well. There behind the bar hung his portrait, goring eye and all.

In temperament, success, and tone, Healy's only true business rival was Belinda Mulrooney. Both were born in Ireland, ruthless negotiators, unapologetic barons, and as stubbornly unmovable as a pile of frozen tailings.

Like Healy, Mulrooney was an entrepreneur from an early age. As a young woman she had left Ireland to join her parents in the coal-mining town of Archbald, Pennsylvania, then struck out on her own at just nineteen, to Chicago for the World's Columbian Exposition of 1893. Using a little bit of money she had saved, she purchased a cheap restaurant just outside the Midway Plaisance and the colossal steel wheel of G. W. G. Ferris. In fact, Mulrooney told her customers that Mr. Ferris himself rented a small lot behind her building, to store a model of his fascinating wheel, which may or may not have been true. She made $8,000 at the lunch counter in Chicago. Not bad for selling 25-cent wienies.

She took the money and moved west, landing a job as a stewardess on the *City of Topeka*—the same ship Jack London would crowd onto, as part of the stampede, years later—making the run between Seattle and the Alaskan panhandle. Mulrooney liked Alaska because it was faraway and new, the kind of place where a person had to take care of themselves first and last. She also liked that she could bootleg whiskey to thirsty miners on the side and there was no lawman to stop her. Mulrooney was in Juneau when the first whispers about Klondike gold flitted from the interior and she arrived in Dawson in June 1897.

The city was a chaotic mess, full of slipshod log cabins and newly crowned Klondike Kings who went from flat broke to royalty after only a few days of cleanup. She opened an import business, and her first shipment consisted of long tin cans full of petticoats and nightgowns. The soiled doves in the tenderloin on Second Avenue couldn't get enough of the silks, touching them softly, gently, as if they might break.

She took the profits from her first sale and opened a restaurant on the waterfront, a place to get a real meal at a counter, not on a bench in the cook tents that had serviced prospectors thus far. She hired the best woman cook in town to tend the stove and bought up all the outfits of new arrivals. "The boys will love it, no more chopping bacon with an axe," she thought. She sold all their supplies back to them for $2 a meal and they were happy for it.

Mulrooney had a knack for anticipating the market. Soon after opening the restaurant, she began buying lots and constructing log cabins out of old boats that had been broken apart for the boards and nails. They sold so fast she doubled the price overnight. At the junction of Bonanza and Eldorado creeks she built a two-story hotel called the Grand Forks: a loft for sleeping upstairs, a bar downstairs with black bottles of rum and cigarette lithographs to add charm. It was a roadhouse bigger than anything in Dawson and the miners thought she was crazy to open it so far from town. That is, until they realized how enjoyable it was to drink at a saloon nearby rather than walk the sixteen miles to Dawson and back. The bunks had curtains and the blankets didn't have fleas and it sold out in a hot minute.

At the Grand Forks she learned about new strikes before competitors in Dawson, and she traded picks and whipsaws for portions of four mining operations. At the time this was her only way to stake her share of creek bed. According to the law, "every person" eighteen years or older was allowed to file a claim, but it was also true that according to English Common Law the only "persons" were men. Eventually the law was amended, but only later when John Healy himself lobbied the Canadian Parliament, the claim of his wife having been denied.

In other cities, more civilized places back east, being a woman would have introduced other, more intrusive, hindrances in the conduct of business. But not in the Klondike; there was too much work to be done.

Still, Mulrooney was clearly different from almost every other woman in town, even on first impression. Twenty-six years old, she was conspicuously and strategically plain. She wore small round glasses and modest tweed skirts and never became intoxicated in public, an occupational hazard for the women working the dance hall. After watching those girls with their packs of stalking men, she insisted on being known as Miss Mulrooney. And when a miner accused her of spilling gold dust on purpose, to cheat him, she threw him out of her restaurant on his ear. He hit the doorjamb on the way out and the whole building shook.

"You will say we are crooks and dishonest?" she yelled.

"Good God! Can't you take a joke?" the man said, picking himself up.

No, she could not.

"I'm credited with being so devilish smart, expected to solve every problem," she thought. "They don't know how little I know, and I never get close enough for them to find out."

The only threat to Mulrooney's restaurants and hotels was a lack of supplies. Dawson had been short of food from the moment of its founding. No outside shipments had arrived in 1896; the initial influx of miners happened in the fall, after the discovery by Carmack in August, and by then it was too late. Most years, navigation on the Yukon lasted only until the first of October. After that, water levels were too low to allow laden steamers to reach upriver. And any steamer caught on shoals would be lost, as the water level would only drop further, winter ice would set in, and then the spring flood would destroy the ships utterly.

By the summer of 1897, though, the ACC and NATT had managed to ship fourteen steamer loads of goods to Dawson, enough for six hundred people for the winter. The population was already swelling past that and the miners themselves were little help, too busy sifting mud to hunt game or plow in kitchen gardens. In reality, farming added little, though. Vegetables grew rapidly in constant sun, but were delicate and turned to mush. To last the food needed to be salted and tinned, and thus came only from the outside.

Healy constructed three steel-clad warehouses on the docks at Dawson City. The project cost $150,000, or about 550 pounds of gold. Normally when a man bought a year's worth of goods he made a separate pile, each man with his own larder, to be drawn down month by month at his own pace. Now with the crisis on the horizon Healy let only one customer at a time into the warehouse and personally supervised their withdrawal. Some talked of stealing food, but Healy wasn't concerned. Up his shirtsleeve he still carried an ace-in-the-hole derringer he called his "swamp angel."

In August, a ship filled with hungry escapees left town, but on the way out passed another, full of newcomers, steaming upstream. "What are you going to eat when you get there?" the emigrants called across the bow. And then the very first stampeders from the Chilkoot stumbled in, baby chicks with hungry open mouths and no food of their own for the winter. The cheechakos pushed the population count to over four thousand with more still on the way and there was no way the supplies would hold.

In mid-September of 1897, with only two weeks left in the summer shipping season, the ACC and NATT stockpiles stood at eight hundred tons of freight, half food and half general merchandise, not nearly enough for the winter. In the grocery stores in town the shelves were empty but the aisles full, aimless loitering men waiting a turn to warm themselves by woodstoves.

Healy started shifting goods from his backup caches at Fortymile. When a boatload of food arrived, he set up a platform in the Front Street mud and distributed a two-week supply at a time to customers. Word came that the river was dropping faster than normal, and three steamers, the *Alice*, *Healy*, and *Hamilton*, with supplies from St. Michael, were stuck on sandbars two hundred miles below Dawson. The news traveled fast up to the Forks and miners from the creeks came into town to ask what they'd eat that winter. The Alaska Commercial Company said they could fill their orders, everything except candles and flour. But the NATT had the bulk of the orders, and Healy assured his worried patrons that the steamers would arrive.

Finally, on the 28th of September, one steamer, the *Weare*, did make it to Dawson, and Healy went out to meet it. It was thirty tons lighter than it was supposed to be on account of the fact that it had been robbed. On the way upriver the men in Circle City had boarded the ship and held the crew at gunpoint, unloaded what they thought necessary, politely marked the bill, and then let the boat proceed.

On the ship was one of Healy's business

partners, Eli Weare. Healy asked what was left on the ship after the robbery, and Weare said not to worry, he brought all the whiskey and hardware the ship could hold.

No food. Just whiskey and pans.

"Nonsense!" Healy exploded as he got his Irish up and reached for his partner, grabbing him around the throat and throttling him. Weare turned red and started to go down. There might have been a murder on the dock right there if the crowd hadn't pulled Healy off the unconscious man.

Two days later, Inspector Constantine, the leader of the tiny outpost of Mounted Police, posted a notice on poles around town. It stated his belief that there was not enough food in Dawson for the winter, that no more was coming in, and so people had to get out, immediately, while the river still ran. A thousand people had to leave.

"For those who have not laid in a winter's supply, to remain here longer is to court death from starvation," the notice read. "Starvation now stares everyone in the face who is hoping and waiting for outside relief."

The posting caused a sensation. J. E. Hansen, the local manager of the ACC, walked all over town, yelling at whoever would listen. "Go! Go! Flee for your lives!"

But not Healy. He was calm, still as a forgotten grave.

Healy took Hansen by the shoulder and pulled

him aside, saying they should work together. Hansen now had plenty of flour, having just received thirteen hundred gunnysacks of the stuff, but was missing everything else. Meanwhile Healy was in the opposite position, plenty of bacon and beans but no flour.

"If there is trouble, as you say there will be," Healy said to the hysterical man, "before anyone starves those who have none will take it from those who have."

Healy had seen the strong eat and the weak shrink and die. And plenty worse besides. In Montana in the leanest years men got a certain look in their eye before they broke the ultimate taboo in the faraway mountain places. Famine had nearly taken Healy once. He was in the wilderness, pursued by Bannock Indians, running along the Salmon River, every secret Mormon food cache claimed long ago, villages abandoned from the Indian wars. One of Healy's comrades took out his pistol and eyed his mates up and down. "I will never die while I can eat that fellow," the man said, pointing the barrel meaningfully. "It's pretty hard to eat him, but I am going to eat him." Healy wrestled away the man's gun and they managed to walk out, but by the time they were finally discovered at a wagon trail, Healy's shoes were worn through, the soles of his feet covered in the thorns of cactus and prickly pear. Better than being eaten.

So Healy knew he'd survive. He could handle a mob and would do so again. This was about saving others, why didn't Hansen see that? "It is better that we take the matter into our own hands right now," Healy pressed his counterpart.

But Hansen wouldn't listen. "I must fill my orders," he said, and that was the end of it.

Dawson City held a miners' meeting then. It was an old-time meeting, the last real miners' meeting ever held in the Yukon. The topic of discussion was how much of the town to send downstream to Circle City and Fortymile. Healy refused to attend; he called it all nonsense. Instead, he sent a lieutenant, to say that the only safe place was outside, back in the continental United States, and unless everyone went there then simply shuffling hungry mouths around Alaska just wasted the little reserves they had. Overall his counsel held, and the miners decided to collect all the food currently in town and ration it out, bit by bit. Belinda Mulrooney's restaurant in Dawson had to close, and while the Grand Forks was allowed to remain open, anyone who stayed there had to turn in their provisions to be centrally stored for equal disbursement. Some suggested going further and reducing the number of mouths by opening the jails and banishing the crooks into the wilderness. But Healy fought against that as well. Better to keep the criminals where they could be watched; creating a band of brigands who would steal food would help no one.

Despite Healy's objections, hundreds did leave. A few score went upstream, to try their hand at getting out over the Chilkoot. The sourdoughs thought this certain death, that ice and hunger alone awaited in that direction. Two steamers, the *Bella* and the *Weare*, left in the other direction in early October, with two hundred passengers. But they got no farther than Circle City, where they were caught in the ice. Some walked for days without provision to reach Fort Yukon, where Healy's prediction came true and there were not sufficient stores either.

Healy canceled all of his contracts and rationed everything in the warehouse, no matter who had purchased it. Already the ACC's remaining stores consisted of little but sugar and axe handles. Healy made a promise to Dawson. "Some may go hungry, but none will starve," he said.

But then, he added, "If there is starvation, it won't be until spring."

Grudgingly, Healy assented to Constantine, and agreed to an armed guard on the warehouses. When the Mounted Police started shooting bread thieves, Healy sent out a runner to the coast, to ask the U.S. government to send soldiers over the border and declare martial law.

Tappan Adney, the correspondent and photographer for *Harper's Weekly*, reached Dawson on

All Hallow's Eve 1897, on one of the last boats to arrive before the river became impassable.

A total of six thousand souls endured that winter in Dawson. Adney figured about five thousand of them didn't expect the town's food stores to last until spring. Healy was a stern ration-master and demanded an interview with every miner who wanted to draw grub from the warehouse. "A new kind of trader," Adney thought, with admiration, an implicit fairness hidden beneath the gruff and occasionally violent exterior. Some entrepreneurs tried to cross the ice with dog teams, to reach the coast and return with food and make a fortune. For $1,000 they would let you walk behind them, in the path cut by the sled. But the vast majority of those hungry in Dawson were broke as well, having spent their last dollar and eaten their last can of beans just to reach the Klondike. As Healy feared, some did try to flee on their own, into the teeth of winter, only to be turned back by the cold and snow. One such man was Joaquin Miller, the "Poet of the Sierras," who had joined the stampede with great media fanfare, just before Adney got his *Harper's* assignment. Miller's ill-fated escape attempt cost him dearly: all of his fingers save one, parts of his toes, cheeks, and ears, plus debilitating snow blindness.

Two enterprises conducted a slew of business that winter: the saloons of Front Street, and St. Mary's hospital, run by the skeletal Jesuit, Father

Judge. The privation of the season and wanton disease produced a tremendous harvesting effect upon the feeble and aged. Sawdust for beds, no sheets but the ones brought by the sick themselves, Judge did not so much care for the patients as ease their passage to the charnel house. Pneumonia. Hemorrhagic typhoid. Malaria. Frostbite and gangrene. Rheumatic fever. Dysentery. Discharge from the ears and eyes that none had ever seen before. When a man died, the next sickest man got his pallet. It was a short wait. During the height of the plagues, three or four perished a day.

Father Judge refused to admit women until the Sisters of St. Ann finally arrived months later. And care improved significantly once a veterinarian agreed to act as a surgeon. Judge died soon after. Forty-nine years old, sunken and frail, he looked far older. On his deathbed he said, with relief, "This is the happiest moment of my life." By then he was only the husk of a person, his thin spark of life like a frayed rope that finally snapped under its load.

When the nuns took over, they discovered the hospital, in a land of gold, was $45,000 in debt.

Tappan Adney was interested in writing magazine stories on miners, not drunkards or starvelings, so he left Dawson and moved to a cabin up Bonanza Creek to spend the winter with prospectors burning out permafrost. On the way up, he stopped at Belinda Mulrooney's Grand Forks hotel and found it unusually well supplied. The whiskey house was packed with outsiders, distinguished by their new red-and-black-plaid Mackinaw jackets. The old-timers wore moosehide, with fur caps of sable or lynx, gauntlet mittens to the elbow. Mulrooney charged $12 a day for meals and a bed, most of a man's daily wage when mining out a dump on another's claim. It was expensive locally, but beyond the bounds of reason anywhere else, ten times Jack London's wages when working in the pickle factory in San Francisco.

Adney moved into a cabin in a deep black valley that shut out the light for three months. In the northern sky the aurora borealis would come as a soft yellow glow followed by waving bands of pink and green that seemed to make a shifty noise that unnerved him. "The light seems very near," he thought, as if it were a thing within reach, "the rustling of the light or the rustling of the river beneath the ice I can never tell, it is so subtle and illusive."

Many days the air was so cold it was too painful to go outside. He saw even the brutish dogs slept curled for warmth, "instead of lying straight like a Christian." Adney and the miners sat inside their hovels and thought about food and how much was left. Many ate one meal a day, bacon twice a week. Adney's neighbor wrote a poem entitled "The Lone Flapjack." One man left in the fall, planning to return with a turkey for Christmas; he did not arrive back in Dawson until April.

Adney himself had enough food but no variety. His butter turned to cheese and they had no soda for sourdough so he could only manage to mix up an inedible flour-and-water-paste concoction. "Not even the passing dogs will eat it," he admitted. Adney craved condensed milk, but "none to be had, for love or money." Of the three essential Bs—bread, beans, and bacon—he had only the last. "Bacon three times a day loses its zest in the course of time," he thought.

As 1898 began, the city of Dawson was famished, destitute, and rich beyond its dreams. Like sailors adrift on an ocean with empty freshwater casks in the hold. "Millions are frozen fast in the dumps of Eldorado and Bonanza," observed Adney. But even if they had the cash, there was little food to buy.

The city withered but did not die. Healy's thriftiness made him the most unpopular man in Dawson, but the rationing worked. The stocks held, with the help of local Tagish hunters who provided timely additions of moose and caribou. When the calendar called spring and the sun had re-exerted its prominence in the sky, the snow melted early in Dawson, in April, though ice still bound the rivers and lakes and the furnace of every hotel still roared away. Men walked around town in wide felt hats and high rubber boots, the mud melting in the long spring sun and then freezing tight at night.

The dog teams made their last runs of the year. The inbound mushers provided reports on life outside. Seven thousand stampeders in Skagway, nearly the same in Dyea, several times that held back at Bennett and Lindeman. And more coming in all the time, a stream of men collecting behind the dam of the icy lakes. The pressure was building. Upon breakup, Dawson would be flooded.

Later, they heard the U.S. government had learned of the food shortages in Dawson and tried to send relief in the form of herds of reindeer. The animals barely made it farther than the coast. "If reindeer had failed, there was no means under heaven by which help could have reached us," Adney thought. In February, 539 Norwegian reindeer and 114 Finn and Lapp herders arrived in New York City. A week later they were in Seattle by freight train, and soon sailed up to Haines Mission, at Pyramid Harbor, Alaska. But none of the reindeer's normal food was available on the trail, and they made it only a short way up the Chilkoot Pass before they started dying rapidly. Three hundred and fifty reindeer were lost before the project was abandoned. The rest were so scrawny they weren't worth eating.

As April closed, muddy water at last began to run in Bonanza Creek. Two days later it spilled over the bank and into Adney's cabin, an ankle-deep slosh with every step. He had to wear rubber boots even when inside and the mosquitoes were merciless, so after a few days he returned to Dawson.

Every day the ice popped and cracked and groaned and jammed. Dynamite was required to free the Klondike itself, as ice floes the size of cabins tore out a bridge that spanned the river. A few days later the Yukon began to rise as well, a tremendous swelling, a leviathan awakened from a long sleep.

Finally, on May 8 at four o'clock in the morning the ice started to move and a cry went up all over town. Breakup had come. And then, only minutes later, Peterborough Canoes from outside beached on the muddy bank.

Cheechakos.

The first man had eggs, and sold them for $18 a dozen. The circus had arrived.

On May Day, Dawson City had been on the edge of starvation.

A fortnight later, the markets were as stocked as a Parisian emporium. "Everything is for sale here," Adney saw, "fresh grapes to opera glasses, safety-pins to ice-cream freezers." A bag of flour, when one was for sale at all, had been worth $150. Now it went for $3, less than cost, because the disgusted newcomers just wanted to liquidate their outfits and go home. When the local newspaper suggested opening a sausage factory and supplying it with packs of stray dogs, it was not for lack of food but merely to clear the streets clogged with canines.

For still the mob kept coming. "This crowd, it is a vast herd," thought Adney. "It is at once curious, listless, and dazed, dragging its way with slow lagging steps. Can this be the rush that newspapers describe?"

Many looked disappointed. "This is not as big as Skagway," said one newcomer to Adney. He was wrong. In a few short weeks Dawson would be many times larger.

That summer, Adney met Robert Henderson, the gaunt man who lost out to George Carmack on the Klondike discovery. Henderson looked ill, stringy as the gristle off a two-bit steak. He had spent the winter in his sickbed and the limp in his leg was pronounced. Henderson told Adney his whole story, about being the first to find gold in the Klondike valley and then losing his chance to stake on Bonanza or Eldorado because Carmack broke the miners' code and never told him about his discovery. And how he had even lost his claim on Gold Bottom Creek, which was now named for Hunker.

Adney asked Henderson if all that made him discouraged.

"No," said Henderson. "There are as rich mines yet to be discovered as any that have been found."

But the man's face told a different tale.

Adney realized he had found his lead for his *Harper's Weekly* story. Adney wrote the tale of Henderson's woe and sent out a manuscript and hand sketches to *Harper's*, three pounds of paper in total. In time, after Adney left Dawson City, the two men would begin a correspondence, and later Henderson would give Adney a small golden pin, the insignia for the Yukon Order of Pioneers, the badge that certified Henderson's status as a pre–gold rush sourdough. "That is all I have got after two and half years prospecting, living on meat straight," Henderson said. It was a prized possession for any man, which is why he handed it over.

"You keep this," he said to Adney. "I will lose it too."

Few worked so hard for so little, but in truth most prospectors in the Yukon left disappointed. Not Jack London. He was happy to escape. When he arrived in Dawson in May, he went immediately to St. Mary's hospital, to get treatment from Father Judge's nurses. London's right leg had retracted against his body. "Now almost entirely crippled," he thought. At the hospital they gave London potatoes to eat and told him to leave Dawson to save himself. Doc Harvey sold the logs of their raft for $600, and London spent his share of the money on two things: a little boat to sail to St. Michael, and whiskey at the bar to collect stories from the old-timers.

London would stay in the city three weeks. "Dreary, desolate Dawson," he called it. "Built in a swamp, flooded to the second story, populated by dogs, mosquitos, and gold-seekers." In that order. And too much of all three.

The mob had swollen the town to bursting. In the early summer of 1898, Dawson City was already home to ten thousand people. And yet the cheechakos kept coming. The tramway was running at the Chilkoot. The White Pass would become a railroad. Tiny steamers began to arrive from the lakes of the upper watershed, specialty boats just eight feet wide, narrow enough to skirt the rapids at White Horse and Five Fingers. Though the initial rush was over, ever more newcomers poured in. In those first heady days, Adney guessed there were eighteen thousand new faces and still by the end of 1898 the population of Dawson would more than double yet again. Forty thousand wannabes and could-bes and used-to-bes in one boomtown.

Colonel Samuel Steele tried his damnedest to make Dawson orderly and safe and boring. He failed. "Simply a hell upon earth, gamblers, thieves, and the worst of womankind," he concluded.

He had finally arrived in Dawson in September

1898, after finishing his supervision of the passing of the mob from Lake Bennett and the upper headwaters. He could not wait to start scrubbing out corruption and grift, but no matter what he tried, any area outside of his immediate vision remained slovenly and inept. "Villainy, licentiousness, robbery and corruption," he griped, and even among his own men. One died of syphilis. Another of his sergeants was arrested for being drunk on duty. Steele buried one and sent the other out.

At the barracks in Dawson, prisoners, not Steele's men, worked on construction of a new quarters, though not nearly fast or well enough. Every government official seemed to want to skim their share rather than do their job, and Steele was frustrated he lacked the power to remove them all. To get gold royalties paid, Steele would resort to sending undercover detectives to the mining camps upstream.

To the irritation of Healy, Mulrooney, and the rest of the business community, Steele remained aloof. Healy knew Steele because he had once written to the man, asking for relief from an 1894 miners' meeting that didn't go his way. Predictably, the by-the-book Steele refused to intervene. Likewise, Mulrooney invited Steele to Thanksgiving dinner at her hotel, but Steele refused. "She is sharp," the colonel had to admit, but he wanted no part of her favor currying.

"Mixed up with certain officials in the way of money making," Mulrooney was corrupt for sure, Steele thought, and declining her invites was a way to display integrity and condescension, avoiding both impropriety and an unpleasant mingling with commoners in a single act. "I am not going to make myself cheap," he decided. "She can't get my legs under her mahogany."

But Belinda Mulrooney had no need of Steele's legs to build an entire empire of mahogany. Her ambitions were fully realized in this boomtown. The Grand Forks hotel was so successful it funded the rest of her expansion. When it was time for the spring cleanup of 1898, she prepped for a rush, hiring more staff and building an addition to the Grand Forks with more counters for extra scales to weigh gold dust.

"Get an assistant," she told the girl who helped manage the hotel. "For heaven's sake get someone who hasn't the gold fever. Tons of gold will go through this place in less than a month and we mustn't let anything disagreeable happen." Mulrooney used the hotel as a bank. The same tin cans that had shipped in silk dresses now stored sacks of gold dust, $50,000 and $100,000 at a time.

Mulrooney rolled the profits from the cleanup back into her sprawling network of properties. One day, before the main flood of cheechakos arrived, the Klondike Kings and tycoons got together at the Alaska Commercial Company warehouse to decide what to do, how they would handle the housing and other material needs of the newcomers. Swampy ground needed to be drained, new log cabins built, but that would take time.

As an immediate solution, Mulrooney suggested that every business on Front Street add another story. Building up, she figured, would be much faster than building anew.

But the men laughed at her. How could you possibly heat the third floor? they asked. It was impossible, everyone knew it, which is why every building in the Yukon had always stopped at a second floor.

Mulrooney's most vocal opponent was a creaky sourdough named Bill Leggett. He had been around as long as anyone and was already rich off a claim on Eldorado Creek.

"That camp will be worked out before you get that three-story building built," he said. "If you ever did get it built, you couldn't get it heated afterwards."

"Bill, old man, if I was as rusty as you are, I'd never get it built," Mulrooney replied. They said she had a tongue like a lawyer, a compliment, as long as it wasn't directed at them.

"Bet you five thousand dollars you won't have that three-story building built by summer," Bill said.

"That sounds like easy money," she replied.

Not only did Mulrooney take the bet, she would lend money to her carpenters and other craftsmen to make their own side bets with Bill Leggett. She brought on Clarence Berry as an investor and bought land at the corner of Front and Princess streets, two blocks from the saloons to avoid the worst of the drunkenness and debauchery. To keep the transaction a secret from Bill Leggett, she negotiated the deal on the dance floor.

"I bought it while old man Ladue and I were dancing the Virginia Reel on Patrick's Day," she told her shocked assistant. "Didn't you think we were a kittenish pair of little devils? I know as much about dancing as a pet bear, and old man Ladue knows less."

The three-story hotel was completed on June 22, 1898. Motivated by the endless sunshine and Mulrooney's bet, of which they each shared a piece, the workers finished in record time. In the end, Bill Leggett owed a total of $100,000 to his many betting rivals, most of whom were secretly bankrolled by Mulrooney.

She named this new hotel the Fairview, as it was on the southern edge of town overlooking the river. Unlike most rough dwellings in Dawson, it was no log cabin, but rather a fine structure, framed with studs and insulated with sawdust. The barroom alone made a thousand dollars a night, serving oyster cocktails to a city that had faced food shortages a few months before. To

Leggett's chagrin, it had a central heating plant in the basement that toasted the whole building. The Fairview also had painted murals, Brussels carpets and lace curtains, a telephone to call the Grand Forks, and novel electric lights—powered by a steamboat, moored in the river nearby—that everyone wanted turned on all day long even though the midnight sun raged. The Yukon Order of Pioneers wouldn't let Mulrooney join, since she was a woman, but the fraternity did recognize luxury when they saw it and rented the dining room for Christmas dinner.

The *Klondike Nugget* newspaper called it "by far the most pretentious structure now in Dawson." Mulrooney paid a fortune to get all the necessary accoutrements shipped in and still she wasn't satisfied. She wanted glass windows and real china, and she didn't trust the transportation companies, even Healy's, to deliver on time. So she took $30,000 and went to Skagway herself on a buying trip, back over the Chilkoot for the first time in a year.

Many of the old-timers and Klondike Kings were leaving as well, but all the way back to the United States with their fortunes. The steamers arrived full of cheechakos and left loaded with gold. Healy himself left Dawson in September 1898, to winter in New York. By then he was worth $1.5 million, representing about 10 percent of the gold mined that year.

But Mulrooney was staying, to keep mining the miners. She just needed a quick trip to get her furnishings. The journey out of Dawson could be harder than the journey in, weeks of frustrating labor against the current. Mulrooney took a little steamer upriver, a rickety underpowered boat that was owned by a company so spendthrift they required the passengers to cut down trees and chop the wood for the boiler. At the White Horse rapids she changed to a canoe, poled by two Indians. At Lake Bennett, she saw that crowds still lined the shores, whipsawing boats, fighting and cursing, same as they had the entire stampede, as if Bennett was a timeless limbo for those seeking salvation in Dawson. "What a dissatisfied, heart sick, unfriendly, restless bunch of people," she thought. All the talk was of thieves in Bennett, that a man had had his head caved in and all his money stolen. Not like the old times at all, this new crop.

In Skagway, all the construction materials coming in were being taken by the railroad, to house workers laying track over the White Pass. No one would sell to Mulrooney, until she threatened to stay and build a competing hotel. Then suddenly she was allowed to take all she wanted, and the railroad barons of Skagway were happy to see her go.

Mulrooney paid a man named J. H. Brooks 40 cents a pound to get all her newly acquired furnishings to Lake Bennett in three days. Brooks had the men and the mules but also a reputation for unreliability due to his devotion to gambling. So she hired additional manpower to protect her investment, including a former con man named Broad, the theory being that he'd steer them out of trouble as he would recognize every scam. "He's got a brain like chain-lightning," she thought. "He can see everything before it arrives."

Mulrooney watched Brooks load her goods on twenty-two mules, then she rode up to Lake Bennett to supervise the acquisition of the fleet required to move her precious glass windows. She left Broad to watch over Brooks and his men and in this she was the one with foresight and intuition. A few days later Broad reported to Mulrooney that Brooks had dropped one load of goods at the summit and then quit the job. Another saloon operator in Dawson had offered Brooks more money to run whiskey over the pass.

"Bill Leggett will be laughing his head off," she thought. She couldn't fail, she just couldn't, not in front of Leggett.

Mulrooney and Broad returned to the summit and surveyed the mess. Her purchases were tossed in an undignified pile. Such a slight could not stand. If Brooks would not cart her goods over the pass then she would do it herself. And what's more, she decided, she would do it with Brooks's men and Brooks's mules. She would commandeer the pack train. All she needed was a gang.

Mulrooney looked about at the hopeless and exhausted boys and men loitering at the summit. "There are desperate looking fellows on this trail," she thought, "hard as iron."

Mulrooney told Broad to raise a posse. "Pay them anything they ask for," she said.

At first, Broad was skeptical, saying Brooks's foreman was pretty tough.

"Then hire some men just as tough," Mulrooney replied. "This isn't your old game of three little silly shells. You got to use your head and muscle too."

Recruitment turned out to be easy. This pack of late-stage stampeders, disillusioned and poor and hungry, would do just about anything to escape the misery of their daily existence and Mulrooney knew it.

"We have a dirty job on hand," she told them. "I will take the lead and won't ask you to do anything I wouldn't do. I'll pay you well." But they didn't require much convincing.

Mulrooney didn't want the Mounted Police interfering with her plan. "Colonel Steele has a splendid bunch of men," she knew. "The crooks get religion or move on." Getting arrested would be bad, but drawing the sustained attention of

Steele's inspectors would be worse, so she led her gang down the trail a bit on the American side and waited for Brooks's mules to appear. She picked a spot in the road that was narrow enough to hem in Brooks's men but wide enough so they could see the gang she had raised. When the pack mules appeared in the distance, she rode out, high in her stirrups, and her hired thugs stood behind her.

The mule train halted, and the foreman rode up. He was a rude and angry man named Al.

"Is that my stuff you are packing?" Mulrooney asked, though she already knew the answer.

"No," Al said. "Get out of the way in a hurry." He looked ready to give his horse the spurs.

Mulrooney wouldn't budge. She told Al that according to her contract with Brooks, all the mules were forfeit when he quit her job, as per the default clause. But Al was unimpressed.

"We're not bothered with a contract, woman," he said.

Woman.

"This is no place to talk paper," Al continued. "Don't give a damn what your business is." Their horses were right next to each other now, so close Mulrooney could feel his breath. "You'll have a hell of a chance taking this pack train," he said.

Mulrooney's gang turned giddy with the tension and were tickled by the show, a little woman on her horse. Maybe they didn't mean anything by it, but she never did take a joke. Her own men, her chaps, laughing just like Bill Leggett would; she hated the idea of that more than anything.

Mulrooney drew her pistol and pressed the business end into Al's crotch. "Well, old man," she said. "I hate to do it, but I must. You better get off."

No one was laughing now. Now it was all eager anticipation, an energy, a lightness in the buoyant air before the first shot comes. "They'll follow me into any devilry," she thought, and she liked it.

Al eased off his horse and then Mulrooney's hard men seized him and dragged him back to the camp and beat him bloody as they had been hired to do. "Make him think it was a real holdup," she told Broad. They beat the foreman because Brooks wasn't there but the message was for him, and for all of Skagway even. From then on, all of Mulrooney's shipments would arrive in Dawson unmolested.

After the beating, she told the rest of Al's men in the mule train that they had a choice, either work for her or get the same as their boss. To a man they chose the work, and Al crawled on his belly back home to Skagway, a place simmering in every kind of deceit and depraved violence, thanks to the outlaw Soapy Smith.

CHAPTER EIGHT

I beg to state that I am no gambler. A gambler takes chances with his money, I don't.
—JEFFERSON RANDOLPH "SOAPY" SMITH II

When new wide-eyed cheechakos disembarked at the wharf in Skagway in the early summer of 1898, by then nearly a year into the stampede, they were met by a throng of buyers and sellers and advice offerers and an ostensible welcome committee's worth of busybodies.

A transporter offering to carry a greenhorn's goods by horse up over the pass. Eager boys begging for news from the outside, looking to buy any newspaper for 50 cents a copy. An old sourdough commenting on the state of a man's outfit. The preacher seeking new congregants. Push past one, another took his place. They came in waves.

Say a newcomer trusted the packer. It would be good to get someone to take his outfit over the pass, after all. So he paid the man, loaded his food and gold pans on the horse, and then never saw his worldly possessions again.

Maybe another trusted the reverend, who somehow knew the solemn handshake from the Moose Lodge back home, and warned that the docks were replete with sinners and villains. Together the two men walked up to the Information Bureau, where a helpful clerk provided an exclusive list of hotels and restaurants and banks where it was safe for godly men to lock away their valuables.

A third was approached by a thin pale man with a dark mustache who called himself Foster. Newcomers needed to be careful, Foster whispered, the town was full of scoundrels. In fact, how did they know they had not been swindled already, and purchased the wrong gear down south? Better head to the Merchants Exchange to get an honest outfit. The salesmen at the exchange agreed, said that the stampeder had been led astray, that the goods he bought in Seattle were the wrong supplies. But no fear, he could turn in his erroneous outfit as a small down payment on the correct new gear for sale. Note that after the transaction, when the newcomer was well on his way up the trail, much of the "wrong outfit" would be reshelved and resold as the "correct outfit" for the next customer.

Perhaps the last newcomer off the ship was suspicious and avoided them all. Each hawker warned the cheechako that every other man was a swindler. How could a greenhorn know who to trust or what to believe? So they skipped the sales pitches and instead they chatted with the boys, sold them the requested newspaper, and then followed the youngsters into town to get a drink at the recommended saloon, Jeff Smith's Place. One drink followed another, and then lo and behold a fight broke out between drunk prospectors at the bar. Regrettably—and, in an unlikely twist, uniquely, among the other spectators—the cheeckako found himself caught up in the brawl and robbed of his wallet.

That all of these hucksters, impostors, shills, steerers, and ropers all worked for the same man was just too fanciful for most to believe.

The ticket office sold fake steamship tickets. The Skagway Real-Estate and Investment Company sold phony land deeds and titles. The Telegraph Office hosted the most successful continuous theater in town, busy switchboard operators communicating with no one, the wire leading out of the building going nowhere, buried right in the ground.

The consortium of crooks and thugs who ran these rackets possessed every possible skill to defraud or hoodwink or simply outmuscle their victims.

Slim Jim Foster was a classic confidence man, guiding the gullible into the gang's establishments. Wilson Mizner was a singer, medical lecturer, and card cheat. The sickly-looking Billy Saportas was an editor at the *Daily Alaskan*, where he could ensure his boss got good press.

"Reverend" John Bowers was a grip-man because he knew the secret handshake of every Masonic and Odd Fellows and Knights of Pythias lodge across the country. The Reverend would stalk the docks for newcomers, spot the heraldic crests of a fraternal order and then—as a pin-man as well, this was key—root in his stash and find the matching emblem to affix to his suit jacket lapel, meet and greet his society fellows, welcome the strangers to their new home, instantly receive their trust and confidence, and then lead them to criminally minded businesses where they could be fleeced for every dime.

Old Man Triplett, in a bowler hat and a full gray walrus mustache, often played the fool, impersonating the men he suckered. Sometimes he dressed like a stampeder with a sled loaded down with bags of feathers. Or perhaps a well-to-do merchant, approaching a cheechako who presented a similar profile, telling a tale of woe and offering to sell his home in Skagway at a bargain. In these late Victorian times, throwing suspicion on such a gentlemanly figure would have been unthinkably rude. So the wealthy newcomer trustingly followed Old Man Trip to the out-of-the-way cabin, where he was robbed at gunpoint.

There were heavies too, for that kind of work. Reddy Gallagher, a former boxer. Walsh, a brute. Big Ed Burns, a former member of the Wyatt Earp gang during the shootout at the O.K. Corral. Burns did the same work in Skagway as he did back then but since he had switched sides now it was called murder.

And over them all was a single gangster holding court at his eponymous tavern.

Jeff Smith's Parlor consisted of a wood-planked storefront with an interior hall that stretched into a long, telescoped saloon. In a city like Seattle, it would be considered barely more than a shack, but in Skagway it was a destination, with a proper door and a double-hung glass window in front and a finely stenciled sign decorated in patriotic bunting. The proprietor could often be found standing at the bar drinking whiskey, or perhaps winning a game of faro, as per usual.

"It's a sure thing," he always said, collecting his winnings.

Jeff Smith was slim, well under six feet tall, with an out-of-fashion furry beard. He spoke with the drawl of a gentleman farmer off a Dixie plantation, and preferred black hats and three-piece suits and a pearl-handled revolver on his belt. "Three things make a man look disreputable: one old hat and two old shoes," he said. Smith had small soft hands, nimble, almost feminine, that could flip a pea under a walnut, or tip a die, or swap a card right under your eye, or pull the trigger on anyone who stoked his famous temper. Suckers, rivals, cops.

But Smith didn't rule through threat of violence. It was ingenuity and intellect, his keen creativity for ever-more-sophisticated schemes, plus a fierce devotion to his men that kept his band together. With his tripe and keister—tripod and suitcase—he perfected shell games and three-card monte and lottery scams, his streetside pitch employing the rhetorical logic of his lawyer father, the lofty vocabulary of his preacher ancestors, and the high-speed prattle and sleight of hand of that celebrity of the frontier: the traveling bunco artist. So thoroughly did he ingratiate himself to his victims, they often thanked him even as they were being swindled.

In Skagway this grift attained yet new heights. Smith was a master of dissembling debauchery and shameless flimflam. He established fake auction houses, fake stock exchanges, fake armies with fake guns and fake military rank for himself. The town lawmen, both of the local newspapers, and fully two thirds of the city council were in thrall to him, though none of them understood the reach and breadth of the scam.

Soapy Smith was the shadow king of Skagway.

It started simply, with a briefcase full of carefully wrapped bars.

"How are you fixed for soap?"

Smith called his cadence to unsuspecting pedestrians passing his Denver street corner.

"Move on up to the box, boys! How are you are fixed for soap?"

Armed with a legitimate business license, Smith hawked the packages out of a faded valise, 10 cents a bar of Sapolio brand soap. His oratory was rapid-fire and alluring, a Pied Piper for the naive, and when a sufficient crowd had gathered, lured by nothing but his extolments regarding simple household soap, Smith upped the ante. He reached inside his coat and pulled out a wad of greenbacks, and after flashing the biggest bills, a hundred-dollar note on the outside of the roll, he quickly wrapped a few around individual soap bars and then covered them with the cake's original blue paper packaging. A lucky few were now hidden in his pile of merchandise.

"Who will give me a dollar for a pick?" he called. "It's a sure thing!" And the crowd responded. He wasn't selling soap anymore, not really. Now it was a lottery.

One man paid the fare and picked a bar of soap and found a winner right away. He waved the five-dollar bill in the air and then another man paid and picked and he won too. Now Smith could auction the soap for more than a dollar each. There followed a string of unlucky choices, the crowd's mood slumped, and then came a winner, the biggest yet. The mob was begging to hand over their money. The price of a bar of soap rose higher and higher, in direct proportion to how Smith's pile shrank. Ten dollars, twenty, even thirty. The crowd was sure the hundred-dollar bill must still be hidden somewhere. Which, in fact, it was not.

Eventually all the soap was sold. The crowd ebbed away. Those winners of the lottery, so vocal during the auction, were suddenly absent. No one on the street could identify anyone who won a prize. The salesman and his suitcase were gone.

Around the corner and out of sight, Smith met up with the winners. They were all his own crew, part of the show, shills to drive the mob. He collected the false winnings back again and then dealt out each man's share from the auction take. He always paid his men first, their loyalty both bought and earned.

Then Soapy Smith and his gang moved on to the next frontier boomtown, where suckers outnumbered lawmen a thousand to one.

Soapy's ascendency in Skagway was no accident. It was a calculated hostile takeover, one he had been preparing for his whole life.

Jefferson Randolph Smith II was born in Georgia in 1860, on his family's cotton plantation known as Shoal Creek. Four years later, the

Smiths' one hundred chattel slaves were freed, and by the end of Reconstruction the family found themselves homeless and destitute. Young Smith's alcoholic father, barred from practicing law and unable to find other work, struck out west, moving the family to the frontier town of Round Rock, Texas, in 1877.

He was seventeen years old, his mother dead, his father next to worthless. To feed his younger siblings, Smith took a job at the dry goods store in town and soon discovered that he was a natural salesman. Not as a neutral shelver of provisions, but as a high-intensity pitch man, pressuring buyers to stock up lest all manner of ills befall them. Smith realized that the item to be sold was almost immaterial. The idea was the thing, to instill in the buyer a fear of calamity or missed opportunity. Soon Smith moved on to street-side jam auctions, selling essentially worthless merchandise at high speed to confuse the buyers. Then came confidence schemes, the bunco dice games, and straight-up scams. By 1879, still a teenager, Smith had moved to Denver to ply the packaged soap racket for which he would become famous.

"How are you fixed for soap?"

In the 1880s, Smith moved all over the West, buying legitimate business licenses and defrauding customers through the rigged lottery. "My business is selling prize packages. No one is obliged to buy," he would say until he was run out of town. Nebraska City, Gonzales, Salt Lake, San Francisco, Tombstone. But it was to Denver where Soapy Smith would return again and again, and ultimately build a criminal empire.

In 1892, Soapy was jailed in Denver for murder, but he beat that charge. People said he outthought the law by never killing a man when alone. Soapy always had a few henchmen with all the same guns, all the same bullets. Five shots fired, four misses, one killing blow. But who pulled the trigger on the deadly round? The police couldn't prove it and the judge threw out the case. Soapy was a crime boss above the law and everyone knew it.

As for so many, it was the Panic of 1893 that did Soapy in. Denver fell into a depression, and with so much less money on the street to swindle, infighting among the gangs and police scrutiny intensified. Soapy's brother was jailed, along with members of his gang, and so Smith fled town. He moved about aimlessly. Jailed in Dallas, run out of Creede and Cripple Creek, harassed by one lawman or another wherever he went.

By 1897, Smith was too well known across the West to operate effectively. He needed a new headquarters, a tabula rasa he could seize and make his own.

Then on July 18, he saw the newspaper reports about gold in the Klondike.

"I expect to be a millionaire," he announced, "in no time at all."

Soapy knew a mark when he saw it. A chance to seize some gold rush town up there from the moment of its birth. And he could set it up every way he wanted, not just gambling dens and corner hustles, but also what he called the big store con, front businesses of every type. "We'll open up a real estate and mining office," he planned, "and I'll gamble they'll tumble like tired doves." Yes, just like a worn-out whore.

This was his final shot. If he could just make enough money now, he could leave and buy a real business, a straight business, and then settle down and be a family man, with his wife and children who lived in St. Louis, far away from him for their own safety.

"This is my last opportunity to make a big haul," he thought. "Alaska is the last West."

Soapy arrived in Skagway on August 22, 1897, less than a month after the first cheechakos. Three longtime members of his gang came with him, and they immediately started their bunco racket on the trails. Meanwhile, Soapy entered into a partnership with John Clancy, who ran one of the first saloons on Broadway. Clancy's establishment would offer drinks in front and Soapy's brothel in back. In the first three weeks the gang had wrung $30,000 from the newcomers.

In these early days, Skagway still consisted of a few wood-frame houses, a blacksmith, a sawmill, four whiskey dens with crap tables and card games. The dentist advertised with a painted sign stuck on a tree: "Teeth Extracted." An unofficial tally of the population counted two thousand men, four wives, and thirteen sporting girls. By the next year, the city hosted seventy saloons and five breweries. Skagway grew rapidly as a city simply because many of the people who arrived could not leave, as the White Pass was first blocked by bloated dead horses and then by winter snows. And that was just the start. "The rush of the people next spring will be something unprecedented in the annals of the world," Soapy predicted.

The gangster knew the score. Very few of those passing through Skagway would get rich and he intended to be one of them. More than that, he'd be on top.

One by one, other members of his gang, old hands from Texas and Colorado, trickled their way up north. There were so many stampeders, no one could tell they were all together. Slim Jim Foster ran a saloon called the Grotto. Bill Saportas took a job at the newspaper. Old Man Triplett posed as a sourdough and warned wealthy stampeders that the snows in the White Pass were ferocious and they were better off staying in Skagway a bit. Other gang members opened storefronts, using gimmicks Soapy had perfected swindling the nouveau riche in Denver. The Telegraph Office, Reliable Packers, Information Bureau, Merchants Exchange, Cut-Rate Ticket Office. Most were complete shams. In a double dip, the fake telegraph office offered to wire money around the country for a $5 fee. Only a very few Skagway businesses advertised reliably. At the Red Onion Saloon there was a line of tin dolls behind the bar. If the doll was upright, the corresponding girl was available upstairs. If the doll was lying down, then so was she.

Soapy's overarching scheme ran like this: shakedown offers of "protection" for those merchants outside of the gang, scams and cons via his storefronts on the inside. And all the while, he paid off police to look the other way and promised the legit local business community that he would target only transients. In fact, Soapy argued that any cheechako so dumb as to be duped by his games was not clever enough to survive in the wild, and he was in fact doing a public service by culling the weakest of the herd.

Violence rose in proportion to the gang's power. To deflect the bullets at night, one resident surrounded his bedroom in boiler iron. In another case, during a shell game along the trail, one victim of the bunco fought back against the dealer. To his surprise, he discovered that six of his fellow gamblers were actually Soapy's men as well. The victim swung and connected with the first man, struck a second, then a third. The dealer drew a pistol and then so did every other man and everyone started firing. By the time the gunfight was done, three innocent packers had been hit and a horse killed.

Soapy always promised local officials that without him, things would be worse. They didn't realize that the extortion and theft and cruelty were all finely calibrated, that Soapy was in control. If the whole gold rush was setting up to be a get-rich-quick scheme, then Soapy's racket was a scheme within a scheme. Or, as the disillusioned cheechakos would learn, a bunco within a bunco.

Once in a while, miners did come out with gold, of course, which stirred in Soapy an occasional desire to go to Dawson himself. But this was fleeting; the urge soon passed and right sense prevailed. "I hate the trip," he reflected, "800 miles in a little canoe and sleep out at night." He was a city man, always had been. Plus, why tangle with Sam Steele and his inspectors, when he had such a good thing going in Skagway.

Soapy was a displaced Southern aristocrat, a genteel man about town. At the Thanksgiving masquerade ball, Soapy attended in costume as a Tin Goblin. Day to day, he was no less dapper, dressed with an air of sophistication and elegant success. As he told his son, a man who couldn't read and write and count, who did nothing but drink, would never accomplish anything, sure to be a bum. Which is why, his whole life, he hated the name Soapy. It was classless. His closest friends called him Jeff, his gang and business associates Mr. Smith.

Thus Jeff Smith's Parlor, on Holly Street, a manicured establishment decorated with plate glass mirrors and electric lighting and a thousand-dollar roulette wheel specially ordered and shipped from Denver. He advertised the finest extravagances, Havana cigars and fine wines and oyster dinners, though he also hung a sign over the gambling hall that read *Caveat Emptor.* Let the buyer beware.

"A cure for the gambling habit," he thought, tongue in his cheek. "In my games, the player cannot win."

At key moments the dealers in Soapy's establishments were known to switch to cold decks, the cards pre-stacked in the house's favor. A shuffle, a cut, the dealer scooting his chair forward so he could drop his hands below the table and swap one stack for another.

Soapy himself had a weakness for playing cards, especially faro, an especially popular and addicting game that players described as "bucking the tiger." In faro, all thirteen cards of a certain suit are laid out to form a playing board. The dealer then draws two cards at a time from a fresh deck, a loser and a winner. Gamblers place chips on the betting board, to try to predict which two cards would come up, doubling or losing their money as appropriate. Every card that had already been drawn remains faceup for all to see, granting the illusion of control. If you could count cards fast enough and had just a little luck you could make money at faro.

Soapy was known to occasionally play in gambling dens not under his control. In such cases, he played alone—against the dealer, the table hastily emptying as he sat down—and he played for keeps, until either he or the house was broke.

When he won, he was generous with his new wealth. When he lost, his rage sent thugs scurrying.

Soapy's success was undeniable and news started to leak out, not always to his liking. Broadsheets on the American West Coast spoke of lawlessness, shootings and theft, disease and frozen bodies on the Chilkoot. The papers put the blame for all this on the same man, and the *San Francisco Examiner* even exposed his sordid past in Denver.

This would not do at all, Soapy realized. He could rule the town only if no one knew what was going on. He sent letters to the editor, defending his reputation. "I have never had any trouble in my place of business; was never convicted of any crime in my life, and don't think that I am being treated right," he wrote in the *Seattle Daily Times*.

But such protestations did little to change public perception, and as Soapy's profile rose there was an unintentional dual effect. Not only did the newspaper coverage encourage official scrutiny from government, but it also served as a beacon to outlaws. By the spring of 1898, too many ruffians had been drawn to Skagway, and Soapy started to lose control. Robbers and gunmen would say they worked for Soapy, whether true or not. And Soapy's gut instinct was to protect them, no matter how unfamiliar or tenuous the bond. It would prove his downfall.

On the last day of January 1898, after a long night of drinking with a good-time girl on the second floor of the People's Theater, a day laborer of low morals named Andy McGrath found himself in a fatal argument. McGrath felt cheated—by both the working girl and the bartender, a man named John Fay—and his belligerence was only exceeded by his drunkenness.

McGrath said Fay had sold him poisoned liquor and the saloon's girl had stolen from him. Fay would hear none of it, nor would the owner of the club, Jake Rice, who got involved in the quarrel. McGrath may have started the row but Fay and Rice and his heelers ended it, beating the man to the ground and tossing him from the bar. McGrath picked himself up from the cold road and shouted "I will come back and settle for this!" at his pummelers before stumbling away.

McGrath made his way across the street and found the deputy U.S. marshal, a man named James Rowan, who was in town looking for a doctor for his deeply pregnant wife. The drunken McGrath asked Rowan if he could borrow the lawman's pistol, in order to go back to the saloon and shoot the bartender. Deputy Rowan declined, but did offer to go see what the trouble was about.

The two men entered the saloon, and the aggrieved McGrath walked straight to Fay and swung a fist at him. Fay staggered and then pulled a pistol from his pocket and fired and McGrath fell and bled a torrent of red where he lay. Rowan reached for his own weapon and Fay pulled the trigger again. Rowan took his shot in the stomach and stumbled backward and outside, where he was rushed to a doctor. No matter. Both men died and Fay escaped out the back of the saloon in search of a hiding place. Who had the power to keep him safe, after he had just killed a U.S. marshal?

The citizens of Skagway were incensed. That Rowan's widow gave birth that very day only added to the public furor. Members of the local vigilance board—the officially constituted, but rarely acting Committee of 101—met in a church to decide whether to hang Fay from a tree, the new bell ringing to call members of the community who wished join the posse. Soapy himself answered the summons and addressed the assembled. In his practiced polished manner, he called for calm. He also said he would shoot any man who tried to lynch Fay.

In the end, Soapy went to the U.S. Commissioner, the ranking federal official in the region, who intervened so that Fay was whisked away by boat to Sitka, where he would face trial and, using an argument of self-defense, force a hung jury. Half of Skagway said Soapy helped a double murderer escape justice. The other half praised Soapy for starting a fund to assist Rowan's widow. Soapy himself gave $50, and charged the bank only $119 for accounting expenses related to organizing the fund. The widow got $305.

Soapy had interfered with justice, and business leaders in Skagway felt emboldened by the public venting of frustration. Soapy's gang was starting to be known derisively as the Pallid Pimps. The businessmen were sick of paying bribes to the gangster, and fearful for the survival of the town if it earned a reputation for lawlessness in the newspapers of the continental United States. Soapy's crew was growing and threatened widespread violence. It was time for the Committee of 101 to get more organized.

On March 8, 1898, the day after yet another murder on the White Pass, the vigilance committee posted signs around town that bunco and confidence men were no longer welcome in Skagway. Anyone involved in shell games and sure-thing cons needed to leave town immediately. The posters were signed "101."

In response, Soapy called a meeting of his newly formed and newly named Law and Order Society, which he claimed had 317 members, far more than the Committee of 101. New posters went up, saying that the law-abiding citizens of Skagway would rise up against the 101 vigilantes. Confusingly, deliberately, these posters were signed "The Committee."

Only the most astute and careful readers may have noticed that Jeff Smith's Parlor stood at 317 Holly Street. In a personal and ominous note, Soapy hung some of the posters on the front doors of prominent members of the 101.

His next opportunity to undermine his opponents came a month later, on April 25, when the United States declared war on Spain. Having lost the USS *Maine* in a Cuban port two months earlier, America got its blood up, a thirsty zeal for revenge it had not felt in decades. And Soapy knew how to exploit it for his own purposes against the Committee.

Soapy proposed the formation of a unit of Alaskan volunteers, the Skagway Military

Company. Naturally, he would be voted captain and Jeff Smith's Parlor would serve as headquarters. In a time of war, security on the home front was of supreme importance, everyone knew, and there was no room for vigilantes like the 101.

"Spain will send her battleships to seize our ports, and they will try to capture our ships," Soapy warned his company, "but, be damned to them and we'll stake our lives against their plots." They must defend their port against all enemies, the Spanish from the sea and troublemakers from within. On paper, eighty-five men joined the company, including several of Soapy's gang.

Soapy personally wrote to President McKinley, offering the services of his volunteer company that he promised was already drilling regularly, and asking only for the War Department to provide the arms to allow them to fulfill their duty. The president's secretary wrote back a one-sentence telegram, simply acknowledging receipt of the original letter, which Soapy promptly framed and hung on the wall of his parlor, showing anyone who would look that the White House had addressed him as "Captain Smith."

On May Day, Soapy organized a parade, a patriotic display to celebrate the declaration of war against Spain. He marched at the head of his command, everyone singing "Yankee Doodle" and wearing a bright red, white, and blue badge that read "Freedom for Cuba. Remember the Maine! Compliments Skagway Military Company, Jeff R. Smith, Capt." Hundreds more identical badges were distributed to citizens in attendance. The day ended with the hanging and burning of an effigy of "Butcher" Weyler, the governor-general of Cuba.

Some citizens thought it all a fraudulent jingoistic display. Others listened to the adulatory speeches from dignitaries and swelled with patriotic pride for their military volunteers. Mostly, no one was sure what to believe, and that's how Soapy knew he had succeeded.

Ella D. Wilson never made it as a singer. Maybe she lacked talent. Or maybe it was her dark skin and kinky hair, which left her no way to pass as white though by blood she was only half a Negro. Whatever the reason, it was hard to believe she left the stage and took up the oldest profession completely by choice. She was twenty-eight years old when she was murdered. A beauty.

Wilson's body was found in her bed, though whether she was dressed, as it were, in the manner befitting her occupation, the newspapers politely did not say. They did report, though, that she was tied up, hand and foot. Tightly wound bedsheets bound her wrists and ankles, her pillowcase cinched around her neck and the ends stuck in her mouth as a gag. The feather pillow itself was found on her face. She had been smothered.

Besides the mussed bed, the only item in Wilson's room disturbed in any way was a large steamer trunk, which was found open and pilfered; the thieves knew exactly where to look. The newspapers said $2,000 was taken, though how anyone knew exactly the amount of money a transient sporting girl kept hidden was not clear.

Wilson's small cabin, on Holly Street, lay only a few doors down from Jeff Smith's Parlor. Fitting, as some people said the mulatto girl was Soapy's mistress. In fact, it wasn't a robbery at all, they said, he simply tired and disposed of her.

On May 31, two days after Wilson's body was discovered, Deputy Marshal Taylor formed a grand jury to conduct an inquest. Taylor was a creature of Soapy's, and two of the six members of that jury were affiliates of Soapy's gang. Unsurprisingly, the jury failed to identify a culprit and returned a finding of unintentional murder. The case was dropped.

But not ignored. Soon after the murder, a woman known as Madam Silks, who ran a bawdy house competing with Soapy's establishments, heard the gang leader talking through the thin walls of the Occidental Hotel that he had killed and robbed Ella Wilson and would do the same to Silks next. The madam fled Skagway and was happy to tell a newspaper reporter in Seattle exactly why. They ran with the story.

Soapy would eventually sue newspapers in Seattle and San Francisco for defamation of character, but the increased notoriety no longer curbed his actions. Fear of being found out was ebbing. He was getting bolder now, and more dangerous.

In early June, Colonel Steele of the North-West Mounted Police ordered the transfer of $150,000 in customs duties from Dawson to the outside. In command of the shipment Steele named Inspector Zachary Taylor Wood, great-grandson of the twelfth American president. Using a cover story that Wood was being transferred to Calgary, the inspector and a small team of heavily armed men packed the gold dust in ordinary saddlebags, so as not to draw unwanted attention, and made their way overland to the south. Steele provided an escort to the American border, but from there on, Wood and his men were on their own. They would descend the Chilkoot Trail down into Dyea, board a private vessel, sail the few miles to the harbor at Skagway, and then transfer to an oceangoing steamship without ever setting foot in town. All of this in order to avoid Soapy's gang.

The plan worked until the last moment. As Wood's small tug made its way into the Skagway harbor, the inspector saw that several members of Soapy's gang were rowing out to meet them in a skiff, the two boats on a collision course. Beyond lay Wood's objective, the *Tartar*, a Canadian Pacific Railroad ship manned by the Royal Navy, tied up to a dock that was crowded with Soapy's hoodlums.

The tug pressed on. Wood gave the order and two of his men raised their .303 Lee-Metford carbines to the shoulder and stared down the incoming boat. With their shabby pirate ruse discovered, Soapy's rowers laid down their oars and slowly floated off. In the distance, Wood could see *Tartar* sailors out along the hurricane deck, covering the pier with their rifles. Wood and his men tied off, and more sailors disembarked the *Tartar* and held the dock while the Mounted Police cross-loaded the 550 pounds of gold.

The wharf was full of men with guns. One kit bag after another, Wood's troopers transferred the dust as the thugs looked on.

Then Soapy Smith himself stepped out of the crowd. He smiled and called to Wood and invited him to visit Skagway as a guest of honor.

The *Tartar* steamed for Canada immediately.

Later, Soapy's people would say the inspector had it all wrong. Who would try to rob armed police in the middle of the day on a public dock? How gauche! Why, Soapy just wanted to invite Wood back to his parlor, engage in a few games of faro.

Confidence had edged into recklessness, and by midsummer, Soapy's tight grip on Skagway was increasingly on garish public display. Gangster, power broker, commander of the local military volunteers, the pesterings of the Committee of 101 fading away, Soapy joined in sponsoring a Fourth of July parade to outdo even the May Day celebration. There would be drinks and floats and an eagle in a cage, a curiosity that on a daily basis was used by Soapy's thieves as a lure to get gullible marks alone behind Jeff Smith's Parlor. From morning to shining night, the town shook from shotgun blasts and dynamite and firecrackers that Soapy handed out to children.

Naive parade organizers, ignorant to the dynamics at play in town, originally gave Soapy the lowly role of fourth marshal, where he would have to ride in the back, twentieth, behind the children's float with the Goddess of Liberty, the City Brewing float, the Chilkat Indians, and the blackface mummers of the grotesquerie.

Such would not do. Indignant, Soapy elbowed his way up and took over as grand marshal. C. W. Everest, the Commercial Club president and original holder of that honor, did not voice a peep of protest as Soapy rode his dapple-gray gelding at the front of the parade.

John Douglas Stewart was an experienced miner in his early fifties, thick and fit, with a light mustache that belied his age. He had done one stint in the Klondike and another in Atlin, in far northern British Columbia, and after an exhausting but successful cleanup, in the summer of 1898 he decided to return home to his family, with $87 in cash and a full poke. Ten pounds of gold dust.

Stewart arrived in Skagway on July 7, and finding no ship leaving that day he made plans to stay the night. Fearing robbery, he put his gold in the safe at Kaufman's store, and then took a room at the Hotel Mondamin.

Soapy Smith's room at the hotel was just a few doors down.

In the morning, Stewart was approached on the street by two men, the Reverend John Bowers and Slim Jim Foster. They said they were new to Skagway and knew nothing about mining or the Klondike. Stewart was such an experienced prospector, could they buy him a drink so he could teach them all about it? In fact, there was a saloon very near his hotel: Jeff Smith's Parlor.

The three men were walking along the alley next to the saloon when another stampeder approached. It was Old Man Triplett, and he told Stewart that he had lost his money to a crooked gambler until the man taught him how the trick was done. Did they want to see? Before Stewart could respond, Bowers and Foster eagerly joined the game.

Triplett pulled up a crate that just happened to be lying nearby and started to deal three-card monte. Foster said he was sure he knew the trick and asked Stewart to borrow $5 to place a bet. Stewart was hesitant, but when he pulled out his folding bills Foster snatched the entire wad of $87 and bet it all. Triplett flipped the cards; the old man had won.

Stewart was angry, so Triplett offered them a second game, a chance to win it all back. But Stewart turned on Foster.

"I should hold you for the money," Stewart said, growing upset.

Triplett then breathed soothing words and offered to return their cash, saying he was just joking the whole time. But still, he wanted to know, if they had gone ahead and played another round, "Supposing you had bet that in earnest, did you have the money to put up."

Foster admitted he did not, but then turned to Stewart. "You have the money, you have some dust."

Stewart begged off, but Foster insisted, show the old man your dust, so he can see we would have been good for the bet. After all, everyone knew it would be unseemly for a gentleman to make a bet he could not keep.

Stewart relented, and went with Reverend Bowers to Kaufman's store to retrieve his poke. Triplett and Foster stayed in the back of the alley. Stewart fetched the sack and returned, Bowers standing behind him. The miner held up the heavy poke for everyone to see.

"I don't know if that's gold," said Triplett.

"Open it and show it to him," Bowers said, "as he don't know gold dust unless he sees it."

Stewart hesitated and then suddenly Foster reached for the poke and pulled it away and passed it to the old man. Stewart threw a punch at Triplett but missed and then both Foster and Bowers grabbed him and held him fast and whispered in his ear, "Make a noise it will not be well for you." Stewart pulled free but Triplett had already disappeared out of sight around an alley corner and then Foster and Bowers melted into the crowd.

Stewart staggered back into the daylight. Across the street he saw a policeman with a badge.

"I've just been robbed of $3,000," Stewart said.

Deputy Marshal Taylor, who had recently exonerated the killers of Ella Wilson, told Stewart that he would see what he could do. Then Taylor turned up the street and returned to oversee construction of his brand-new home.

Everyone agreed that this time Soapy had gone too far.

Business leaders could tolerate Soapy preying on newcomers when they were all relatively poor and headed inland. But this was different. The flow of stampeders was beginning to reverse, and now that the Dawson miners were leaving, the merchants and hoteliers and barkeepers of Skagway wanted their legitimate share of that Klondike gold.

If prospectors coming back down the trail were robbed and harassed, and if word leaked back to Dawson that Skagway was unsafe for any miner with means, then everyone would leave via Dyea or St. Michael instead. Skagway would become a ghost town in no time.

Soapy Smith heard the ruckus and rumors of his involvement and he sought out a few town politicians to assure them of both his personal innocence and the innocence of his men. In fact, no robbery had occurred at all, Soapy said. Stewart lost his poke in a card game. Perfectly fair. Though, to calm tensions, Soapy offered to return the gold to Stewart as a gesture of goodwill, as long as he kept quiet and didn't make a fuss in the newspapers.

But Stewart did make a fuss, to all who would listen, and by six o'clock that evening, the presiding commissioner—who was based in Dyea, not Skagway, and who after receiving the news of the robbery by telephone, took the first boat available—had approved three warrants, for the arrest of Foster, Bowers, and Triplett. He delivered the paperwork to Deputy Marshal Taylor, who took as much interest in the case as he had upon hearing the original news. But the die was cast.

Word on the street was that Soapy thought himself above the law, a coward who hid behind a gang of thugs, that if the deputies would not serve the warrants then the vigilance committee would have to. In his parlor, Soapy started drinking. The company constructing the railway in the White Pass handed out rifles to their workers. The leaders of the Committee of 101 announced that a meeting of concerned citizens would take place that very night. Soapy's spies kept their boss informed of each development and as afternoon became evening a *Skagway News* reporter approached the intoxicated gangster to suggest that if the gold wasn't returned there would be trouble. Too late, Soapy would hear none of it.

"By God, trouble is what I'm looking for," he yelled, and he took another drink, stepped out on Broadway and harangued the gathered crowd. "I'll litter the street with corpses," he vowed. But then he returned to his bottle in his bunker.

Promising to serve the warrants themselves, men of the Committee of 101 started to gather at Sylvester's Hall. So many attended, though, that they ran out of room, and so they moved to the Juneau wharf, one of four long jetties that thrust out over the mud flats and into the harbor on the far southern edge of town. They thought it was one of the few places Soapy would not have ears listening. They were wrong.

Four were chosen to guard the entrance to

the pier, though only one man, Frank Reid, was armed. Reid was from Illinois, but after the Civil War he moved west, where he volunteered to serve in a militia fighting the Paiutes in the Bannock War in Oregon. Reid was no angel, nor above violence in the name of pride; he had once killed a neighbor with a shotgun in a petty feud. Now into his fifties, Reid had first worked as a bartender in Skagway in one of Soapy's many saloon-fronts, a minor satellite in the crime boss's orbit. But Reid had since switched sides and became the town surveyor, a member of the closest thing Skagway had to a government. He was old and tough and perhaps crooked, though only as crooked as any other man who would travel so far and under such hardships, prizing gold above all else.

The agenda of the meeting of vigilantes was clear: how to drive Soapy Smith from town. As one allegation after another was aired, the size of the conspiracy was revealed. As if everyone in the Committee of 101 finally understood what had been going on in town the whole time. The deputies were on the take, the newspaper was on the take, half the businessmen and councilmen too. It seemed like almost everyone was in on the scam. But that time was over now. Soapy was exposed, and the mob would have satisfaction.

The reporter Bill Saportas, Soapy's source at the *Daily Alaskan*, attended the start of the vigilance meeting and then snuck back to the gang leader in his parlor, passing Soapy a small slip of paper. It read: "The crowd is angry, if you want to do anything do it quick."

It was after nine o'clock. Soapy had been drinking half the day. If he didn't stand up now, he knew, he'd be run out of town again, same way he had in Creede and Denver and all over the West. He needed to make a stand.

Soapy drank another whiskey and checked his old heavy Colt revolver on his belt and then reached over the bar and took his 1892 Winchester .44-40 rifle in his free hand and left for the docks.

"You have a lion by the tail," he reasoned. "Swing it, don't let it swing you."

When Soapy strode from his parlor his men hung back, like a slipping shadow. No one stood beside him. His gang was already splintering, melting, fleeing into the hills surrounding the bay. Soapy marched to the port alone.

Reid and three other guards stood at the end of the wharf. In the full sunlight of a northern summer, they could see Soapy coming down State Street directly to the harbor. He had his rifle over his shoulder and was cursing loudly. The crowd fell back and the men's nerves tingled as Soapy marched down the jetty toward them.

Men shrank, revolvers clanked, bootheels planted on each plank, the sound of sharp steps banking across the docks as Frank Reid's heart knocked in his breast.

Soapy shouted for the guards to get out of the way and they did, stepping aside or jumping off the wharf to the mud flat below. All except for Reid.

"You can't go down there," Reid said, and he held his ground.

The gangster didn't hesitate. Soapy swung his rifle off his shoulder, hard, and Reid raised his left arm to ward off the blow. The barrel struck Reid and opened him but he managed to grab the muzzle with his left hand and jerk the rifle down and toward him as he reached for his revolver with his right. They were in the clinch now, tight. Reid drew his .38 Smith & Wesson, an old heavy snub-nosed five-shooter, his trusty sidearm from many a militia ride on the Western frontier, and pressed it against Soapy's rib cage.

"My God, don't shoot!" Soapy yelled. Reid pulled the trigger.

Click. A misfire. For an instant, silence. Then both men squeezed at once and two shots rang and echoed off the canyon walls surrounding the town.

Soapy's rifle had been pushed low in the scuffle and his bullet struck Reid in the left leg. At the same moment the revolver round entered Soapy under his left armpit and shredded a lung and upon exit blew out the left side of his back.

Gore sprayed the dock. Reid fired again and then a third time. One bullet grazed Soapy's left arm, the next kneecapped him. Soapy staggered, fell back, but still managed to cycle his rifle, raise the barrel, and fire. Soapy's second round hit Reid in the gut and tore him out. His hip shattered upon impact and Reid crumpled forward and cherry-red blood geysered from his groin. Both men fell to the wharf.

Soapy died abandoned there on the dock, his blood dripping through the slats and into the sea below. His gang fled town and no one came to collect the body.

Men from the Committee ran up to Reid and rolled him onto his back. He was sticky and wet and they could smell his open bowels.

"Did I get him?" Reid asked. One of the vigilantes nodded as they called for a stretcher.

"I got the son of a bitch," Reid said. There was venom.

"He may have got me, boys, but by God I got him first.

"I got the son of a bitch.

"I got the son of a bitch."

A little weaker now.

"I got the son of a bitch.

"I got the son of a bitch . . ."

It took Reid twelve days to die.

CHAPTER NINE
1898

You must howl with the wolves, when
you are with the wolves.
—ANNA DEGRAF

Autumn was in free fall, and winter waited at the bottom. It was late in 1898, the bedraggled mob's momentum slowing, and those left on the trail were worn and thin, like the frayed knees in a pair of old work pants. The stampeder Anna DeGraf thought she could actually watch the ice build on Lake Laberge even as they sailed the small boat across the water. She sat in the bow and broke the frozen crust with an oar, swinging the wooden stick over and over, but progress was minimal and the effort wasted. "We're never going to get through," she worried. Night came on, the midnight sun a distant memory, and when a light appeared on the horizon the boys who paddled her boat steered for shore.

But to DeGraf's frustration, this glow proved to be no Mounted Police outpost or cheechako cooking fire to share in solidarity. It was an Indian encampment, and plenty hungry. "Young squaws and a lot of whiskey," she saw. The women seemed eager to sell themselves for a little food and the boys hooted with delight, running off without a care in the world.

The longer this journey went, the more easily distracted these boys became. They were good boys. Or good enough anyway, back in Skagway, when she hired them to carry her goods to Dawson. In the warm sun on the coast they had displayed the required motivation, but the hardships of the trail and the cold and snow had run them down, and she feared that none had the fire in their belly to reach the Klondike. Not like her.

Her packers were all white and they carried her outfit on their backs; one had a little mule at the start, but the beast never made it over the pass. True, she was slower than they, and why not, she was fifty-nine years old after all. She had lived three lifetimes already compared to these boys. And while her face looked much younger— smooth and kind, rounded like a porcelain doll's—she was dressed in burlap rags and walked with a limp, the result of a badly broken leg that had never healed quite right.

But it would be unwise to judge her from this outward appearance. She was not a broken doll. Her frame was sturdy from decades of labor, and she was not scared of hard work. She could put in twenty-five miles a day, using a crutch to pick among the boulders, and still by evening be pushing the boys to go but a little farther.

She had to get to Dawson. Her son George, missing these past six years, he would be there, she was sure of it. She knew her child, and she knew George would find and follow the stampede. And so she must go too.

"Are you looking for gold?" everyone asked her.

"No, I am seeking my son," she would reply, and everyone on the trail called her Mother, even the other women and old men.

Sometimes it took the packers several days to leapfrog her outfit ahead, so in the mornings she'd have time to bake a few loaves of bread and other stampeders would smell it from far away and come to her. These men were hungry as wolves and so tired they couldn't even speak, and she would just feed them and never take any money. How could she? They all looked just like her son.

"Wherever you are, George, I hope they are being kind to you," she thought.

That's all any of them wanted. Kindness. And comfort. There was precious little of either to be had. When men saw that she'd cook for them on the trail, many offered to pack for her for free, just to eat a square meal. And at night the boys she hired would lie on the ground right where they fell from exhaustion, their moccasins and feet both torn to ribbons. Then she'd melt snow and wash the blood and bind their feet with strips of cloth torn from blankets. Making them a new pair of moccasins took only a few days.

One cheechako, who didn't last long before quitting, she could see his courage fail a little more every day. All he talked about was his wife and his feather bed. Another group of young men all wore patent leather shoes. They were hopeless. "My sons, you should go home to your mothers," she told them. She bought their whole provision, so they had cash to buy steamer tickets for the passage south. They all slunk home, gratefully.

"They just want to have a good time in a wild country," she decided. But they weren't cut out for it. "This is a strong man's country, and gold-seeking is the hardest kind of real work."

She had no doubt she could make it, she had survived this far. Food was tight on the overburdened ferry north, as the captain had left cargo on the dock in Seattle, including much of her own, to make room for more passengers. In Skagway she got a job at a lunch counter to earn her keep while waiting for her provisions to be delivered two weeks later. And none too soon. Before she left, one of Soapy Smith's gang tried to crawl into her tent under the flap. She blew out the candle and then stomped on his hands with both feet and yelled for help but the man got away. She knew what he wanted; she had fought them off before.

In Dyea the music and racket from Arizona Charlie's dance hall was unbearable. "Surely a bedlam camp." So she set up her tent on the hillside above and convinced her disappointed packers to join her. And still, somehow, in the small hours of the morning she was awoken by a loud noise that she couldn't quite place. "I've never heard that before," she thought. Not carousing, drinking, or the work of sporting girls. No, she didn't recognize it at all.

She opened the tent flap and looked up into the dawning twilight. Something black and enormous filled the canyon and was rushing right at them.

"For God's sake, boys! Get up and see what this terrible thing is coming toward us!"

Everything shook. The air was alive. Below them, in the valley, a miner dipped his bucket in the creek, stood up to drink, and then his skull was dashed to bits by a falling rock. A wall of inky water followed and scoured everything in its path. Camps and tents were flattened, the dance hall was ripped from its foundation, and half-dressed girls fled in all directions. DeGraf watched safely from her high perch, the rocks and trees and mud burying the approaches to Dyea. And then all of a sudden it was quiet, a stillness hung, and she could hear nothing except for the sound of stampeders searching for their drowned comrades among the avalanche debris.

She and the boys pressed on. It was no safer on

the Chilkoot. She had learned that "it takes the trail to find out what kind of stuff is in a person." At the summit the rain began, then snow, then a mix of both. Her gumboots filled with creek water and her feet turned to stone and hurt so bad from the cold she could see stars. She prayed to God every night, thanking him for deliverance from that day and asking for protection from roving men at night. The rain soaked her outfit and washed away her salt and she could no longer make bread. The temperature fell further, and the snow piled up around them. She swaddled her feet in gunnysacks, as her shoes had long worn out. Lunches were hardtack and snow water. It was so cold and the boys were so tired carrying her outfit they would sit in the snow and say they didn't care if they ever moved again.

"Boys, it's just a little further," she would say, but they all knew it wasn't true.

Eventually her packers were done. Getting stuck in the ice on Lake Laberge was the last straw, and the boys refused to be hurried any further by their "mother," not when whiskey and the warm beds of Indian girls were so readily available.

She was beside herself with the delays, and in constant sorrow for her son George, and oh so frustrated to be stuck again. She knew it would soon be too late in the season to get through. The despair was like a thing alive inside of her and she thought she might explode from the pressure of it.

Finally, she had had enough. She walked into the camp where the boys were drinking and lying with the squaws and broke up their revelry and gave an ultimatum. DeGraf told them that she was leaving, at once, and with all the food. If they didn't come with her at that very moment they'd all be stranded.

The boys laughed at her, laughed at that limping old woman with rags for shoes. And then she reached into her clothes and pulled out her revolver.

"I will go, just the same," she said to them.

Her heart bumped, but her voice was level and flat, this mantra in her head, over and over: You're so brave you're the bravest thing that ever was the bravest thing in the whole world.

"And the first one that stops me will be shot."

First the boys stared at her in shock. And then, slowly, at gunpoint, they started to gather the outfit.

George had to be in Dawson. He just had to, she couldn't bear the thought that he wasn't waiting for her in the Klondike. She would get these packers over the Chilkoot through sheer force of will if necessary.

She knew she could do it because she had done it before. This was not Anna DeGraf's first stampede.

• • •

George DeGraf went missing in July of 1892. It had been a cool and dry summer, and Seattle was booming, the Panic still to come. George could have just gotten a job like so many other young men, but it wasn't enough for him.

"He is a restless and venturesome man," she thought. He was only twenty-three years old and she knew he yearned to leave and live.

Even then stories about Alaska were creeping into the newspapers, miners and business rivalries and Mr. John J. Healy building a new paddle-wheeler to ply the Yukon River. Young men whispered tall tales about the riches to be had. As the main embarkation port, Seattle stood to benefit, but George wanted to be in the thick of it. Steamers left for Alaska every week.

So one day George kissed her on the front stoop of their Seattle home and said, "Good-bye, Mother, I'll see you in fourteen days," and then he was gone.

Three weeks after he left, Anna DeGraf got news from a friend that George had been spotted in Juneau. Her husband was dead, her other children long buried or moved away. She didn't have to think hard about what to do next.

Hardships did not intimidate her. She was born in 1839 in Alsace-Lorraine, and then as a child moved to Saxony, in central Europe. As a young woman she had survived the Seven Weeks' War, and then, in 1867, she crossed the Atlantic to join her husband, who had emigrated to New York ahead of her, just in time to fight in the American Civil War. Her first child died an infant, she and a daughter survived cholera, and after her husband went bankrupt in the depression of 1873, they moved west, where he was murdered while placer mining in the Yakima valley.

George was going to be a prospector too. She thought of him, swinging his bag, whistling as he walked to the pier. She sold her sewing business and got on the next boat north to Alaska.

In 1892, Juneau was a mean town of a thousand hardened miners. She intended to search the nearby camps for her son and then go home, but she ended up staying, working as a seamstress but always keeping an ear to the wind for any whisper of George.

That whisper took two years to arrive, and it came from Joe Ladue, the old-timer who grub-staked Robert Henderson and other prospectors besides. Ladue had been running a sawmill up in Sixtymile, providing lumber for sluice boxes at claims up and down the Yukon, and while passing through Juneau he told DeGraf that a young man with the same name had come past his place on the way to Fortymile. Anna made up her mind then and there. She would go to Fortymile, and take her sewing machine with her.

The first time she took the Chilkoot Trail she was a spring chicken of fifty-three years. There were no stampeders then, only Indian packers and whiskey bootleggers, and when the two met there was blood. One night, after a bout of drinking, DeGraf saw one Indian woman, her baby strapped on her back, attack her husband with nothing but her hands, tearing off chunks from his face and throwing them on the ground. DeGraf fled into the woods and afterward carried her outfit herself, thirty pounds at a time, a crutch in one armpit and her leg throbbing.

She found Ladue's sawmill at Sixtymile, but no one was around save for an Indian woman who had heard of George but didn't know if he'd gone upstream or down. DeGraf pushed on to Fortymile; no word of George. At that time, the fall of 1894, all the prospectors were heading to Circle City and so Anna did too. She arrived at the end of October in a heavy snowstorm, the flakes the largest she had ever seen. The next day the Yukon froze and she was trapped for the long winter.

No, no one in Circle City had seen her son.

Juneau was a bastion of civility and integrated with the enlightened world compared to Circle City. She was at the far edge now, the extreme frontier. Anna DeGraf wasn't the first white woman over the Chilkoot. That honor belonged to Dutch Kate, half a dozen years before. No,

DeGraf figured she was the seventh white woman in Circle City. All the men had Indian wives that they purchased from the tribe outside of town, some of the girls as young as twelve. DeGraf thought the Indian women good and peaceful and industrious, everything she valued, which was one reason it was such a shame when the dance hall girls showed up. Then the white men abandoned their Indian wives, beat them or shut them away in their cabins alone, and spent every last grain of gold dust on whiskey and dances and what came after.

"These men are fine, as a rule," DeGraf thought, "except when they drink." Which was every waking moment when they were in town and away from the mines.

The fact that she was twice the age of the prospectors did not keep their lust at bay. One man came into her home and locked the door behind him, trapping her. She hit him with a heavy quarter of firewood, right across the face, and when he yelled in pain and anger the neighbors heard and the man ran off.

"Boys, come out here, and look at the man who barred my door, and see what he got for it," she shouted. "Now, you go back to the creek and tell the miners that the dressmaker gave you a licking."

The constable gave her a Colt six-shooter and told her to use it next time. And DeGraf did, only a few days later.

That particular night there was only a single girl selling herself in the saloon, and after work, once she returned to her cabin, six men came for her at once, as a gang. They broke in and grabbed her and she knew what was coming. One took the front and a few more the back and the others waited their turn, their eyes trained on her. She yelled again and kicked and one grabbed her ankles and another her shoulders and they threw her across the room, where the woodstove glowed like the devil. Then they picked her up and seated her right on the stove. The poor girl screamed so as to wake the whole city. It was a cattle brand, and the stove burned through what little clothing remained, through her hands, her legs, her indecent areas that no man but her husband should see. She screamed in agony and they would not let her off the stove even in the midst of her suffering.

Somehow she got away and ran straight to DeGraf's cabin. "For God's sake, open the door, quick!" the girl yelled. "They are after me, don't let them get me!"

DeGraf opened the door and saw the girl covered in burns. Mother put her in bed and doused the lamp and told her to be quiet and then stood in the darkness with the revolver. She could hear them coming. She waited, silent. They were at her door.

"We want that woman in your cabin," they

called. "We won't bother you if you let us have her."

"You won't get her, as long as I am in here with my gun."

"Open this door!"

"I will shoot the first man that comes in here!"

They smashed her door so the hinges nearly snapped. She could scarcely believe it, they were really breaking in and coming for her. She cocked the gun and pointed it at the door and fired. The heavy half-inch bullet blew easily through the wood planks but the men didn't stop and the frame rocked again. She fired a second time, and then a third, and finally she heard them run.

The Circle City old-timers held a miners' meeting after that. All the men said it was just a roughhouse, meant nothing really. Still, shouldn't happen again. But it did.

Those men who threw that girl on the hot stove faced no trial, no conviction, no punishment. But take a bit of a man's outfit, swipe some sugar or flour, and you're banished, sent floating on the first log out of town.

Those miners' meetings were just a way to pass the time in a long winter. Consider that poor Negro girl, Mary Aikan. The miners put her on trial. They called it the coon trial. The jury drank two gallons of whiskey before declaring her guilty of being both a coon and a harlot. They ran her out of town just for something to do. She may have starved. If the miners' meetings ever were legitimate, they were no longer.

DeGraf's first winter was cold like she didn't know possible, 70 below zero. The freeze was so deep and so enduring that the Yukon barely thawed and ran low the next summer. No steamships came in or out. She was so disappointed, she said, "It's like I'm locked up in Siberia and the key lost." DeGraf was stuck for a second year, whether she wanted to be or not.

When a steamer finally did arrive, a full twelve months later, all the white men and Indians and dogs ran out to greet it, and the malamutes howled as it docked.

"After two long, hard, dark, winters, I am good and ready to go," she thought. She booked a steamer to Seattle but found that over the years she could not shake thoughts of the Yukon. It stayed in the front of her thoughts. Then in 1897 Dawson appeared all over the newspapers, the headlines never stopped, and she was sure her son would be drawn to that place.

She had escaped that icy prison but she knew she needed to go back.

Her boy. The boy was still missing.

Anna DeGraf did not make it to Dawson City until the spring of 1899. She moved into a small cabin next door to one of the major hotels, and almost immediately left the crowded city to walk the creeks and interrogate each claim in search of her son. Every day, among the windlasses and tailings, in Belinda Mulrooney's Grand Forks hotel, in the mean sod cabins and at each lunch counter, one by one she looked every miner in his frostbitten face.

None were her George.

"Still no news of my son!" Her misery was unbounded, and in her heart a wail of pain.

She resolved to wait for him. She had brought her sewing machine, she could stay and work as a seamstress, just as she had in Juneau and Circle City. Dawson was like those Alaska towns but magnified in every way imaginable, like a fully inflated hydrogen balloon stretching at the seams. So many people, so many enterprises, so much gold. They said nineteen million dollars would come out of the Klondike that year. The streets may have been full of sewage but they were lined with modern electric lights.

Mulrooney's three-story Fairview set the pace. Soon every proprietor was ripping off their roofs and building up. The Bonanza, the Monte Carlo, the Tivoli, the Mascot, the Criterion. Huge wooden gambling halls and pleasure palaces lined Front Street, filled with burlesque dancers and minstrel shows, whiskey and absinthe, seven-foot-high oil paintings of Greek nudes and banners proclaiming "Fresh cheechako girls, just in over the ice."

DeGraf was Mother on the trail and stayed Mother in Dawson. The working girls needed her, they needed advice and counsel. DeGraf thought they were so strong and beautiful, they had the glow of the young, part energy, part potential, all earnest enthusiasm. Ethel Berry had told women not to go to Klondike. Lone women, she had seen them do anything for the miners, to the miners, to get a big payday. DeGraf had seen it as well, knew that too many of these poor girls hid a desperation behind their bright eyes. They were troubled long before they came north. Why come otherwise? But this was why they needed her.

She would sew for them, make all their beautiful dresses and costumes, and she fitted them very early in the morning when they got off of work. Those were the evil hours, in the dim light of the early morning, when the liquor covered everyone's mind like a wet darkness. DeGraf would see all the evidence of the worst excesses from the night before. One time, on her way to fit a dress, she saw something odd sticking up out of the deep water-filled ditch that lined the sidewalk. When she got closer she saw it was one of the girls for whom she sewed. DeGraf grabbed a stick and pulled her out, took her home, put her in bed to sober up.

"What do you mean, getting drunk and throwing yourself away like this?" DeGraf asked.

The girl was in tears. "Oh how can I help it?"

she sobbed. Her job was to drink and dance and dance and dance. She was a good-time girl.

Onstage, in their whalebone corsets and bloomers, the variety girls performed melodramas and sang all the popular songs, "Put Your Arms Around Me, Honey" and "All Coons Look Alike to Me" and "Just a Little Lingerie" with a lifted skirt. As the owner of the Tivoli said, "We don't go in much for talent. All we want is plenty of lungs and legs to make the show a go."

Everyone knew the girls made the gold dust fly. "The poor ginks just gotta spend it. They're scared they'll die before they get it out of the ground," said Diamond Tooth Gertie, the famous performer with the eponymous smile. Sing well and all the miners threw nuggets; girls would run off or be injured by the stinging hail. Charlie Anderson, the "Lucky Swede," dropped ice-cold nuggets down blouses, and when a stripteasing Gertie taunted the audience—"Boys, ain't it pretty. The diamond, I mean."—they would toss gold at her with notes attached propositioning her for after-the-show activities upstairs, which made her a wealthy woman.

The work was about stamina and ruthlessness. After the shows the variety girls spent the rest of the night walking the floor selling whiskey. So too the percentage girls, named because they earned a commission on each dance and drink sold. These women were not known for their adornment—on the dance floor, revealing clothes meant mid-calf petticoats that showed ankles and high-buttoned shoes—but rather for their staying powers of drink and merriment. A caller would yell, "Come on, boys—you can all waltz—let's have a nice long juicy waltz," and the orchestra played "Blue Danube" and "Merry Widow" and they three-stepped with barely a stop, often 150 dances a night, earning 25 cents each. These were girls built for endurance.

In the largest halls, a series of mezzanines and balconies rose on either side of the stage, tiers of booths to watch the show. A white man from Alabama known as Nigger Jim owned a theater called the Pavilion. Jim had grown up near the Dixie plantations and could sing and dance as well as any Negro and when he blacked up and crooned in his Southern drawl he brought down the house. Everyone loved those minstrel shows. Even Belinda Mulrooney wore blackface and performed in a "coon show," as a benefit for Father Judge's St. Mary's hospital. Or they held boxing matches—one waiter, known as "The Black Prince," was a crowd favorite—though Colonel Steele put an unpopular ten-round limit on prizefights, and there was little point in betting on the Negro if he fought a white man, as the outcome seemed preordained.

The Klondike Kings reigned in the balcony boxes, the Berry brothers in vests and sleeve garters buying champagne at $25 a pop. Bottles cost twice as much in these rooms but the girls gave personal attention and service. You could close the curtains for privacy, and the girls called you honey, kissed your cheek, sat and talked and touched your leg all night as long as you bought champagne. You were the favored beau for the evening, the object of every other miner's jealousy.

The variety girls called this "wrestling the boxes," cozying up and drinking fast so the men would do the same and keep the bottles coming. They'd find a willing victim for the night, the model candidate possessing an abundant combination of unsteadiness and wealth. The drinks would arrive, a miner's back would turn, and the girls would pour their whiskey in a spittoon so he'd order another round. The waiters were in league with the girls, sometimes returning with the same half-empty bottle again and again for the woozy sucker to repurchase. And if the girls could get the men drunk enough and stay sober themselves, they could cinch the drapes and roll the miner, cleaning out his pockets after he passed out.

This was ideal, empty the man's poke without having to go upstairs to do it. But if the men stayed on their feet, they'd want to meet up again, as dawn broke.

Good-time girls went a dollar a dance and

three dollars a trick. Only straight tricks. None of those French tricks turned by vulgar two-way girls. Every dance hall had at least a few spare stalls above for the impatient ones, a place for the percentage girls to become sporting girls with barely a lick of discretion or privacy. All the knots in the planking of the wooden walls were pushed out, so peepers could watch.

When the miners weren't too drunk, at least it was over soon and they didn't hit too hard.

Many of the full-time sporting girls lived in semiproper rooms above the saloons. It was respectable cover to meet customers, not to mention efficient, less distance to travel to finish a man off and then get back downstairs to find the next one to roll. The rest rented cribs a block over, on Paradise Alley, between Queen and Princess streets. Little hutches with crimson drapes, in the window a divan or tear-stained bed where the girls would pose in chemises pulled up to the thigh, tap on the glass as the men walked by. Absolutely scandalous, all the bare arms and scooped necklines. Bow-tied waiters strutted out the back doors of hotels on Front Street with trays of champagne and shiny clean glasses, to serve their customers across the alley in the tenderloin.

The most popular girls had a queue outside eight men deep. "Guys, if you're not ready, don't stand in line," came the call.

Many took on noms de guerre. The youngest

was called "The Virgin" because she may have seen one once. The "Grizzly Bear" had only one eye. Edith Neil was known as the "Oregon Mare." Yes, she did imitate a horse onstage, but she earned her name when she bragged at the Monte Carlo about how many men could ride her at once.

After Madam Silks fled Skagway, fearful of her life due to the threat from Soapy Smith, she eventually moved to Dawson and opened a disorderly house on Second Street. Each of her eight girls averaged $50 a night, giving half to the madam. This was less than a girl with her own crib could make, but was far better than working as a $10-a-night streetwalker. And Silks took good care of her girls, kept on hand all required tonics and medicinal powders. Quinine, belladonna, chloroform, laudanum, Vaseline. Belladonna comes from the plant known as deadly nightshade. It was a wicked poison but if you took the right amount it would make your pupils dilate so your eyes widened liked a child's, sparkling and open and willing.

In 1899, when DeGraf arrived in Dawson, over half the women in town were working in the demimonde in some way, as full-time employment or to make ends meet. Living in Dawson was so expensive, costing at a minimum $180 a month. Men could make $15 a day hoisting permafrost from a mine, but not women.

Laundresses and maids earned $12 a week. Nurses only made $25 a month, for a two-year contract. A dressmaker like DeGraf could hope for $100 a month. Meanwhile, the most attractive girls charged four ounces of gold, or $68, for fifteen minutes of private attention.

There were so few opportunities, girls got creative. Many sold themselves as live-in "housekeepers," to service just one man full-time. One girl made $20,000 as a "wife" for two years. Three other girls sold themselves for their weight in gold, filling their corsets with buckshot when getting on the scale. But these were all temporary arrangements. Women could marry legally, and lovelessly, but so few miners were getting rich it made no sense to hitch your wagon to just one.

Colonel Steele thought the whole *maison de joie* business a necessary evil, and in fact less detrimental than most of the other entertainments in the saloons and showhouses. He told his Mounted Police that women could solicit on the street as long as they didn't wear bloomers. He also arrested 150 women a month for prostitution and fined them $50 each, but not, in his mind, as punishment. It was a tax, to fund the hospital. The first eighteen men serviced by each girl every month paid for Father Judge's sick wards. And a good thing too. Ten dozen stampeders a week were dying from typhoid, also consumption, scurvy, pneumonia. And syphilis, which rots the body till your hair falls out and your nose collapses into a horrid pit. Steele ordered medical inspections. For $5 a woman could get a letter declaring her healthy and free to ply the trade. Otherwise, she had to take mercury, ointment when she could get it, otherwise mercury pills, or pure mercury, of which the miners had plenty, to separate out gold. One doctor who treated the girls for venereal disease said that there were two or three queens, but most were nothing but sluttish painted creatures.

DeGraf was more than a mother to the girls. She was a confessor and kept their secrets. And they were always getting in trouble. Sick. Drunk. Preyed on by the macques, those weak soft men could do no real work and so pimped the girls. Worse trouble too. Anytime a single woman disappeared for a few days it was always suspicious. Many girls just wanted the "problem" to go away but not every girl survived such fixing. Spoons, curling irons, glass rods, wax candles. Everyone knew it shouldn't be done after quickening, but it was, and then it was worse. They'd find the results at the base of Moosehide Mountain, near Father Judge's hospital. One time the fetus was wrapped in a Seattle newspaper, put in a pasteboard box, and hidden under a rock. When a stampeder first found the carton he assumed it was hidden treasure.

The men beat the women, the women beat their bellies, the women killed themselves. Myrtle Brocee came to Dawson to perform in the theater but she grew to hate her life, doing nothing but constantly fulfilling the basest of needs, so she put a .32 caliber Smith & Wesson against her head and pulled the trigger.

A few days after her funeral, nineteen-year-old Kitty Stroup got drunk and then walked to a waterfront pharmacy and said she needed an eight-ounce bottle of strychnine to kill the rats that were eating her gaudy dresses. The druggist gave it to her without question. Then she went back to the Monte Carlo, locked herself in her room, and yelled goodbye through the thin walls. When they broke down the door she drank a glass of clear liquid and said, "I have taken care of myself and now it is all done." Soon she was spasming. A small crowd watched in fascination as she died. It was four days before Christmas.

"Oh what men," DeGraf vented in frustration. They were the cause of so much of this trouble. She had seen it herself. One night, DeGraf dropped off a new dress for a stately brunette—"voice like a nightingale"—who had a headline song in the show. But when she opened the door, she found the girl in agony in bed. Her chest was a mass of purple welts in the pattern of boot soles. "These are prints like a horseshoe," thought DeGraf. Some drunk man had kicked down her door and then stomped and trampled her. The girl never recovered, and was dead six months later.

Another night DeGraf dropped off matching blue dresses for two girls bound for the masquerade ball. But when she arrived at the hotel there was an anxious stirring in the air. DeGraf realized something was amiss and went upstairs and found one girl weeping, the other fair thing cold and very still. A man walked in, her companion. He was quiet, looked about the room, lit a cigarette, and left without speaking. DeGraf was furious. "Life goes on," she lamented, "and nobody bothers about her."

All the men said it was so safe to be in Dawson City, Colonel Steele kept everything in line, that you could drink and pass out and upon waking find your poke of gold on the counter right where you left it. Well, of course they would think such. They were men. Their gold was all important, and their grub and gear so they could keep digging for it, and so thievery was severely punished. Colonel Steele kept twelve men on patrol in Dawson day and night, and anyone caught stealing was sent to chop firewood at the Mounted Police barracks. Fifty men at a time worked those axes.

But Dawson was safe only for men. It was the women who suffered. Gold lay in abundance and food was sacred. But the exclusive company of a good-time girl, this was in short supply. Finding a girl to turn a trick? Simple. Cheaper than flour. But finding a girl to turn her tricks only for you? Impossible. Jealousy enraged the men, the thought that their girl was with another man while they worked the mines. No way they would stop digging for gold, that was unfathomable. Better to make sure no one else could ever have her.

The stories were in all the newspapers. Dave Evans was young, good-looking, and engaged in public wrestling matches that drew crowds of spectators. Libby White was older, had been married several times, and knew that keeping several men satisfied was a good way to keep from going hungry. Evans thought he might marry her, until he met one of the other men in White's life. She begged forgiveness, and swore off seeing the other men, said she would live with Evans alone. Cohabitate, before marriage? Unthinkable to Evans. He couldn't believe how promiscuous she was, this woman whom he thought he knew and loved.

It was the small hours of the morning. Evans sat in his room on the second floor of the Monte Carlo and the whole hotel shook from the dancing downstairs. He thought only of Libby.

"I still have that .44 calibre," Evans told his friend who sat by him. "The one I borrowed some weeks ago, to take a trip up the cricks."

"Maybe you ought to return that," his friend

said, with meaning, and Evans nodded and stood and walked out into the hallway to take the revolver back to its owner. But there instead, at the head of the stairs, he met Libby.

Evans grabbed her and forced her back into her room and closed the door. He held her with his wrestler's strong left hand and went for the revolver with his right and then she screamed such that even the musicians below could hear. Libby kicked and struggled. Evans pushed her against the wall, held her down, put the gun to the top of her head and fired. The bullet entered her skull, tore through her brain, and then lodged in her broken spinal column. She flopped forward, her face dropping in a pail of water that turned pink and then red.

Evans stood. He looked at what he had done. Her hair was matted and slick. She looked like she was drowning in the pail but her body was still and there was not a single spark of life within her.

Evans sat on the bed, put the revolver to his right temple, and squeezed. The bullet passed through him and lodged in the far wall. He slumped and tipped to the floor and lay as silently as she.

On the second floor of the Monte Carlo, patrons and girls took a break from their sporting. One man, Eddy Dolan, knocked on the door to room number three. No answer. The constable was called soon after, but the music never stopped.

• • •

Helen Holden was a dance hall girl who lived on the second floor of the Bodega. As was true for most of those in her profession, her days ended late and started late and so it was often evening time before she wanted lunch. So it was on April 26, 1899, a typical day. The calendar said spring and the sunshine was robust but it was still deathly cold, especially in the upper story of a drafty log-cabin saloon. To heat her room Helen had a little oil lamp and a stove, next to which she hung her clothes to warm and dry. Small comforts.

Helen left her room about six o'clock and got lunch out at a counter and then returned to the Bodega to begin drinking, get an early start on the day's dollar waltzes. An hour later the bar was short on whiskey, so George Harris, a porter at the hotel, went upstairs to get more liquor.

Walking down the hall, he heard a crackling at the door of Helen Holden's room. Harris had just seen Helen in the barroom, chatting with friends, so he knew she wasn't inside. What would make such a ruckus, with Miss Holden away?

He put his hand on the wall of her room. It was hot as an oven.

Harris opened the door and flames leapt to the ceiling. He ran downstairs into the dance hall and yelled fire and grabbed a bucket of water. But when he returned, the flames had already spread to the top of the landing and the heat pushed him back. The bucket looked small and pathetic in his hands.

The girls, the dancers, the bartenders, the gamblers, everyone ran for their lives. Fire leapt from the roof of the hotel. On the street, Helen grabbed a man who worked at the nearby Northern restaurant, and begged him to run into the Bodega to save her clothes. It was not the silliest request of the evening, but it was close.

The air was still, not a breeze, as always seemed to happen on the most frigid days. So the tongues of flame and smoke just rose straight into the sunlit sky. The air above the Bodega shimmered, wavy above the flame. And yet, a stone's throw from the burning hotel it was still so cold, somewhere south of negative 45 degrees.

Everyone in the streets began to move at once. Some men grabbed buckets for water but found only frozen muck. Others hefted axes and ran to the Yukon to break through to the flowing river but the ice was so thick they exhausted quickly. Still more called for the fire brigade. But the newly organized company was on strike for better wages, and so the coal fire in the boiler of the mobile engine had been allowed to die. It took many precious minutes to restart the pump. The fire in the Bogeda would burn.

The adjacent Northern restaurant burst into flame from radiant heat alone. The Tivoli Theater, on the other side of the Bodega, caught next. The Tivoli burned so hot that the Rutledge building on the far side of the street spontaneously ignited as well. For twenty-five long minutes crews fought the fire by hand.

Clouds began to form. Hot air rose from the burning hotels and billowed into steam and when the wet air cooled a fog of hoarfrost settled over the town. The bucket men lost sight of one another and the flames too. With an icy chill in the misty streets and a firestorm in the dance halls everything seemed either frozen or alight, nothing in between.

Then the wind came in off the river and grabbed the fire and threw it all about Front Street. It was a holocaust, a cataclysm, a force of elemental hunger and heat that descended upon them like something from legend, eating the town in block-sized bites.

Dawson had known fire. All wood-framed frontier towns had. But Dawson had never seen a conflagration like this. The whole city was about to be swallowed.

Residents began emptying the hotels and cabins of their valued possessions, clogging the streets with their accumulated sundries and obstructing the paths of rushing bucket crews and the delayed fire brigade. George Noble, the owner of the Tivoli, knew almost immediately that the situation was hopeless, and ran back in his hotel for the most expensive items in the place. Namely, three large plate glass mirrors he had just installed. Men with horses and wagons plied the streets to help saloon owners save their most precious belongings, not out of charity, but for $100 an hour. It was futile. Everything out of doors got covered in mud and soot and ruined anyway. Barkeepers carried barrels of whiskey into the street but the temptation for free booze was unbearable and the bucket men stopped to drink. Soon, many of the volunteers were roaring drunk, stumbling through the inferno.

Anna DeGraf was asleep in her cabin when a crackling woke her. "A great commotion outside my window," she thought, getting out of bed. She walked into the street and saw disaster. The Pioneer, Opera House, and Dominion were all ablaze. Saloon owners stalked their rooflines, desperately trying to brush sparks from their dry shingles. The wind was throwing the embers everywhere, even onto her own little cabin.

DeGraf ran about her home, grabbing her sewing machine and other belongings. She even tried to save her feather bed, but soon her shack was overwhelmed and she quit. A scorched chair stood in the center of the street. She sat down. Her cabin burned to the ground. She just sat. She had nowhere to go.

Belinda Mulrooney ruthlessly prioritized what was to be saved. She and her men moved from establishment to establishment collecting gold dust, giving every poke to Steele's Mounted Police for safekeeping. At the Pioneer Saloon she busted open the safe that was red hot. The owner was Bill McPhee, an old competitor of Mulrooney's, the very man who had hired away Brooks and his mules in Skagway the year before, forcing her to seize the caravan. In the tumult of the moment, though, all was forgiven.

"For heaven's sake, Bill, help us with the gold, to get it down to the Fairview," she begged.

"To hell with the gold dust," McPhee said. "Save my moose horns." From the day the Pioneer opened, the massive rack of antlers had hung over the bar like a pair of guardian angel wings. "They're the pride of his life," Mulrooney thought, before she helped rip them from the wall and carry them outside. Only then would Bill abandon the Pioneer.

Back at the Yukon River, crews had finally broken through the ice and started to pump water. They punched through the frozen barrier the way they sank mine shafts through the permafrost, by building fires and burning their way down. With labor, the fire engine's pumps began to draw and fill the hoses. But the boiler in the steam-powered Clapp and Jones engine was still far too cool, and the river water deathly cold, and so in mere moments the hoses froze and the pumps jammed under the pressure and the leather lines burst along the seams as the ice expanded and that's when they knew Dawson was truly lost.

In Paradise Alley, behind Front Street, the tenderloin was engulfed, the hotel fires spreading easily to the back walls of each shanty, their sumptuous chiffon curtains reduced to soot in an instant. The women fled into the street wearing nothing but pink silk and slippers.

"These girls don't have enough clothes to wad a shotgun," thought Mulrooney.

"Boys, I think we got a new job—rescuing those women," she said. They gathered the shivering girls and took the coats off any man who passed and wrapped them up as quick as they could and carried them to the Fairview. The girls were screaming from the pain in their bare feet.

"What the hell are we going to do with that bunch?" asked Cooke, Mulrooney's hotel manager, looking at fifty or so half-naked working girls.

"This is where they stay, Cooke," Mulrooney said. "I'll be the boss of this hotel tonight anyway." Later, the Mounted Police would take in the homeless girls, somehow managing to find room in their cramped barracks.

By now the fire was burning south, consuming the Northwest Trading Company, then the Madden house, a grocery, the Ryan boot and shoe store, Graf the jeweler, the Douglas mercantile, the M and M newsstand, the Arlington saloon, and the Montana. The Fairview lay right in its path. Mulrooney had turned the hotel into a shelter and a base of operations for the fire brigade, handing out cups of coffee mixed with brandy to keep everyone awake and warm. The concoction proved motivating; everyone wanted to save the Fairview and the source of free liquor. A few times sparks landed on the roof, but they were quickly doused by buckets of half-frozen muck. Mulrooney eventually had to tell the men to stop, to go save another building or the hotel would be ruined by the mud. But nobody wanted to leave. The coffee was too good.

Still the fire spread. The entire business district was in flame, from the river in, and nothing would stop it. The buckets were pitiful. The fire engine had broken. The volunteers were drunk or useless or both. No one knew what to do.

Except for Colonel Steele. The commander arrived on scene with the full strength of the Mounted Police and soldiers from the newly deployed Yukon Field Force auxiliary. "A terrific fire," thought Steele. True battle, finally, for an officer trained to fight. Steele ordered every one of his men into the fray and bystanders joined them, out of duty or fear, as Steele himself arrested every able-bodied sourdough and cheechako who refused to pitch in.

"Blow the buildings in front of the fire!"

yelled the captain of the guard. They had to make a firebreak, to sacrifice some for the good of all. And they knew how to do it. Dawson was a mining town, after all, and the Alaska Commercial Company warehouse held a stockpile of blasting powder and dynamite.

The police started tearing down buildings in the fire's path. "Almost superhuman effort," Steele swelled with martial pride for his men. They were in the heart of it now, put hard to the line. They blew the Aurora and Big Alex MacDonald's home and Nigger Jim's cabin and every remaining structure between the fire and the Fairview.

The whole town shook from the dynamite blasts. Hundreds of Dawson's stray dogs ran away and joined wolf packs and were never seen again. The glowing hot steel vault of the Bank of British North America ruptured and threw diamonds and pocket watches and melted nuggets into the dirt road.

In wagon ruts on Front Street, the molten gold mixed with whiskey, flowing from broken hogsheads, to form a coagulation of vices, freezing solid in the rock-hard mud.

In the morning light, the residents of Dawson looked upon their ruin. The demolition had worked, but at what a price. One hundred and eleven hotels, saloons, cribs, and cabins burned to the ground. Another fifteen were demolished by Steele's Mounted Police to stop the blaze. Over one million dollars in damage.

On the north end of Front Street, a blackened Monte Carlo. On the south end, the Fairview was a house of muck. In between, a wasteland of smoldering coals in the liminal dawn.

But even there, among the charred remains of the ravaged town, ash-stained men stooped with their pans, as they would in Bonanza Creek, sifting gold dust from the cinders.

The fever.

CHAPTER TEN
1899

I sent you a letter last fawl telling you
of the strike I made. Well, it has growed
wonderful since then every body
here are millionaires.
—LYING GEORGE CARMACK

But the fever wouldn't last. Broke in less than three years. George Carmack told the prospectors in Fortymile he had staked the discovery claim on Bonanza Creek in August of 1896, and by the time Dawson City burned in April of 1899 the great flood of stampeders had already receded, reduced to the dribble in the bottom of a gulch.

The mob's last stragglers came in on the much ballyhooed "all-Canadian" routes from Edmonton. Those few poor souls said they left with everyone else, in the summer and fall of 1897, but it took them nearly two years to complete the journey to Dawson. The vast majority never made it; the lucky ones turned back, the unlucky died of scurvy along the trail. Arctic leprosy, as that disease came to be known, killed more all-Canadian stampeders than all the cataracts and avalanches and brigands combined, fully half of those who set out from Edmonton. They had been promised an easy trail and provisions along the way. Instead, the track was a thicket, and all the Hudson's Bay Company forts along the route turned out to be abandoned and ransacked long ago. So the walkers of that road just died out there, slowly and painfully, one step at a time, always hoping the next promised outpost would be stocked. But they never were. Of the two thousand who set out, fewer than a hundred would reach the Klondike. Many had lost their noses to frostbite, and survived on the rations of the dead they found along the trail.

Such daunting odds faced all who took inland routes. Fifteen hundred men and three thousand horses attempted the Telegraph Trail through interior British Columbia; not a single animal survived the journey, and only a handful of prospectors. The Stikine Trail, near the coast, was attempted by five thousand men and women, and fewer than three hundred would arrive in Dawson, where they wandered confused into a burned-out boomtown that was emptying even as they arrived.

Those on the all-Canadian routes certainly felt like they missed the party. But in fact, they were more typical then they knew. When all was said and done, most stampeders never even reached Dawson.

The newspapers reported that in the initial

rush of 1897, a mob of over 100,000 people set out, more than the populations of Los Angeles and Seattle combined. Less than half made it to the headwaters of the Yukon, and of those, only another half reached the Klondike. Three quarters of those who left on the stampede were shipwrecked, shot, suffocated, frozen, starved, drowned, or demoralized to the point they gave up and went home.

Of the thirty thousand or so who reached Dawson, less than half bothered to stake a claim and actually do some mining. The majority found as much gold as Jack London, about $5 worth. Only a few hundred dug out enough to call themselves rich.

One hundred thousand set out on the stampede, less than one percent got rich or anywhere close. The inequities of the Gilded Age and the Panic of 1893 that had spurred the disastrous mass migration in the first place were re-created in the Klondike.

Dawson was never the same after the fire. Like a man struggling to reconstruct the events of a boozy night, an official inquest was held to determine the source of the conflagration. Jurors would ask Miss Holden if she smoked cigarettes, or used a hot iron to curl her hair. And she very seriously said no to both questions, she was vehement about abstaining from cigarettes, and said Mother Nature provided her lustrous curly hair. She had certainly not left her oil lamp lit either, as it gave off the most horrendous black smoke.

Surely no one could blame her for starting the great fire of Dawson City.

But the papers did blame Helen Holden. She had faked a suicide once before, and the commission decided this was just another case of supreme carelessness and selfishness. And it wasn't just Helen. All such loose women were magnets for trouble, the papers maintained. So the town passed a new law, that women be excluded from all public buildings except licensed hotels. Cultured, honorable women were still welcome, of course. It was the good-time girls who needed to go. Their low morals were the cause of so much ill in society. Everyone knew it. And so the tenderloin was dismantled and moved across the Klondike River, to Lousetown, the old Indian camp, which was free to burn as fate deemed fit.

Yet one more example of how Dawson was changing. The town was built back, but official and standardized, no longer a disorganized frontier menagerie. Dawson became a nostalgic echo of itself. Hotels and saloons began to sell themselves as a tourist attraction even as the last all-Canadian stampeders were still arriving; tragedy and then farce indeed. Gone were the log cabins and tents, replaced by only grand palaces. Everything was being shipped in from all over the world, the telegraph and the railroad would arrive shortly after. Thirty-five thousand men were blowing the White Pass to kingdom come to make the path straight. Thirty-five thousand.

And for what? Rumor was they found gold on the sand beaches in Nome. There would be a new stampede, to the coast. Get to Nome before all the choice spots were taken.

The party had moved on and Dawson was left behind. No more boomtown. No more of the old ways. No more miners' meetings or coon trials or running thieves out of town on a log. Now if justice was to be handed out, the executioner wore a uniform.

Everyone came out when those boys got hanged in August. They made a big deal of it, like it was the first one. And it was, officially. The first conviction in a court followed by a proper hanging at the Mounted Police barracks with all the officers watching. Law and order had come to the Yukon, and three were hanged that day. The first, a prospector named Edward Henderson, who was known to piss blood. When he spilled a bottle of the stuff on his tentmate one night, the two men fought and Henderson shot his stampede partner dead. The other two hanged were Indians, the infamous Nantuck boys. There were in fact a total of four Nantuck boys who had killed a white man and stolen his outfit, but two of the brothers had already died of consumption while shackled in prison and so you knew they had to swing the last two while they could.

The gibbet consisted of three ropes hung from a rough crossbeam and a platform with a double trapdoor held in place by an iron bar. Edward Henderson kept vigil on his death watch, joined by the local pastor who read him the Word and assured him of his forgiveness and reward. The two Nantuck boys were left solitary, to pass the night as they would.

They killed them after dawn. The blood-pissing Henderson had been bedridden the last year, and as he was unable to stand the executioners put out a chair for him to sit on as they looped his neck. The faces of the Nantuck boys were the color of a morning ash heap. Jim Nantuck, the older of the two, said "Tell my mother I died bravely." But when the rope came for him Dawson Nantuck began to quiver and his knees buckled, so his brother had to hold him up when they put black bags over their heads and bound their hands with thongs. As they cinched the noose tight, Dawson trembled with whimpering sobs. Coward, said the crowd. The boy was a teenager.

The sheriff nodded and the door dropped. Three figures fell and bobbed like a jigged fishing line. The timber groaned and held. Henderson and the older Nantuck boy jerked once, twice, and then went limp with snapped necks.

But Dawson Nantuck was too thin, a waif on a

string, and when he dropped his throat crushed and closed but the bones of his spine held and he started to kick and gurgle and fight. In his struggle his left hand broke free of the ties and he reached for the rope and pulled. He was too light to die and too weak to relieve the gagging throttle of the noose and he gasped for breath behind the black hood. Dawson pulled harder and somehow raised himself and sucked a frothy bloody breath but then the hangman reached out and struck his hand away and the boy dropped and began the strangle anew. His body convulsed as if possessed. Minutes passed. It took a long time before the fight left him.

The hanging was done precisely at eight o'clock in the morning, August 4, 1899. Colonel Samuel Steele of the Mounted Police dutifully noted it so in his daily journal as he did all administrative tasks. Steele had built the gallows and made the arrangements but didn't pull the drop. It wouldn't be seemly. Steele believed any adjudication of the law should be remote and reserved, and decorum would never allow his attendance at public hangings, no matter how popular.

The execution would be one of Steele's last official acts. He was reassigned by the end of the month, removed from command early and sent home humiliated. The reassignment had nothing to do with the stampede or the Dawson City fire or any of his official acts, as far as he could tell. It was petty politics, he learned, parties bickering back in Ottawa. "Because the correspondence I had with some friend favoured the Conservatives," he thought it might be. "I cannot remember such a thing. I think it is only a pretext."

Steele felt betrayed. He had come north out of a sense of duty, obligation, and both he and his family had sacrificed. Back home in Alberta his young son, not even one year old, was gravely ill, and the Mounted Police had stopped giving his wife food rations for the family since he was no longer assigned at the fort. And this is how they repaid his dedication? "Curse the day I ever served such a country." Steele was furious and shamed as he boarded the steamer for passage south.

The Klondike was emptying, to Nome, to the outside. Willingly or not, three quarters of the population of Dawson City left by the end of the year.

On his way out of town, the writer Tappan Adney staked his own section of creek, a bench claim 56 Below Bonanza. But the paperwork was lost by the office, and he never saw any gold. Adney filed his magazine story, naming down-on-his-luck Robert Henderson the rightful discoverer, for making the initial find in the Klondike watershed and telling Carmack where he had panned. "Siwash George would be fishing yet at the mouth of the Klondike if it hadn't been for Bob Henderson." That's what the old-timers said and that's what Adney reported.

The story appeared in the April 8, 1899, edition of *Harper's Weekly*, too late to grab the headlines. All the newspapers, which had given wall-to-wall coverage of the Klondike for almost a year, had moved on first to the romantic Rough Riders on San Juan Hill in Cuba, and then to Manila Bay and the war in the jungles of the Philippines. Adney's report was buried deep in the magazine, behind a new story by the futurist fiction writer H. G. Wells. Likewise, when Adney's book on the subject was published in 1900, no one talked about it. There were dozens of other titles in the stores by then, and Adney's appeared no more authoritative than any potboiler written from the writer's cushioned divan.

Adney never struck the jackpot, and neither did the vast majority of those who went north. Even Soapy Smith was worth only $148.60 when he died. For those lucky few who did get rich, most gambled it away, or lost it in speculative investments, or, like Belinda Mulroony, got caught riding the wave too long, wealthy in the boom and then losing it all in the crash.

A few managed to keep their money. Business tycoon John Healy died well-to-do, Clarence and Ethel Berry as well. George Carmack managed to keep the bulk of his wealth, but more importantly, he kept a secret, from the press, from official historians in capitals, from any outsider and cheechako.

Until his dying day, Carmack never admitted who it was that truly found the gold in Bonanza Creek.

It certainly was not Lying George.

George Carmack never was a great prospector. When he first arrived in Alaska in 1882, he was a disgruntled U.S. Marine aboard the USS *Wachusett*. He would soon desert the corps for his sister's sheep farm in the dusty San Joaquin Valley of California. It was a homecoming, of sorts. Carmack's parents had died when he was young, and his barely older sister, Rose, married a rancher nearly three times her age and raised George from then on. But the California farm was never a good fit. She was a strict hardworking Baptist, he just wanted freedom.

From the time he landed back in Juneau in 1885, Carmack never took white man's work. He packed with the Indians over the passes, fished and dug clams and shot deer and tried to speak Tlingit and Tagish. He put aside canvas pants and leather boots for caribou moccasins and followed the seasonal hunts. But his brief forays into prospecting never lasted long or amounted to much.

In time Carmack learned the local languages,

but not well, and he always struggled with pronunciation, making a habit of bestowing English equivalents when he couldn't say proper names.

In those early days Carmack packed over the Chilkoot with a Tagish man named Keish, whom he called Jim. This was before the strong man earned the name Skookum. And Carmack met Jim's nephew named Káa Goox, also known as Charlie. And he met Jim's sister, named Shaaw Tláa, whose first husband and infant daughter had died of influenza.

In 1886, while he wintered over with the Tagish people near Marsh Lake, Carmack married a young girl that he renamed Kitty. But she died only a few months later, and so according to Tagish custom, George was given a new wife, Kitty's aunt, who had also recently lost her spouse. And this is how Shaaw Tláa became Kate Carmack.

Kate was a proud woman. Her mother was of the Dakl'aweidi people, the killer whale nation. Her father was of the Deisheetaan, the beaver clan. She was raised to be a leader and a bridge between nations. Soon the Carmacks had a daughter, whom Kate called Aagé but George named Graphie Grace. The little family moved up and down the Yukon River valley, cutting trees, catching and drying fish, running a trading post for a time, staking a claim and panning here and there, sometimes with Skookum Jim and Tagish Charlie, sometimes alone, as the seasons waxed and waned.

By 1896, all of Carmack's ventures had come to naught. The post was closed, his previous claims just dry holes. That summer Carmack was back to netting salmon to sell for dog food, and in July, as he and Kate and their daughter were foraging for blueberries and drying fish at the traditional place at the mouth of the Klondike, Skookum Jim and Tagish Charlie and a few other relatives arrived at their camp. Jim had not seen his sister in several years while she followed Carmack on his failed projects and he had grown concerned about her welfare. He had brought his family to join hers for the summer, after which time they would all head back upstream before the lakes froze.

A month later, in August, Robert Henderson arrived with news of his nearby claim on what he called Gold Bottom Creek. After Henderson told Carmack that Indians were not welcome to stake their own share, and left the group to fish their weirs, it was Skookum Jim who was angry and motivated to prove Henderson wrong. And he knew he could.

Two years before, while he lay sick with a delirious fever, Jim was visited by Wealth Woman, a shining figure who nursed him back to health by sending her kindred, the frogs, to bring him food and medicine. Wealth Woman told him that from then on, for the rest of his life, Jim would be lucky, and that if he went to the mountains and put his face in the waters of a certain creek, he would find something special there.

The morning after Henderson's visit, Carmack and Jim and Charlie packed their boat with axes and shovels and some small provisions and went upstream a few miles to cut logs to float down to Fortymile for grub money. They took their pans as well, to find their own creek to prospect. Carmack let Skookum Jim lead, and near a stand of good timber he soon found a creek full of quartz. Carmack gathered some gravel and swished it around in the pan. None of the three men had ever been successful prospectors, but even they could see the little flecks of gold settle out of the fine black sand.

A decent find, but Carmack wanted to explore further, moving up the gully to higher elevations. "If we find nothing better, we can always come back here," he said.

The next day they worked a few creeks and their pups, one of which would come to be known as Eldorado. They found only colors on each, and kept pressing on for something better. At the top of the hill they turned east toward the Dome, cleared the ridge and saw, off in the distance, a line of smoke rising from a rocky gulch. It had to be Henderson.

"Well, boys," said Carmack, "we've got this far, let's go down and see what they've got."

It was the working mine on Gold Bottom, where Henderson and his four white companions had been digging out eight-cent pans for the last two months. All summer, Carmack's salmon fishing on the Klondike had gone poorly, and the three men were nearly out of provisions. Knowing they could use the resupply from the mining camp, the men scampered down the ridge and met with Henderson.

Jim asked for food and tobacco, even offering to pay. Henderson refused.

Henderson asked if Carmack had seen any prospects. Carmack said no.

The miners' code failed, neither man living up to their obligations, though Carmack harbored not a shred of guilt. "Childish, unreasoning prejudice," he called it. If Henderson weren't so against the Indians, if he hadn't said Jim and Charlie were unwelcome to stake on Gold Bottom, Carmack might have shared the news about the colors on the creeks they passed. As far as Carmack was concerned, it was bigotry, plain and simple, that cost Henderson a chance to be part of everything that was about to happen.

Carmack, Jim, and Charlie left Henderson, and headed back toward the Klondike on a new path, across the rim and then down a ravine, where they reached a bog. Mosquitoes swarmed

Carmack's face and he swatted them away while attempting to stay upright on the wobbly tussocks of grass. By the time they were on the other side, they were exhausted, and their moccasins slimy with slick frozen mud. Stumbling down the wet draw, out of food now, pushing through thickets of spiny Devil's Club, weary in the unfading light. Carmack and Charlie collapsed in fatigue, but Jim pushed on through the bush with his Winchester, determined to find some game to relieve their hunger.

And then his luck returned. A moose crossing the stream gave him an open shot. Jim fired his rifle but missed, so he quickly cocked the weapon and put it back to his shoulder and dropped the beast with a second shot before it could break for the treeline.

Jim called to Carmack and Charlie, to come help gut and clean the animal, but they were some distance away. So Jim worked his way down to reach the moose, dragged the carcass aside, and in the heat and his exhaustion, lowered his face to the clear water and dipped his hand to slake his thirst.

It was just as Wealth Woman had said. There before him in the sandy creek bed lay more shining gold dust than he had ever seen in his life.

Skookum Jim was the one who discovered the Klondike gold.

He called again to Carmack and Charlie, and fetching them, showed off what he had found. And from that day forward Carmack never treated his Tagish family the same way again.

They remained two days in that place, feasting on the moose and panning up and down the creek to identify the richest sections. But when it came time to stake, Carmack told Jim and Charlie that he was the one who must make the discovery claim, granting him double the normal land. He would take a thousand feet of creek, Jim and Charlie could each claim five hundred.

It had to be this way, an Indian would never be allowed to claim discovery, said Lying George.

Carmack named the creek Bonanza. He measured out two sections for himself and one each for Jim and Charlie. Four parcels that, in time, he would come to think of as all his own.

A few days later, Carmack was in McPhee's saloon in Fortymile, showing off Skookum Jim's Winchester cartridge filled with gold dust, and telling the assembled prospectors what he, and he alone, had discovered, setting off the greatest stampede of the age.

Kate Carmack did not settle into mining camp life. Separated from her extended family and the rhythms of her traditional migrations along the Yukon, she found her homeland increasingly unfamiliar as it swelled with strangers. The few white women were either prostitutes or wives too proud to speak to her, and the many white men did nothing but drink and dig holes in the earth.

Carmack grew embarrassed of Kate. He said that his wife was Irish, which explained her poor English. Immune to public shame, Kate would shout at him in Tagish from the cabin doorway, drawing a crowd of onlookers.

"What's going on?" asked one miner.

"Oh, that woman," Carmack said, dragging up a sled. "She's just telling me no wood, no fire, no dinner. She thinks her screaming will make me move faster."

In private, they were no better. At night, when Carmack snored, he would startle awake in pain, to find Kate twisting his right ear to get him to stop fussing in his sleep.

"I don't know when I will get out of this country," he thought. He just needed to see the work through while he could. "One chance in a lifetime."

Early on, Carmack sold Tagish Charlie's claim for $13,750, a fraction of what it would ultimately produce. But the men labored hard for two years on the remaining parcels, and once they had completed the spring cleanup in 1898, Carmack was ready to leave. By then they had washed out a total of $150,000, to be divided among the three men. Carmack wanted to get out, go on a holiday, enjoy a little of his new money, so he leased the three claims to other miners and loaded Kate and his daughter and the rest of his Indian family on a boat and went south to the States.

To the Tagish, Seattle seemed wholly alien. After they checked into a hotel, Kate took a hatchet and chopped divots out of the walls, banisters, and doorframes, marking blazes to guide her trail from the lobby to her room. Tagish Charlie threw gold half-dollars out the window just to watch the crowd fight over the bouncing coins. Later Kate bought a side of beef ribs at a local butcher shop and cooked them over a fire made from wooden packing crates in the alley next to the hotel. When Jim went gambling and was overtaken with drink, Kate found him and started in on his bottle and caused such a scene that both were arrested and sent to jail. At the time Carmack was out of town, checking on his new Washington mining investments, but the incident was covered in the papers, which claimed that all had succumbed to "firewater," and Kate, called "a wild animal" and Carmack's "dusky spouse," was said to have performed "an aboriginal Yukon war dance" in the corridor on the second floor of the hotel.

So. "All hands got drunk and some of them got in the cooler," Carmack concluded. "I am disgusted with the whole outfit." And humiliated to read about it in the *Post-Intelligencer*. "I feel like taking an ax and smashing something." It wasn't the first time the law had come for Kate. A few weeks earlier, the bellboy called the police when he entered their room and saw Carmack's face cut open, his pants in tatters, and finger wounds around his throat. Officers subdued Kate, but she was never charged and Carmack dropped the matter. "If Kate's trunk were here I would ship her back to Dyea mighty quick, she is getting so unreasonable," he now thought. He had rescued her from poverty and barbarism, tried to introduce her to proper manners, modern civilization, and this is how she returned the favor? "I am simply too good to her that's all."

In the summer of 1900, while Carmack was back in Dawson settling business, he went to a dinner party and met a woman named Marguerite Laimee. She was twenty-six years old and a veteran of gold rush demimondes all over the world. In Dawson, Marguerite ran the "cigar store" at the Green Tree Saloon on Front Street, where a man with an oral fixation could be satisfied in ways that did not involve tobacco. In a corset and gown, oglers said she looked like she was hiding two ostrich eggs in the front of her dress. Carmack asked her to marry him the night they met.

Marguerite had come north on the Klondike stampede to make a million dollars by marrying a millionaire. Carmack appeared qualified. She said yes.

Carmack decided then that he had never really been married to Kate after all. There was no ceremony, no paperwork, she couldn't prove it. And he had money now, investments, real estate holdings, a new mobile steamer automobile with a plate that said "Discoverer of Gold in the Klondike." And he had found Marguerite. He had improved himself. He deserved better.

Carmack was done with the Klondike for good. He sold the three remaining shares of Bonanza Creek to Skookum Jim, essentially selling the Tagish man back his own claim. He avoided any contact with Kate or his daughter, whom he had sent to live on the California ranch with his sister, her invalid husband, and her squabbling children. "I can never live with Kate again. It is simply a misery for me," he wrote to his sister, while never sending so much as a telegram to Kate.

But that illiterate woman had the gall to send him a letter, dictated to someone or other. It said things that made his blood boil.

The letter said: "I think, maybe, you are mad with me. I want to learn to read and write."

The letter said. "If I could play on the piano, and talk good English, you would like me better."

Kate said that she heard she was being divorced, but she didn't understand what that meant. That they would never see each other again?

The letter ended: "When you get tired of the false world come to your own faithful Kate."

Carmack would have none of it. She wanted money, of course. That was it. "You can't get an Indian to look across the creek without pay," he always said. He would marry Marguerite, be done with Kate, and she couldn't stop him. "Just let that old hag go ahead and do her dirtiest," he decided, "the judge will get disgusted with them and throw them all out of court."

Eventually, as he grew older, Carmack sat down and began to write his story, his version of the famous events of August 1896. In the twenty-four-page testimony that he delivered in 1922 to the hallowed Yukon Order of Pioneers, the fraternal society who admitted only old sourdoughs who had preceded the gold rush, he never made a single mention of his wife Kate. He never said that Jim and Charlie were family by marriage. He wrote that prospecting the Klondike had been his idea the whole time, no one else's. And by way of explanation for his good fortune, he told a story of a dream, of a fish with gold nuggets for scales and gold pieces for eyes, appropriating Skookum Jim's vision of Wealth Woman for his own.

In his address to the fraternal order, Carmack said that he had told Henderson everything, about every prospect. That he was the one who found handfuls of gold nuggets in Bonanza Creek. And that when he got to the saloon in Fortymile, placing the gold dust on the bar and telling all the miners about his incredible find, he was regaled. In fact, the biggest toughest miner in the saloon came up to him and shook his hand and said "Put 'er there, George, I've known you since '88, and I've never known you to lie to white man or a Siwash, and I can lick any hootch-guzzling salmon-eating son-of-a-gun that says you lie now."

Carmack was determined to set the official history. So everyone would know, that's how it went, that's how all the miners thought of him. He wasn't a squaw man any longer. He wasn't Lying George. He was respected, because now he was one of them.

One day the Klondike Gold Rush was the talk of the whole world. And then, seemingly overnight, everyone stopped paying attention.

The stampede ebbed, Dawson burned, and America moved on. The dark days of the Panic were behind them and the country's swagger had returned in the form of a newly discovered appetite for empire overseas. Young Teddy Roosevelt, the hero of the Spanish-American War, was now president, and everything was fresh and future-facing, full of potential, the Great White Fleet and Panama Canal, both wonders of the age.

Once the century turned, America was interested in the Klondike only as a matter of nostalgia, a heroic story from a primitive time. And in the hills above Oakland, the epicenter of a different gold rush, one author in particular rode that sentiment to national success.

Jack London had returned from the Klondike determined to be a writer, and he succeeded. Before 1899 had come to a close, London was publishing short stories—"To the Man on Trail," "In a Far Country," "The Men of Forty Mile," "The White Silence," "A Thousand Deaths"— and getting ready to release his first book, *The Son of the Wolf.* An incredible pace, and one that only increased. Novels followed in torrents. *The Call of the Wild*, *The Sea-Wolf*, *White Fang*, all by 1906.

London's fiction was filled with the hard-won experiences of his time wintering over at the Stewart River and the characters he met along the way: Goodman, Thompson, Sloper, Tarwater, Father Judge. The Chilkoot Trail appeared in *John Barleycorn*, the rigors of packing in *Smoke Bellew*, the numbed helplessness and silent death in "To Build a Fire." America couldn't get enough, reminiscing about a time just past.

Others kept that past as their present until the very end. Only a few score miles away from London's home, across the valley past Sacramento, where the mountains begin to rise, another Klondike veteran kept panning, kept digging, kept cleaning. Even in the last years of his life, as America watched the Great War in Europe, Carmack's gaze never wavered from the dirt.

Marguerite ran all the real estate investments, hotels and apartments, while Carmack moved from venture to venture. Snoqualmie Pass, the northern Cascades, and finally the western slope of the Sierra Nevada. His claims abutted Canada Hill, near Westville, just north of where the 1849 California rush got its start.

"It is nice in the mountains in the summer," he thought. He had three claims where he poked and prodded, panned coarse gold out of the creek, smoked a cigar, swung a pick, and puttered about. He was nearly sixty years old and losing his lifelong battle with rheumatism in his hips and back. His teeth ached in his swollen gums, and the only way he walked was with a cane.

But there were black bear in that country. Warm winters. His young grandchildren came to him and picked fool's nuggets out of the tailings.

The three claims were called Snowshoe, Outbreak, and Pacific Blue Lead. All three lay in Placer County, pored-over gold rush territory, land that had been squeezed and wrung out for seventy years by the time he arrived. Every last fleck had been accounted for, but Carmack persisted. He was sure he saw something that other miners did not. There was more to be found. A hidden trove.

Sometimes he took a new powered Star drilling outfit and bored a hole straight down in the ground, as he would have burned a shaft through permafrost, to find the pay streak he was sure still lay below. Maybe there were even two down there. But other times he dug pay dirt the old way, and ran it through the sluice box fed by the high mountain springs.

When the bloodred sun dropped behind the rolling piney ridges of the Sierra foothills, and the light played off the rocks of the deep canyons so they glowed, Carmack bent over the creek again and gathered the gravel and swished it along the rim of his pan and cleaned it so the dust would glitter and sparkle as he once dreamed.

Carmack was looking for the mother lode. He finally wanted to be the one who discovered the gold.

But he never would.

Afterword

August of 2021 marks the 125th anniversary of the discovery of gold at Bonanza Creek by Skookum Jim, more appropriately known by his Tagish name Keish. In the years since, investment firms estimate a total of twenty million ounces have come out of the ground, about $34 billion worth in today's dollars and prices.

Only the tiniest fraction of that wealth has stayed in the Yukon valley, and the legacy and artifacts of the Klondike gold rush lay unevenly across southeast Alaska and the Yukon Territory. Dyea is no more. Skagway is a port-of-call for cruise ships, four and five at a time, and when the passengers unload the line at the Red Onion Saloon Brothel Museum runs out the door. The White Pass railroad carries mostly sightseers. In 1958, a dam swallowed the White Horse Rapids. Hikers can brave the Chilkoot Trail, but only with a permit from the National Park Service, the terms of which require camping at specific designated points and prohibit the disturbance of any rusted pickaxes and boot soles found along the way. The descendants of Keish, Káa Goox, and Shaaw Tláa—Jim, Charlie, and Kate— are now known as the Carcross/Tagish First

Nation, and live in towns across their traditional indigenous lands.

Today Dawson City is a small town of about 1,500 people, a side jaunt for tourists in RVs and campers traveling the famed Alaska-Canadian Highway. You can gamble at a hall named for Diamond Tooth Gertie and take in the view of the Yukon from the shops on Front Street, but the creeks have been disfigured, dredged for every molecule of gold, the tailings remaking the landscape. On the *Gold Rush* reality television show, the "Klondike" mining location is actually across the ridge on Quartz Creek, where Robert Henderson panned and worked in the last days of 1895.

The decline of Dawson began quickly, the circus left almost as soon as it arrived. At its peak, the city was the size of Dallas, Texas, but by the turn of the century, Dawson had lost three quarters of its population, and was down to nine thousand residents. In a census in 1911, it had barely three thousand.

One of the first to leave was John Healy, the business tycoon, who resigned his position as general manager of the North American Transportation and Trading Company and took off in 1900. He moved back to the Alaska coast and tried various ventures, fishing and mining, financing schemes, and, by far his most audacious, a railroad that would connect to Siberia via a forty-four-mile tunnel on the floor of the Bering Sea. He stayed in regular correspondence with Tappan Adney, even hiring the journalist temporarily to produce geological prospectuses. Adney wanted to write a biography of Healy, but the book, like the tunnel, was never completed. After years trying to work political deals and secure funding, Healy gave up the Trans-Siberian dream in 1907, when land negotiations with the czar fell apart for good. A year later, Healy died of liver disease at St. Winnifred Hospital in San Francisco. He was sixty-eight years old.

Belinda Mulrooney lived the high life in Dawson too long. In 1900, in a ceremony at the Fairview Hotel, she married a man named Charles Eugene Carbonneau. He claimed to be a count, royalty from Bordeaux. But he was a bunco man like so many others, and after he nearly bankrupted her, she divorced him and left Alaska in 1908. She moved to Yakima, Washington, and bought an orchard and an enormous home that she called a castle but she couldn't afford them and lost it all again. During the Great Depression she worked as a seamstress for the Works Progress Administration, and in World War II, by then in her early seventies, she labored in a Seattle shipyard as a scaler, scraping rust from the steel decking of minesweepers. She died in 1967, at the age of ninety-five. On her death certificate, her occupation was listed as "housewife."

Clarence and Ethel Berry didn't stay in Dawson long. By 1902, they had pulled $1.5 million out of Eldorado Creek, and immediately started investing the money in other ventures: mines in Fairbanks and Circle City, the Los Angeles Angels baseball team, and, most importantly, land in McKittrick, California, where so much oil was bubbling from the ground it stuck to your boots. Berry Petroleum would ultimately own oil fields throughout the southern San Joaquin Valley, including the Ethel D field near Maricopa that broke the ten-million-barrel mark in 1989. Clarence died in 1930, of a burst appendix. Ethel, a bejeweled matriarch, followed in 1948. In 2013, Berry Petroleum was acquired by Linn Energy for $4.3 billion.

One who stayed the longest in Dawson was Anna DeGraf. She lived there, working at her sewing machine, until 1915. Every Sunday, when the summer sun ruled, she woke early and walked the creeks to look for her son. She never found him. The birth of a great-granddaughter enticed her to move to San Francisco, where she worked in the wardrobe department of the Pantages Theatre and wrote her memoirs. She died of pneumonia in 1930, at the age of ninety-one.

Colonel Samuel Steele was not out of favor long among his superiors. In 1900, he was sent to South Africa, to lead Lord Strathcona's Horse, a mounted rifle regiment, in the Boer War. In 1914, Major General Steele took command of the 2nd Canadian Division and prepared to head off to the Great War. His health was failing, though, and he lied about his age so the politicians in Ottawa would not think him too old to go fight. Steele was pushing seventy, and when it was clear his reduced vigor would be a liability at the front, he was given administrative training duties in the rear, and made it to the trenches in France only to hand out medals for bravery to younger men. He died in his bed in England in 1919. It was diabetes and drink that killed him, though his children told the press it was the Spanish Flu cutting him down in his prime.

Sam Steele's fight against the Cree in 1885, at a place now called Steele Narrows, remains the last military battle fought on Canadian soil.

After Tappan Adney left the Klondike, he continued to sketch and write. He covered the stampede to Nome for *Collier's*, and illustrated Teddy Roosevelt's 1907 book *Good Hunting*. In the Great War he enlisted with the Canadian Army and served as an engineer at the Royal Military College in Kingston, Ontario, where he designed and made small models of field fortifications, bridges to span trenches. In time, Adney became devoted to saving the wisdom and culture of the Maliseet people with whom he had spent his youth. He compiled their language and place names, and made tiny models of birchbark canoes and tried to sell them to the Smithsonian in Washington and the Field Museum in Chicago. No one was interested. Academics looked down on him as an eccentric hobbyist. Eventually, Adney moved back to the forests of New Brunswick, where he was known to spend time in the woods with no clothes on. He died in 1950, at the age of eighty-two.

The writer John McPhee credited Adney's meticulous sketches and collection of 150 models with no less than saving the birchbark canoe from the oblivion of lost human knowledge. Several of Adney's paintings, of sled dogs and canoes and the Hudson's Bay Company, still hang in the famed Explorers Club in New York City.

Jack London's first books mined his Klondike experience for material, but after he attained fame and wealth, the focus of his writings shifted to more political matters. He went undercover to investigate deplorable conditions and health hazards in workhouses for *The People of the Abyss*, he covered the Russo-Japanese War for the *San Francisco Examiner*, and he wrote a dystopian novel called *The Iron Heel* that served as a stealth socialist manifesto. Though a member of the Socialist political party, running for mayor of Oakland as their nominee in 1901 and 1905, he sat uneasily in any camp. He believed in

Anglo-Saxon supremacy and social Darwinism, a theme that he explored in the books *A Daughter of the Snows* and *Before Adam* and would go on to be called eugenics. In time he tired of the class struggle and embraced a comfortable life on his yacht and at his ranch on Sonoma Mountain. He died at home in 1916, of heart and kidney failure, the result of a lifetime of hard drinking. He was forty years old.

Despite not finding a paying streak in the Klondike valley, Robert Henderson continued to prospect along the Yukon and up the Pelly River, though he never made it big. As he got older, Henderson lobbied extensively to be recognized by the Canadian government as the "real" discoverer of the Klondike gold. Politicians and prominent officials publicly took up his cause as well, and in time much of the effort acquired racial overtones, that a white Canadian man was being denied what was rightly his, and he should be the one remembered by history, not an American married to an Indian. Henderson eventually received a small pension from the Canadian government as an acknowledgment of his contribution. He died in 1933.

George Carmack, as we've seen, never wavered in his conviction of what happened on Bonanza Creek. On May 30, 1922, when he told the story to the Yukon Order of Pioneers in Vancouver, the fraternal order cheered him, and passed a resolution declaring Carmack the one true discoverer and initiator of the famous stampede. The next morning, at his hotel, Carmack felt a weight growing in his chest. He died of pneumonia five days later. He was sixty-one years old.

After their temporary forays south, Jim, Charlie, and Kate each were eager to leave Seattle and California and return to their homeland. All three would ultimately settle along the lakes of the upper Yukon valley. Jim and Charlie built large homes, and furnished them with expensive imports. Charlie gambled and drank too much, and the day after Christmas 1908 he fell off the White Pass railroad bridge in Carcross and drowned. He was about forty-eight years old.

Kate was dependent on her brother Jim for support, and lived in a dilapidated cabin along the train tracks near Lake Bennett. When tourists stopped at her cabin to buy trinkets, Kate told them the story of her life, and of Jim and Charlie, and how she was there in the Klondike when her brother discovered the famous gold. She was about sixty-two years old when the Spanish Flu killed her in 1920.

Not everyone at the time believed Carmack's version of the events of August 1896. John Healy considered Carmack lazy and unreliable, and always assumed Jim had found the gold while Carmack napped. William Ogilvie, the area's chief surveyor, was a great admirer of Jim's, being the recipient of the Tagish man's packing services. Ogilvie interviewed Jim and Charlie after the discovery, and likewise became convinced that Carmack did not find the gold. And in any case, the oral histories of the Tagish people always consistently named Jim as the discoverer. That Carmack and Henderson dueled in public for recognition, and Jim's role retreated from prominence for decades, says more about how history is written than the truth.

Skookum Jim largely kept his money, and honored his people and his responsibilities as a recipient of Wealth Woman's luck, placing much of his gold in trust funds for the betterment of generations of Tagish still living on the lakes. He was about fifty-five years old when he died in 1916. The Skookum Jim Friendship Centre in the city of Whitehorse currently offers a shelter for youth, after-school tutoring, prenatal nutrition, and legal advocacy for the indigenous communities in the Yukon, and continues to keep alive the memories and traditions of his nation's elders.

From Skookum Jim's discovery to the burning of Dawson, it took only a thousand days for the gold rush to go from madness to myth. The story has always focused on grizzled prospectors striking it rich, rather than the human cost.

There is no official death toll. Add up the high-profile shipwrecks and avalanches, you get over a thousand fairly quickly. Add in everyone who disappeared along the various overland trails—from Edmonton, along the Telegraph, or up the Stikine—and the toll surges to over ten thousand. All of these estimates are just that. Many of the deaths involved individuals drowning or freezing on the Chilkoot, the White Pass, on the lakes of the upper Yukon. They were just swallowed by the trail and died anonymously.

This history of futility is lost in the fairy tale of dancing girls and Klondike Kings and friendly Mounties. The most lasting cultural reference to come out of the rush, the Klondike ice cream bar, is literally sugarcoated. Many of the official histories published in the decades immediately following the stampede emphasized how safe it was. That a man could fall asleep at the bar and his gold poke would still be there when he woke up. Even a surprising number of recent academic treatments focus on particular crime statistics in Skagway and Dawson City to make this same point generally. And if one focused only on murders reported to the police, then this might be true for a subset of white men. But the era was considerably more violent and dangerous for the women and indigenous people who experienced the stampede.

Much economic theory of the twentieth century

is built upon the idea of the Rational Actor, that a person is able to weigh the costs and benefits of decisions and then logically make the choice best for them. Likewise, it has become an article of faith in contemporary culture that wisdom is to be found in crowds. This concept, that the sum of us is smarter than any one of us, has been applied to everything from investing to military intelligence to Wikipedia.

Yet it is hard to find much rationality or wisdom in the stampede to the Klondike. The limitations of crowdsourcing were keenly felt by those seeking a solution to the problem of passage to Dawson City. And the economic interest of very few stampeders was ever served by the journey.

Perhaps "Klondicitis" was the best term for the infectious cloudiness of reason that ran amok. The newspapers had the paradigm right from the very beginning. A contagion of hopes and misinformation, a sticky idea that the crowd couldn't shake. The whole thing proved to be a naturally occurring pyramid scheme, where profits flowed to the lucky few at the start and the later arrivals were guaranteed to lose all.

The Klondike stampede of 1897 would prove America's purest expression of this spectacle, bigger than the initial push to California in 1849, deadlier than any American earthquake or cyclone or terrorist attack, the last of the great gold rushes. Other stampedes would go here and there—in Alaska and British Columbia, overseas to Australia and Chile—but never again on the same scale. The earth was running out of places that had not been prospected and picked over. But more importantly, and from an economic point of view, physical gold became less important over time. During the Great Depression of the 1930s, the United States and most other countries effectively moved off the gold standard, giving them flexibility to increase the monetary supply and fight the economic downturn. After adjusting for inflation, gold was cheaper in the year 2000 than in 1900.

And yet the fundamental psychological phenomenon of the gold rush continues, just in different form. Sometimes the rush is virtual, to the latest stock or cryptocurrency, like Bitcoin, which claims to be "mined" at server farms. And sometimes it is trivial and cultural, the 1990s fad of Beanie Babies, which somehow turned into a get-rich-quick scheme. The last few years have shown that gullible Americans continue to succumb to mass delusions and a herd mentality; consider the QAnon conspiracy, for instance.

But many times the mass rush is still physical, an ill-informed and dangerous but deeply human movement across geographies for a chance at economic opportunity. The poor and desperate around the world continue to take unimaginable risks to escape places that bear a strong resemblance to America's Gilded Age. Sometimes gold is even still involved, such as in Darfur, which has seen a number of smaller violent rushes as rumors of riches spread. But more often the promise is ephemeral, the news that a better life exists somewhere else far away. They see it on a smartphone, not in a newspaper. And they are willing to cross the Chihuahua or Sahara deserts, or sail the Mediterranean or Bengal seas, to reach it.

A great migration is under way, a swelling crowd of refugees and migrants seeking work and, with a little luck, their own chance at striking it big. In the early twenty-first century, millions of people face disease and disaster every day, they contend with gangsters and grifters and bunco men, they risk drowning and starvation, to reach a far-off country where they can stake their own claim.

Acknowledgments

This book is the product of four years of work, from proposal to publication, and so I fear any list of appreciation will be woefully incomplete. That said, here we go.

Most importantly, to my wife, Jessie, and my sons, Virgil, Marty, Sam, and Eli: I love that we got to research this one together.

Many thanks to my first readers, Rachel Kambury, Matt Gallagher, and Jonathan Loeb, with double appreciation for Matt Komatsu, whose constant exhortations to send more chapters provided the fuel that kept the writing process on track. Thank you to Bob Mecoy, my agent, counselor, and guide. Also to Tirana Hassan, my boss at my day job, for ceaseless moral and practical support, such as giving me time off for book tours. And many thanks to Don Reardon, Dan Branch, and Jeremy Pataky of 49 Writers, the Alaskan literary organization, for suggesting and encouraging that I, an Outsider, should write an Alaska book at all.

I am grateful for the significant assistance I received navigating archives and libraries during my research. Many thanks to Linda Quirk, Jeff Papineau, and Robert Desmarais at the University of Alberta in Edmonton, to Vivian Belik and Dannie Helm of the Yukon

Archives in Whitehorse, to Ryan Cameron of the British Columbia Archives at the Royal BC Museum in Victoria, to Sandra Johnston at the Alaska State Library, to Alex Somerville at the Dawson City Museum, to Kellyn Younggren at the Montana Historical Society, to Karl Gurcke at the Klondike Gold Rush National Historical Park, to Natasha Khursigara at the Toronto Reference Library, to Fawn Carter at the University of Alaska Fairbanks, to Kathleen De Laney and Laura Perott at the Canisius College library in Buffalo, and to independent researcher Juliet Demeter, who assisted me with the Helen Hawkins Papers at the Bancroft Library in Berkeley, California. Also, thanks to Wendy Bensted, at the Nova Scotia Commissionaires, for working a miracle and providing a copy of Henry Henderson's journal, a book that I thought I had no chance to find. And to Roger Brown, great-great-grandson of Anna DeGraf, who sent me amazing original photos and manuscripts that fleshed out and illustrated her story. And an extra special thank-you to Keith Helmuth and the staff of the Carleton County Historical Society, based at Connell House in Woodstock, New Brunswick, which maintains the only museum dedicated to the life and work of Tappan Adney.

But most importantly, and most generously, I am still overwhelmed by the gift given to me by Rod Macleod, Professor Emeritus of History and Classics at the University of Alberta in Edmonton. First my heart jumped when I discovered Sam Steele's complete diaries and letters in the Bruce Peel Special Collection at his university. Then it fell through the floor when I actually tried to read them: Steele's handwriting is atrocious and nearly illegible. When I asked Rod for tips on deciphering the journals, he simply shared his transcriptions, documents that took years, perhaps decades, for him and his wife to tediously produce. I am completely indebted to them, words fail me.

Thank you to all the good people at Penguin Random House: to Bill Thomas and Todd Doughty and Nora Grubb at Doubleday, to Doug Pepper at McClelland & Stewart, and to Sarah Nisbet at Anchor/Vintage.

And finally, an extra and hearty word of gratitude for Gerry Howard, my editor. We've worked together for nine years. This is our third book, but also, unfortunately, our last. Considering the many truly great writers Gerry has worked with over the years, I feel extraordinarily lucky to be paired with him. His editorial input was always targeted and decisive. Things I learned from Gerry (sometimes the hard way): editors like to know what a book is about, readers don't like to be confused, always strive for clarity. We made a book together that became an opera. It's been an honor, sir, thank you.

About the Author

BRIAN CASTNER is a former Explosive Ordnance Disposal officer and veteran of the Iraq War. He is the author of *Disappointment River* (2018), *All the Ways We Kill and Die* (2016), and the war memoir *The Long Walk* (2012), and is the coeditor of the anthology *The Road Ahead* (2017). His journalism and essays have appeared in *The New York Times*, *Wired*, *Esquire*, *The Atlantic*, and on National Public Radio. He has twice received grants from the Pulitzer Center on Crisis Reporting, and *The Long Walk* was adapted into an opera that has been performed nationwide. He lives in Buffalo with his wife and sons.

Center Point Large Print
600 Brooks Road / PO Box 1
Thorndike, ME 04986-0001 USA

(207) 568-3717

US & Canada:
1 800 929-9108
www.centerpointlargeprint.com